The Authoress
of the Odyssey

The Authoress of the Odyssey

where and when she wrote, who she was, the use she made of the Iliad, & how the poem grew under her hands

By Samuel Butler

With a New Introduction by

David Grene

Phoenix Books

The University of Chicago Press

CHICAGO & LONDON

This edition of *The Authoress of the Odyssey* is
reprinted from the second edition
(London: Jonathan Cape, 1922)

THE UNIVERSITY OF CHICAGO PRESS, CHICAGO & LONDON
The University of Toronto Press, Toronto 5, Canada

Printed in the United States of America

Introduction

DAVID GRENE

Samuel Butler is that rather rare phenomenon, a writer whose own personality is really his best raw material. All the books he has left us are expressions more or less direct of this intensely maverick, intensely iconoclastic, intensely paradoxical personality. The *Erewhon* books are the most stylized, and perhaps the least effective, of the intellectual versions of Butler the individual, though even these have a dry wit and poignancy that are very arresting. But the *Notebooks*, the travel books, above all the ever-famous *Way of All Flesh*, are truly wonderful exhibitions of the talker, the raconteur, the champion of causes, just the plain entertainer, situated somewhere in the middle between the writer of fiction and the Victorian version of commentator journalist, partaking of the character of both but so happily that his hybrid nature seems to enrich him, rather than lead us, as it usually does, to depreciate him in either capacity. Perhaps it might be said that this is to underrate *The Way of All Flesh*, which indeed can and should be recognized as a very important work of Victorian fiction. This is true, but then it is alone amongst Butler's writings as a genuine novel; also, even this is heavily autobiographical, much more so than, for instance, the nearest challengers like *David Copperfield* or *Jude the Obscure*; it appeared only after Butler's death, and his lifetime had been spent in writing essays of the directly critical or expository type. Yet it is impossible to look at any of those essays—and not least this book, *The Authoress of the Odyssey*—without feeling that Butler's gift belongs with that of the original creators, rather than the critics—that

he is much nearer, say, to Laurence Sterne than he is even
to Charles Lamb or William Hazlitt. Sooner or later the
discussions of ideas or facts always lead Butler to im-
agining the facts or the ideas in the mouth of some man or
woman, and then everything acquires a vitality quite dis-
proportionate to its share in the argument.

Here is Butler discussing the—to him—profoundly unconvincing attitude attributed to Penelope by the writer
of the *Odyssey*, and his arguments against the wilful blind-
ness of the classical scholars who have examined the book.

> Sending pretty little messages to her admirers was not
> exactly the way to get rid of them. Did she ever try snub-
> bing? Nothing of the kind is placed on record. Did she ever
> say, "Well, Antinoüs, whoever else I may marry, you may
> make your mind easy that it will not be you." Then there
> was boring—did she ever try that? Did she ever read them
> any of her grandfather's letters? Did she sing them her own
> songs, or play them music of her own composition? I have
> always found these courses successful when I wanted to get
> rid of people.

Of course this is a kind of spoofing. Of course the
solemn-minded will treat it as trivial and frivolous. But the
fact is that if you read this book as carefully as it merits,
this triviality acquires a slightly different tone. For Butler
comes very near to establishing a character for the *Odyssey*
as a work of literature which permits these funny questions
of his to be still funny, still absurd, but also to bear on
certain genuine problems of authorship and meaning. He
convinces one of the ironic, graceful, subtle qualities of the
poem so that the caricature workshop questions of a nineteenth-century writer of prose fiction *have* a suggestive
bearing on the meaning of this remote poem of anonymous
authorship and largely anonymous provenance.

Butler is a master of the art of debunking. The debunking is naturally in the direction of an alleged commonsense,
but unlike much debunking, including that of his ad-
mirer Bernard Shaw, Butler's commonsense has a special
sturdiness. It stands up. It occasionally approaches philis-
tinism; but it never dissolves into verbal trickery and human falsity when we look closer. And in this strangest of

books of classical scholarship and criticism, the paradoxical approach, whether you accept Butler's conclusions or not, makes you look at real things in the poem.

Furthermore, in strictly scholarly terms Butler has been "proved" right—if indeed anything in the whole Homeric problem with all its vexedness can be said to have been *proved*—in several most important respects; some of these scholarly issues, on which he waged a brave champion's battle against the dignified silence of the experts like R. C. Jebb, he has won simply in virtue of his much stronger feeling for literature than his opponents'. It is worthwhile to see how extensive are his winnings.

The book tries to establish three main points—all of them in the 1890's rejected by the classical scholars. The first is that the *Odyssey* and the *Iliad* were written by one author apiece, and that a different one. The second is that the *Odyssey* was composed about two hundred years after the *Iliad* and about the year 1050 B.C. The third is that the writer was a young Sicilian lady who lived at Trapani and that the entire locale of the poem is drawn from Sicily—for the author knew nowhere else. Thus *both* the island over which Alcinoüs ruled *and* Ithaca are in fact Trapani and only very superficially differentiated from one another. Perhaps it is best to say at the outset that Butler's first position has been proved entirely right; that his second has substantial elements of correctness—that is, there is a gap of some considerable length between the *Iliad* and the *Odyssey*, though few would now put it as much as two hundred years, and almost no one would put the writing of the *Odyssey* earlier than 700 or 750 B.C. The third is obviously the most controversial, and I am sure that Butler himself never believed that it could be accepted as proved. Even here he gives us furiously to think. A score of one and two-halves—if one is generous in the reckoning—is very high in the critical and historical estimate of a work the size of the *Odyssey*, and as obscure in origin.

In Butler's day the various scholarly theories about the Homeric poems were in agreement: that both were collections of lays and stories put together sometime in the seventh century by someone who was essentially an editor.

These lays were supposed to be of different dates and exhibited in diction, and also in archeological matters, evidence stemming from widely varying times and places. Butler says that one supreme poet wrote the *Iliad* and one—quite a while later—the *Odyssey*. He thinks of these poets as two of a chain of similar writers who were responsible for the other, now lost, poems of the Epic Cycle—the *Little Iliad*, etc.

Substantially Butler is right—so now at any rate thinks the overwhelming majority of the scholars, with somewhat more objective reason for our accepting them than those of Butler's generation. For Milman Parry and Albert Lord have found out more about how such poems as the *Iliad* and *Odyssey* have been transmitted in this Western civilization of ours than was known in the nineteenth century, and our archeologists have broadly confirmed these findings for the *Iliad* and *Odyssey*. We know now that oral epics have been transmitted, and were being transmitted as late as thirty years ago, in Serbia by the use of metrical systems used as mnemonic devices. That is: the accounts of all ordinary technical processes of ordinary life in such poems—the harnessing of teams, the sailing of boats, the preparation of meals, the putting on of armor—are expressed in a series of traditional lines. These lines and half lines are learned by the minstrel from the time he is a boy from the elder practitioners of the craft. Consequently when he grows up and starts to sing songs on his own, his invention is not taxed in the way in which a completely original poet's would be. When the moment comes in the poem for a description of these processes, there are his two or four or ten lines ready for him. This practice covers much more ground than mere technical processes. There were formulas for most things a man said or did or, to some extent, thought.

But the Homeric poet, to use a phrase which momentarily may be applicable to the authors of both *Iliad* and *Odyssey*, was not identical with the pre-Homeric minstrel, like Phemius, who sings in the *Odyssey*. Such a minstrel had a long line of forebears, probably reaching back into nearer and more remote Mycenaean times, and they forged the hexameter line and the traditional formulas. The authors of the *Iliad* and the *Odyssey* came at the end of the long line of minstrels. They used the minstrels' technique, they inherited their language (which was probably a courtly literary language, rather than a spoken one) and their traditional employment of it, but they each wrote a long poem *of their own composition* in it. The minstrels, as far as we can make out from the practice of Phemius and Demodocus, had restricted themselves to short lays, which they sang at intervals in banquets. The epics were composed somewhat like our novels. In our texts there are probably a few insertions of a later date, but there is really no reason to suspect more than that. The metrical format of the formulas froze them in their expression, and so the early theories, that different layers of archeological and linguistical material are superimposed, are quite correct—but the nineteenth-century scholars' conclusions from this state of things are not. They thought that this meant that the poems were written down and edited at a later time. We think —assuming that we are right in our analogy between the Serbian singers and the pre-Homeric minstrels—that the different layers were taken over bodily via the meter and the artificial literary language which the Homeric poet inherited from his predecessors. This Homeric poet used his language like a great series of prefabricated blocks. The phrase or the line was at his disposal where the poet of our times has only a single word originally conceived and placed in an originally conceived sentence. The Homeric poet was an original composer—but his line was not an original composition in the same way that a line of Keats's is.

Butler, of course, knew none of this. But he had a very sound instinct in his capacity of one writer examining the work of another. He was perfectly sure that both poems showed an artistic creation of an author of the first magnitude. And he said so, bluntly. He enjoys underplaying his originality in this. He points out that no one until Friedrich Wolf in the *Prolegomena ad Homerum* (1795) had had the stupidity to question what he was so daring as to assert in the 1890's. But one must not underestimate his clearheadedness and obstinacy in maintaining his thesis in his own day against the full tide of both German and English scholarship. As far as I know he had almost no scholarly support at all except somewhat dubiously in Andrew Lang.

In a way the correctness of Butler is so interesting because it is so significantly combined with wrongness. Since he has no idea of what a traditional language could mean for such poets, he thinks that every time the poet of the *Odyssey* uses a line from the *Iliad* he (or maybe she—so strong is the impression Butler makes on any reader who surrenders to his charm!) is doing so consciously. He even thinks *she* is building a conscious comparison between her poem and the *Iliad*. In other words, quite apart from the moments when he is teasing us, as in the passages I have quoted where he criticizes the presentation of Penelope's behavior, he really does think that there is no essential difference in methods of composition between himself as a nineteenth-century novelist and the writer of the *Odyssey*. The centuries flee away, and they are left looking directly at one another.

Just *how* far this misleads him is hard to say. He is certainly wrong about the self-conscious use of the *Iliad*. The writer of the *Odyssey* was only employing formulas which the writer of the *Iliad* had also not invented but taken over as part of his stock in trade. Butler thought of the process as plagiarism, whereas the very idea of plagiarism in such a context is absurd. But about Butler's capacity to penetrate the *feeling* of the actual author of the *Odyssey*, one cannot be so sure. He has written one of the most penetrating statements of the character of the *Odyssey* that anyone has yet given us—and that seems to me to say something about the correctness of *how* he saw it. Characteristically it is buried in one of his usual paradoxical arguments.

> If the *Odyssey* enforces one artistic truth more than another [he says], it is that living permanent work in literature (and the same holds good for art and music) can only be done by those who are either above, or below, conscious reference to any rules or canons whatsoever—and in spite of Shakespeare, Handel, and Rembrandt, I should say that on the whole it is more blessed to be below than above.

For after all it is not the outward and visible signs of what we read, see, or hear, in any work, that brings us to its feet in prostration of gratitude and affection; what really stirs us is the communion with the still living mind of the man or woman to whom we owe it, and the conviction that that mind is as we would have our own to be. All else is mere clothes and grammar.

As regards the mind of the writer of the *Odyssey* there is nothing that impresses me more profoundly than the undercurrent of melancholy which I feel throughout it. I do not mean that the writer was always, or indeed generally, unhappy; she was often, at any rate let us hope so, supremely happy; nevertheless there is throughout her work a sense as though the world for all its joyousness was nevertheless out of joint—an inarticulate indefinable half pathos, half baffled fury, which even when lost sight of for a time soon re-asserts itself. If the *Odyssey* was not written without laughter, so neither was it without tears. Now that I know the writer to have been a woman, I am ashamed of myself for not having been guided to my conclusion by the exquisitely subtle sense of weakness as well as of strength that pervades the poem, rather than by the considerations that actually guided me.

Let us disregard momentarily Butler's reference to his central thesis of the feminine authorship, and let us only bear in mind lightly his reading of a book as the personal statement of the author—quite a characteristic view of his, by the way. "There is nothing that impresses . . . more profoundly [in the *Odyssey*] than the undercurrent of melancholy throughout . . . a sense as though the world for all its joyousness was nevertheless out of joint—an inarticulate indefinable half pathos, half baffled fury . . . the exquisitely subtle sense of weakness as well as of strength that pervades the poem."

This is extraordinarily good. It is exactly what one feels through the ironic comedy of the incidents of the games at Alcinoüs' court, when Odysseus tells his stories. It is all over the place in the part of the book devoted to the Return. It is in the relationship of Odysseus and his father and Odysseus and his son—the cold, teasing character of the man with undercurrents of cruelty and savagery, but always seen by the author as triumphant in his inventiveness and dominating energy. Indeed, in his interpretation of the *Odyssey* as the exposition of the author's personal sentiments, Butler lays his finger on something very important. But it is the point of view from which the characters are seen and the stories told that has "the undercurrent of melancholy throughout." Butler is mistaken in his emphasis on the personal element. The author entirely effaces himself—except in the occasion he gives critics for the objective interpretation of his world. Never was there a story—or novel, if we dare call it that—with fewer of the tiny hints of the personal foibles of its creator. One of the remarkable things about Butler's criticism is that he really nails down the quality of the *Odyssey* while he spends a lot of time on thoroughly unconvincing arguments all based on the thesis "only a woman could have written that"!

His translation is masterly, if it is masterly to impregnate every word of the version with the intellectual character you believe the original to have held. Butler leaves no loose threads: he is certain that he knows exactly how the whole fitted in the author's mind, and the translation has a style as particular and definite and systematic as Butler's own.

At its best I think it conveys a picture of the *Odyssey* to the non-Greek reader as deeply significant as any and infinitely more satisfactory in the nature of its execution than most. Its main feature is that Butler saw the writer as someone always given to under- rather than overstatement and relying for effect on a gentle ironic commentary which runs beneath the surface of a commonplace vocabulary, and almost colloquial tone. Here is the meeting of the disguised Odysseus and his father Laertes, before the son makes himself known to his father. He pretends to take the old man for a gardener.

> "I see, Sir," said Ulysses, "that you are an excellent gardener—what pains you take with it to be sure. There is not a single plant, not a fig-tree, vine, olive, pear, nor flower-bed, but bears the traces of your attention. I trust, however, you will not be offended if I say that you take better care of your garden than yourself. You are old, unsavoury, and very meanly clad. It cannot be because you

are idle that your master takes such poor care of you; indeed, your face and figure have nothing of the slave about them, but proclaim you of noble birth. I should have said you were one of those who should wash well, eat well, and lie soft at night as old men have a right to do."

Most people now think that the *Iliad* and *Odyssey* were written by different authors. There is some stylometric evidence for this, though probably this should not be trusted too far. There are some archeological and social matters, much feebler in their impact, that seem to point in the same direction. Rather surprisingly Butler takes no account of Longinus' statement (made about the middle of the second century of the Christian era) which would make Homer, the poet of the *Iliad*, write the *Odyssey* late in life as a kind of sequel. (This certainly fits in very well with the visit to Hades to see the heroes of the *Iliad* and Telemachus' trip to Sparta, with its almost comic study of the homelife of Menelaus and Helen.) Furthermore, while allowing for a gap between Homer the writer of the *Iliad* and the events he describes, Butler makes it much shorter than we would nowadays. He thinks of it as barely two hundred years, 1350–1150. We believe it is nearer four hundred. But with the exception of these two points he has taken into account every aspect of the problem very thoroughly. And even here, most modern authorities feel that the important thing is to see the two authors as different and the two worlds as different, and that is Butler's main point—which he puts with his usual perverseness. He says that *only* the fallacious assumption of a single authorship for the two epics kept people from realizing that the second of them was written by a woman.

The evidence of Thucydides *does* point to the West as a possible locale for the Odyssean stories. He was convinced that the Cyclopes and Laestrygonians, though with his proper rationalism he condemns such monsters as nonexistent, were in Sicily—insofar as they were anywhere. Perhaps he was drawing on local tradition. This was taken up by J. B. Bury, who in his little *History of Greece* in the middle nineties mentions it as a possibility. Otherwise, as far as I know, Butler, who was ahead of him by a few years, is the only person then to work out the possibilities of Sicily as the country of the Wanderings.

Butler is at his weakest—and most amusing—on the femininity of the author. All of his pet theories—the attitude of women to money, the revealing depths of the management of a household, the assertiveness of one sex against the other, the Victorian concept of coquetry—they are all marshaled to do service in the fight to prove that no one but a women—and a young woman, of the best society and not particularly handsome at that—could have written this poem. Yet even here, with all the amusing nonsense, there are two excellent critical observations of detail. Why is the sixth book, the Nausicaä episode, so prominent, so deliciously interesting and funny? Butler is right in saying that it is quite unimportant in terms of the rest of the poem. Nausicaä vanishes at the end of this book, and we never hear of her again. And yet the home circle—Nausicaä, Arete sitting by the fire and clearly the most important person (so that Odysseus is bidden by the daughter to go by the king and supplicate the mother), and the slightly pompous courtly father—*why* do they have such clarity, such vitality? Butler says: because that's her home; because that is where she really knows her way about, and she could not write of it as she did of the rest. You may accept this or reject it—and accept or reject the implications about the writer and his material. But unquestionably Butler has put his finger on something strange and interesting in the workmanship, something that calls up questions.

He also comments that there is really only one woman in the poem, and she is Penelope, who doubles also as Circe and Calypso.

At first sight this seems extremely farfetched. Many people have commented on Calypso and Circe as duplicate figures—the two enchantresses who hold Odysseus against his will on their islands. But no one but Butler has ever claimed that they have any close kinship with Penelope the faithful wife, who weeps on her pillow continually and whose life is made a burden to her by the clamorous suitors who eat up the substance of the household. Butler's notion is that all three show the writer's interest in one sort of woman—the one who can hold men at her feet indefinitely. He believes that the poet has altered and cleaned up the Penelope legend. This he finds to have been a much more sordid one, in which Penelope intrigues with many of the suitors and is disowned by Odysseus when he returns home and kills them. His evidence is the summary of the *Telegony*, which certainly indicates that after his return and vengeance Odysseus leaves Penelope and marries Callidice of Thesprotia and eventually is killed by Telegonus, a son of his by Circe. He assumes that this implies that Penelope had been unfaithful; hence, he thinks, Odysseus came to divorce her.

Now one does not need to work too hard over the evidence for this. The *Telegony* is probably late, maybe later than the *Odyssey*. We have only an account of it anyway, and it is Butler who has put in the significant inference that it is because of her infidelity that Penelope was discarded. Let us not bother as to whether Butler is right or not about the external evidence.

But what it makes one notice about the poem is much more interesting. Is Penelope really being presented simply as patient Griselda? What about her son Telemachus' comments that he wishes she would really make up her mind one way or the other because this way his estate is being ruined through the forced entertainment of the suitors? Or his revelation that he regards sending his mother away to her father's house again as a disaster because he would have to pay back her dowry and that would hurt him? Butler has not invented *these* references. They come straight out of the text. The realism of the *Odyssey*, if we are right to construe it as realism, is always pointed. It makes you not only see the scene more clearly or place it more sharply in context. It does so, with implications toward *another* position. The writer of the *Odyssey* knew just as well as we did that the above comments of Telemachus about his mother are not what you might expect of the heroic age and the legend of the ever patient wife. Butler's extravagant arguments, all bearing to the point that Penelope could have got rid of the suitors if she wanted—but that she did not want—bear fruit. We need not accept the whole of Butler's theory, but it certainly makes us see the curious undertow of satire that is in the Penelope part of the poem. The fixed smile of the archaic statue gives place to something more comprehensible. If we do not then see the self-conscious nineteenth-century novelist (and do not need to), we *do* see a kind of craftsmanship which is much more individual than it at first appears. And it is Butler who makes us see this and probe what we think of it most explicitly.

His own last paragraph is perhaps as good a preparation as any for reading this marvelous essay which creates a sort of Greek Lady Murasaki of the eleventh century before Christ.

> What can it matter to me where the *Odyssey* was written, or whether it was written by a man or a woman? From the bottom of my heart I can say truly that I do not care about the way in which these points are decided, but I do care, and very greatly, about knowing which way they are decided by sensible people who have considered what I have urged in this book. I believe I have settled both points sufficiently, but come what may I know that my case in respect of them is amply strong enough to justify me in having stated it. And so I leave it.

He is even more justified in what he makes us see in the poem, whether or not, in order to do so, one has to go through and reject his factual arguments.

Preface to First Edition

THE following work consists in some measure of matter already published in England and Italy during the last six years. The original publications were in the *Athenæum*, Jan. 30 and Feb. 20, 1892, and in the *Eagle* for the Lent Term, 1892, and for the October Term, 1892. Both these last two articles were re-published by Messrs. Metcalfe & Co. of Cambridge, with prefaces, in the second case of considerable length. I have also drawn from sundry letters and articles that appeared in *Il Lambruschini*, a journal published at Trapani and edited by Prof. Giacalone-Patti, in 1892 and succeeding years, as also from two articles that appeared in the *Rassegna della Letteratura Siciliana*, published at Acireale in the autumn of 1893 and of 1894, and from some articles published in the *Italian Gazette* (then edited by Miss Helen Zimmern) in the spring of 1895.

Each of the publications above referred to contained some matter which did not appear in the others, and by the help of local students in Sicily, among whom I would name the late Signor E. Biaggini of Trapani, Signor Sugameli of Trapani, and Cavaliere Professore Ingroia of Calatafimi, I have been able to correct some errors and become possessed of new matter bearing on my subject. I have now entirely re-cast and re-stated the whole argument, adding much that has not appeared hitherto, and dealing for the first time fully with the question of the writer's sex.

No reply appeared to either of my letters to the *Athenæum* nor to my Italian pamphlets. It is idle to suppose that the leading Iliadic and Odyssean scholars in England and the continent do not know what I have said. I have taken ample care that they should be informed concerning it. It is equally idle to suppose that not one of them should have brought forward a serious argument against me, if there were any such argument to bring. Had they brought one it must have reached me, and I should have welcomed it with great pleasure ; for, as I have said in my concluding Chapter, I do not care whether the " Odyssey " was written by man or by woman, nor yet where the poet or poetess lived who wrote it ; all I care about is the knowing as much as I can about the poem ; and I believe that scholars both in England and on the continent would have helped me to fuller understanding if they had seen their way to doing so.

A new edition, for example, of Professor Jebb's *Introduction to Homer* was published some six weeks after the first and more important of my letters to the *Athenæum* had appeared. It was advertised as " this day " in the *Athenæum* of March 12, 1892 ; so that if Professor Jebb had wished to say anything against what had appeared in the *Athenæum*, he had ample time to do so by way of postscript. I know very well what I should have thought it incumbent upon me to do had I been in his place, and found his silence more eloquent on my behalf than any words would have been which he is at all likely to have written, or, I may add, to write.

I repeat that nothing deserving serious answer has reached me from any source during the six years, or so, that my Odyssean theories have been before the public. The principal notices of them that have appeared so far will be found in the *Spectator*, April 23, 1892 ; the *Cambridge Observer*, May 31, 1892 ; the *Classical Review* for November, 1892, June, 1893, and February, 1895, and *Longman's Magazine* (see " At the Sign of the Ship ") for June, 1892.

My frontispiece is taken by the kind permission of the Messrs. Alinari of Florence, from their photograph of a work in the museum at Cortona called " La Musa Polinnia." It is on slate and burnt, is a little more than half life size, and is believed to be Greek, presumably of about the Christian era, but no more precise date can be assigned to it. I was assured at Cortona that it was found by a man who was ploughing his field, and who happened to be a baker. The size being suitable he used it for some time as a door for his oven, whence it was happily rescued and placed in the museum where it now rests.

As regards the Greek text from which I have taken my abridged translation, I have borne in mind throughout the admirable canons laid down by Mr. Gladstone in his *Studies in Homer*, Oxford University Press, 1858, Vol. I., p. 43. He holds :

1. That we should adopt the text itself as the basis of all Homeric enquiry, and not any preconceived theory nor any arbitrary standard of criticism, referable to particular periods, schools, or persons.

2. That as we proceed in any work of construction drawn from the text, we should avoid the temptation to solve difficulties that lie in our way by denouncing particular portions of it as corrupt or interpolated ; should never set it aside except on the closest examination of the particular passage questioned ; should use sparingly the liberty of even arraying presumptions against it ; and should always let the reader understand both when and why it is questioned.

The only emendation I have ventured to make in the text is to read Νηρίτῳ instead of Νηίῳ in i. 186 and ὑπονηρίτου for ὑπονηίου in iii. 81. A more speculative emendation in iv. 606, 607 I forbear even to suggest. I know of none others that I have any wish to make. As for interpolations I have called attention to three or four which I believe to have been made at a later period by the writer herself, but have seen no passage which I have been tempted to regard as the work of another hand.

I have followed Mr. Gladstone, Lord Derby, Colonel Mure, and I may add the late Professor Kennedy and the Rev. Richard Shilleto, men who taught me what little Greek I know, in retaining the usual Latin renderings of Greek proper names. What was good enough for the scholars whom I have named is good enough for me, and I should think also for the greater number of my readers. The public whom I am addressing know the " Odyssey " chiefly through Pope's translation, and will not, I believe, take kindly to Odysseus for Ulysses, Aias for Ajax, and Polydeukes for Pollux. Neither do I think that Hekabe will supersede Hecuba, till

" What's Hecuba to him or he to Hecuba ? "

is out of date.

I infer that the authorities of the British Museum are with me in this matter, for on looking out " Odysseus " in the catalogue of the library I find " See Ulysses."

Moreover the authors of this new nomenclature are not consistent. Why not call Penelope Penelopeia ? She is never called anything else in the " Odyssey." Why not Achilleus ? Why not Bellerophontes ? Why Hades, when 'Αίδης has no aspirate ? Why Helios instead of Eëlios ? Why insist on Achaians and Aitolians, but never on Aithiopians ? Why not Athenæans rather than Athenians ? Why not Apollon ? Why not either Odusseus, or else Odysseys ? and why not call him Oduseus or Odyseys whenever the " Odyssey " does so ?

Admitting that the Greek names for gods and heroes may one day become as familiar as the Latin ones, they have not become so yet, nor shall I believe that they have done so, till I have seen Odysseus supplant Ulysses on railway engines, steam tugs, and boats or ships. Jove, Mercury, Minerva, Juno, and Venus convey a sufficiently accurate idea to people who would have no ready-made idea in connection with Zeus, Hermes, Athene, Here, and Aphrodite. The personalities of the Latin gods do not differ so much from those of the Greek, as, for example, the Athene of the " Iliad " does from the Athene of the " Odyssey." The personality of every god varies more or less with that of every writer, and what little difference may exist between Greek and Roman ideas of Jove, Juno, &c., is not sufficient to warrant the disturbance of a nomenclature that has long since taken an established place in literature.

Furthermore, the people who are most shocked by the use of Latin names for Greek gods and heroes, and who most insist on the many small innovations which any one who opens a volume of the *Classical Review* may discover for himself, are the very ones who have done most to foist Wolf and German criticism upon us, and who are most tainted with the affectation of higher critical taste and insight, which men of the world distrust, and which has brought the word " academic " into use as expressive of everything which sensible people will avoid. I dare not, therefore, follow these men till time has shown whether they are faddists or no. Nevertheless, if I find the opinion of those whom I respect goes against me in this matter, I shall adopt the Greek names in any new edition of my book that may be asked for. I need hardly say that I have consulted many excellent scholars as to which course I should take, and have found them generally, though not always, approve of my keeping to the names with which Pope and others have already familiarised the public.

Since Chapter xiv. was beyond reach of modification, I have asked the authorities of the British Mueusm to accept a copy of the " Odyssey " with all the Iliadic passages underlined and referred to in MS. I have every reason to believe that this will very shortly be indexed under my name, and (I regret to say) also under that of Homer. It is my intention within the next few weeks to offer the Museum an " Iliad " with all passages borrowed by the writer of the " Odyssey " underlined—reference being given to the Odyssean passage in which they occur.

Lastly, I would express my great obligations to my friend Mr. H. Festing Jones, who in two successive years has verified all topographical details on the ground itself, and to whom I have referred throughout my work whenever I have been in doubt or difficulty.

September 27th, 1897.

Contents

Contents

CHAPTER III

CHAPTER IV

Contents

xxvi Contents

CHAPTER XIV

CHAPTER XV

CHAPTER XVI

List of Illustrations

The Authoress of the Odyssey

Chapter I

IF the questions whether the " Odyssey " was written by a man
or a woman, and whether or no it is of exclusively Sicilian
origin, were pregnant with no larger issues than the determination of the sex and abode of the writer, it might be enough
merely to suggest the answers and refer the reader to the work
itself. Obviously, however, they have an important bearing on
the whole Homeric controversy ; for if we find a woman's hand
omnipresent throughout the " Odyssey," and if we also find so
large a number of local details, taken so exclusively and so
faithfully from a single Sicilian town as to warrant the belief
that the writer must have lived and written there, the presumption seems irresistible that the poem was written by a
single person. For there can hardly have been more than
one woman in the same place able to write such—and such
homogeneous—poetry as we find throughout the " Odyssey."

Many questions will become thus simplified. Among others
we can limit the date of the poem to the lifetime of a single
person, and if we find, as I believe we shall, that this person
in all probability flourished, roughly between 1050 and 1000 B.C.,
if, moreover, we can show, as we assuredly can, that she had

the " Iliad " before her much as we have it now, quoting, consciously or unconsciously, as freely from the most suspected parts as from those that are admittedly Homer's, we shall have done much towards settling the question whether the " Iliad " also is by one hand or by many.

Not that this question ought to want much settling. The theory that the " Iliad " and " Odyssey " were written each of them by various hands, and pieced together in various centuries by various editors, is not one which it is easy to treat respectfully. It does not rest on the well established case of any other poem so constructed ; literature furnishes us with no poem whose genesis is known to have been such as that which we are asked to foist upon the " Iliad " and " Odyssey." The theory is founded on a supposition as to the date when writing became possible, which has long since been shown to be untenable ; not only does it rest on no external evidence, but it flies in the face of what little external evidence we have. Based on a base that has been cut from under it, it has been sustained by arguments which have never succeeded in leading two scholars to the same conclusions, and which are of that character which will lead any one to any conclusion however preposterous, which he may have made up his mind to consider himself as having established. A writer in the *Spectator* of Jan. 2, 1892, whose name I do not know, concluded an article by saying,

That the finest poem of the world was created out of the contributions of a multitude of poets revolts all our literary instincts.

Of course it does, but the Wolfian heresy, more or less modified, is still so generally accepted both on the continent and in England that it will not be easy to exterminate it.

Easy or no this is a task well worth attempting, for Wolf's theory has been pregnant of harm in more ways than are immediately apparent. Who would have thought of attacking Shakespeare's existence—for if Shakespeare did not write his plays he is no longer Shakespeare—unless men's minds had been unsettled by Wolf's virtual denial of Homer's ? Who would have reascribed picture after picture in half the galleries of Europe, often wantonly, and sometimes in defiance of the clearest evidence, if the unsettling of questions concerning authorship had not been found to be an easy road to reputation as a critic ? Nor does there appear to be any end to it, for each succeeding generation seems bent on trying to surpass the recklessness of its predecessor.

And more than this, the following pages will read a lesson of another kind, which I will leave the reader to guess at, to men whom I will not name, but some of whom he may perhaps know, for there are many of them. Indeed I have sometimes thought that the sharpness of this lesson may be a more useful service than either the establishment of the points which I have set myself to prove, or the dispelling of the nightmares of Homeric extravagance which German professors have evolved out of their own inner consciousness.

Such language may be held to come ill from one who is setting himself to maintain two such seeming paradoxes as the feminine authorship, and Sicilian origin, of the " Odyssey." One such shock would be bad enough, but two, and each so far-reaching, are intolerable. I feel this, and am oppressed by it. When I look back on the record of Iliadic and Odyssean controversy for nearly 2500 years, and reflect that it is, I may say, dead against me ; when I reflect also upon the complexity of academic interests, not to mention the commercial interests vested in well-known school books and so-called education—how can I be other than dismayed at the magnitude, presumption, and indeed utter hopelessness, of the task I have undertaken ?

How can I expect Homeric scholars to tolerate theories so subversive of all that most of them have been insisting on for so many years ? It is a matter of Homeric (for my theory affects Iliadic questions nearly as much as it does the " Odyssey ") life and death for them or for myself. If I am right they have invested their reputation for sagacity in a worthless stock. What becomes, for example, of a great part of Professor Jebb's well-known *Introduction to Homer*—to quote his shorter title—if the " Odyssey " was written all of it at Trapani, all of it by one hand, and that hand a woman's ? Either my own work is rubbish, in which case it should not be hard to prove it so without using discourteous language, or not a little of theirs is not worth the paper on which it is written. They will be more than human, therefore, if they do not handle me somewhat roughly.

As for the " Odyssey " having been written by a woman, they will tell me that I have not even established a *primâ facie* case for my opinion. Of course I have not. It was Bentley who did this, when he said that the " Iliad " was written for men, and the " Odyssey " for women.* The history of literature furnishes us with no case in which a man has written a great masterpiece for women rather than men. If an anonymous book strikes so able a critic as having been written for women, a *primâ facie* case is established for thinking that it was probably written by a woman. I deny, however, that the " Odyssey " was written for women ; it was written for any one who would listen to it. What Bentley meant was that in the " Odyssey " things were looked at from a woman's point of view rather than a man's, and in uttering this obvious truth, I repeat, he established once for all a strong *primâ facie* case for thinking that it was written by a woman.

If my opponents can fasten a cavil on to the ninth part of a line of my argument, they will take no heed of, and make no reference to, the eight parts on which they dared not fasten a misrepresentation however gross. They will declare it fatal to my theory that there were no Greek-speaking people at Trapani when the " Odyssey " was written. Having fished up this assertion from the depths of their ignorance of what Thucydides, let alone Virgil, has told us,—or if they set these writers on one side, out of their still profounder ignorance of what there was or was not at Trapani in the eleventh century before Christ—they will refuse to look at the internal evidence furnished by the " Odyssey " itself. They will ignore the fact that Thucydides tells us that " Phocians of those from Troy," which as I will show (see Chapter xii.) can only mean Phocæans, settled at Mount Eryx, and ask me how I can place Phocæans on Mount Eryx when Thucydides says it was

---

* See *Introduction to the Iliad and the Odyssey*, by R. C. Jebb, 1888, p. 106.

Phocians who settled there ?   They will ignore the fact that
even though Thucydides had said " Phocians " without qualify-
ing his words by adding " of those from Troy," or " of the
Trojan branch," he still places Greek-speaking people within five
miles of Trapani.

As for the points of correspondence between both Ithaca
and Scheria, and Trapani, they will remind me that Captain
Fluelen found resemblances between Monmouth and Macedon,
as also Bernardino Caimi did between Jerusalem and Varallo-
Sesia ; they will say that if mere topographical resemblances
are to be considered, the Channel Islands are far more like
the Ionian group as described in the " Odyssey " than those
off Trapani are, while Balaclava presents us with the whole
Scherian combination so far more plausibly than Trapani as
to leave no doubt which site should be preferred.   I have not
looked at the map of Balaclava to see whether this is so or
no, nor yet at other equally promising sites which have been
offered me, but am limiting myself to giving examples of
criticisms which have been repeatedly passed upon my theory
during the last six years, and which I do not doubt will be
repeatedly passed upon it in the future.

On the other hand I may comfort myself by reflecting that
however much I may deserve stoning there is no one who can
stone me with a clear conscience.   Those who hold, as most
people now do, that the " Iliad " and " Odyssey " belong to
ages separated from one another by some generations, must be
haunted by the reflection that though the diversity of authorship
was prominently insisted on by many people more than two
thousand years ago, not a single Homeric student from those
days to the end of the last century could be brought to acknow-
ledge what we now deem self-evident.   Professor Jebb, writing
of Bentley,* says

> He had not felt what is now so generally admitted, that the
> " Odyssey " bears the marks of a later time than the " Iliad."

How came so great a man as Bentley not to see what is so
obvious ?   Truly, as has been said by Mr. Gladstone, if

---

* *Bentley*, English Men of Letters, Macmillan, 1892, p. 148.

Homer is old, the systematic and comprehensive study of him is still young.*

I shall not argue the question whether the " Iliad " and " Odyssey " are by the same person, inasmuch as if I convince the reader that the " Odyssey " was written by a woman and in Sicily, it will go without saying that it was not written by Homer ; for there can be no doubt about the sex of the writer of the " Iliad." The same canons which will compel us to ascribe the " Odyssey " to a woman forbid any other conclusion than that the " Iliad " was written by a man. I shall therefore proceed at once to the question whether the " Odyssey " was written by a man or by a woman.

It is an old saying that no man can do better for another than he can for himself, I may perhaps therefore best succeed in convincing the reader if I retrace the steps by which I arrived at the conclusions I ask him to adopt.

I was led to take up the " Odyssey " by having written the libretto and much of the music for a secular oratorio, *Ulysses*, on which my friend Mr. H. Festing Jones and I had been for some time engaged. Having reached this point it occurred to me that I had better, after all, see what the "Odyssey" said, and finding no readable prose translation, was driven to the original, to which I had not given so much as a thought for some five and thirty years.

The Greek being easy, I had little difficulty in understanding what I read, and I had the great advantage of coming to the poem with fresh eyes. Also, I read it all through from end to end, as I have since many times done.

Fascinated, however, as I at once was by its amazing interest and beauty, I had an ever-present sense of a something wrong, of a something that was eluding me, and of a riddle which I could not read. The more I reflected upon the words, so luminous and so transparent, the more I felt a darkness behind them that I must pierce before I could see the heart of the writer—and this was what I wanted ; for art is only interesting in so far as it reveals an artist.

---

* *Homer*, Macmillan, 1878, p. 2.

In the hope of getting to understand the poem better I set about translating it into plain prose, with the same benevolent leaning, say, towards Tottenham Court Road, that Messrs. Butcher and Lang have shewn towards Wardour Street.   I admit, however, that Wardour Street English has something to say for itself.   " The Ancient Mariner," for example, would have lost a good deal if it had been called " The Old Sailor," but on the whole I take it that a tale so absolutely without any taint of affectation as the " Odyssey " will speed best being unaffectedly told.

When I came to the Phæacian episode I felt sure that here at any rate the writer was drawing from life, and that Nausicaa, Queen Arête, and Alcinous were real people more or less travestied, and on turning to Colonel Mure's work* I saw that he was of the same opinion.   Nevertheless I found myself continually aghast at the manner in which men were made to speak and act—especially, for example, during the games in honour of Ulysses described in Book viii.   Colonel Mure says (p. 407) that " the women engross the chief share of the small stock of common sense allotted to the community."   So they do, but it never occurred to me to ask myself whether men commonly write brilliant books in which the women are made more sensible than the men.   Still dominated by the idea that the writer was a man, I conjectured that he might be some bard, perhaps blind, who lived among the servants much as the chaplain in a great house a couple of hundred years ago among ourselves.   Such a bard, even though not blind, would only see great people from a distance, and would not mix with them intimately enough to know how they would speak and act among themselves.   It never even crossed my mind that it might have been the commentators who were blind, and that they might have thus come to think that the poet must have been blind too.

The view that the writer might have lived more in the steward's room than with the great people of the house served (I say it with shame) to quiet me for a time, but by and by it

* *Language and Literature of Ancient Greece*, Longman, 1850, Vol. I., p. 404.

struck me that though the men often both said and did things that no man would say or do, the women were always ladies when the writer chose to make them so. How could it be that a servant's hall bard should so often go hopelessly wrong with his men, and yet be so exquisitely right with every single one of his women ? But still I did not catch it. It was not till I got to Circe that it flashed upon me that I was reading the work, not of an old man, but of a young woman—and of one who knew not much more about what men can and cannot do than I had found her know about the milking of ewes in the cave of Polyphemus.

The more I think of it the more I wonder at my own stupidity, for I remember that when I was a boy at school I used to say the " Odyssey " was the " Iliad's " wife, and that it was written by a clergyman. But however this may be, as soon as the idea that the writer was a woman—and a young one —presented itself to me, I felt that here was the reading of the riddle that had so long baffled me. I tried to divest myself of it, but it would not go ; as long as I kept to it, everything cohered and was in its right place, and when I set it aside all was wrong again ; I did not seek my conclusion ; I did not even know it by sight so as to look for it ; it accosted me, introduced itself as my conclusion, and vowed that it would never leave me ; whereon, being struck with its appearance, I let it stay with me on probation for a week or two during which I was charmed with the propriety of all it said or did, and then bade it take rank with the convictions to which I was most firmly wedded ; but I need hardly say that it was a long time before I came to see that the poem was all of it written at Trapani, and that the writer had introduced herself into her work under the name of Nausicaa.

I will deal with these points later, but would point out that the moment we refuse to attribute the " Odyssey " to the writer of the " Iliad " (whom we should alone call Homer) it becomes an anonymous work ; and the first thing that a critic will set himself to do when he considers an anonymous work is to determine the sex of the writer. This, even when women are posing as men, is seldom difficult—indeed it is done almost

invariably with success as often as an anonymous work is
published—and when any one writes with the frankness and
spontaneity which are such an irresistible charm in the
" Odyssey," it is not only not difficult but exceedingly easy ;
difficulty will only arise, if the critic is, as we have all been in
this case, dominated by a deeply-rooted preconceived opinion,
and if also there is some strong *à priori* improbability in the
supposition that the writer was a woman.

It may be urged that it is extremely improbable that any
woman in any age should write such a masterpiece as the
" Odyssey." But so it also is that any man should do so. In
all the many hundreds of years since the " Odyssey " was
written, no man has been able to write another that will compare
with it. It was extremely improbable that the son of a Stratford
wool-stapler should write *Hamlet,* or that a Bedfordshire
tinker should produce such a masterpiece as *Pilgrim's Progress.* Phenomenal works imply a phenomenal workman, but
there are phenomenal women as well as phenomenal men, and
though there is much in the " Iliad " which no woman, however phenomenal, can be supposed at all likely to have written,
there is not a line in the " Odyssey " which a woman might not
perfectly well write, and there is much beauty which a man
would be almost certain to neglect. Moreover there are many
mistakes in the " Odyssey " which a young woman might easily
make, but which a man could hardly fall into—for example,
making the wind whistle over the waves at the end of Book ii.,
thinking that a lamb could live on two pulls a day at a ewe
that was already milked (ix. 244, 245, and 308, 309), believing
a ship to have a rudder at both ends (ix. 483, 540), thinking that
dry and well-seasoned timber can be cut from a growing tree
(v. 240), making a hawk while still on the wing tear its prey—a
thing that no hawk can do (xv. 527).

I see that Messrs. Butcher and Lang omit ix. 483 in which
the rudder is placed in the bows of a ship, but it is found in
the text, and is the last kind of statement a copyist would be
inclined to intercalate. Yet I could have found it in my heart
to conceive the text in fault, had I not also found the writer
explaining in Book v. 255 that Ulysses gave his raft a rudder

"in order that he might be able to steer it." People whose ideas about rudders have become well defined will let the fact that a ship is steered by means of its rudder go without saying. Furthermore, not only does she explain that Ulysses would want a rudder to steer with, but later on (line 270) she tells us that he actually did use the rudder when he had made it, and, moreover, that he used it τεχνηέντως, or skilfully.

Young women know that a horse goes before a cart, and being told that the rudder guides the ship, are apt—and I have more than once found them do so—to believe that it goes in front of the ship. Probably the writer of the "Odyssey" forgot for the moment at which end the rudder should be. She thought it all over yesterday, and was not going to think it all over again to-day, so she put the rudder at both ends, intending to remove it from the one that should prove to be the wrong one ; later on she forgot, or did not think it worth while to trouble about so small a detail.

So with Calypso's axe (v. 234–36). No one who was used to handling an axe would describe it so fully and tell us that it "suited Ulysses' hands," and was furnished with a handle. I have heard say that a celebrated female authoress was discovered to be a woman by her having spoken of a two-foot *ruler* instead of a two-foot *rule*, but over-minuteness of description is deeper and stronger evidence of unfamiliarity than mistaken nomenclature is.

Such mistakes and self-betrayals as those above pointed out enhance rather than impair the charm of the "Odyssey." Granted that the "Odyssey" is inferior to the "Iliad" in strength, robustness, and wealth of poetic imagery, I cannot think that it is inferior in its power of fascinating the reader. Indeed, if I had to sacrifice one or the other, I can hardly doubt that I should let the "Iliad" go rather than the "Odyssey"— just as if I had to sacrifice either Mont Blanc or Monte Rosa, I should sacrifice Mont Blanc, though I know it to be in many respects the grander mountain of the two.*

---

* Shakespeare, of course, is the whole chain of the Alps, comprising both Mont Blanc and Monte Rosa.

It should go, however, without saying that much which is charming in a woman's work would be ridiculous in a man's, and this is eminently exemplified in the " Odyssey." If a woman wrote it, it is as lovely as the frontispiece of this volume, and becomes, if less vigorous, yet assuredly more wonderful than the " Iliad " ; if, on the other hand, it is by a man, the half Bayeux tapestry, half Botticelli's Venus rising from the sea, or Primavera, feeling with which it impresses us gives place to astonishment how any man could have written it. What is a right manner for a woman is a wrong one for a man, and *vice versâ*. Jane Austen's young men, for example, are seldom very interesting, but it is only those who are blind to the exquisite truth and delicacy of Jane Austen's work who will feel any wish to complain of her for not understanding young men as well as she did young women.

The writer of a *Times* leading article (Feb. 4th, 1897) says :

The sex difference is the profoundest and most far-reaching that exists among human beings. . . . Women may or may not be the equals of men in intelligence ; . . . but women in the mass will act after the manner of women, which is not and never can be the manner of men.

And as they will act, so will they write. This, however, does not make their work any the less charming when it is good of its kind ; on the contrary, it makes it more so.

Dismissing, therefore, the difficulty of supposing that any woman could write so wonderful a poem as the " Odyssey," is there any *à priori* obstacle to our thinking that such a woman may have existed, say, B.C. 1000 ? I know of none. Greek literature does not begin to dawn upon us till about 600 B.C. Earlier than this date we have hardly anything except the "Iliad," the "Odyssey," and that charming writer Hesiod. When, however, we come to the earliest historic literature we find that famous poetesses abounded.

Those who turn to the article " Sappho " in Smith's *Dictionary of Classical Biography* will find Gorgo and Andromeda mentioned as her rivals. Among her fellows were Anactoria of Miletus, Gongyla of Colophon, Eunica of Salamis, Gyrinna, Atthis, and Mnasidica. " Those," says the writer, " who attained the highest celebrity for their works were Damophila, the Pamphylian, and Erinna of Telos." This last-named poetess wrote a long poem upon the distaff, which was considered equal to Homer himself—the "Odyssey" being probably intended.

Again, there was Baucis, whose Epitaph Erinna wrote. Turning to Müller's work upon the Dorians, I find reference made to the amatory poetesses of Lesbos. He tells us also of Corinna, who is said to have competed successfully with Pindar, and Myrto, who certainly competed with him, but with what success we know not. Again, there was Diotima the Arcadian; and looking through Bergk's *Poetae Lyrici Graeci* I find other names of women, fragments of whose works have reached us through quotation by extant writers. Among the Hebrews there were Miriam, Deborah, and Hannah, all of them believed to be centuries older than the "Odyssey."

If, then, poetesses were as abundant as we know them to have been in the earliest known ages of Greek literature over a wide area of Greece, Asia Minor, and the islands of the Ægæan, there is no ground for refusing to admit the possibility that a Greek poetess lived in Sicily B.C. 1000, especially when we know from Thucydides that the particular part of Sicily where I suppose her to have lived was colonised from the North West corner of Asia Minor centuries before the close of the Homeric age. The civilisation depicted in the "Odyssey" is as advanced as any that is likely to have existed in Mitylene or Telos 600–500 B.C., while in both the "Iliad" and the "Odyssey" the status of women is represented as being much what it is at the present, and as incomparably higher than it was in the Athenian civilisation with which we are best acquainted. To imagine a great Greek poetess at Athens in the age of Pericles would be to violate probability, but I might almost say that in an age when women were as free as they are represented to us in the "Odyssey" it is a violation of probability to suppose that there were no poetesses.

We have no reason to think that men found the use of their tongue sooner than women did; why then should we suppose that women lagged behind men when the use of the pen had become familiar ? If a woman could work pictures with her needle as Helen did,* and as the wife of William the Conqueror did in a very similar civilisation, she could write stories with her pen if she had a mind to do so.

The fact that the recognised heads of literature in the Homeric age were the nine Muses—for it is always these or " The Muse " that is involved, and never Apollo or Minerva— throws back the suggestion of female authorship to a very remote period, when, to be an author at all, was to be a poet, for prose writing is a comparatively late development. Both " Iliad " and " Odyssey " begin with an invocation addressed to a woman, who, as the head of literature, must be supposed to have been an authoress, though none of her works have come down to us. In an age, moreover, when men were chiefly occupied either with fighting or hunting, the arts of peace, and among them all kinds of literary accomplishment, would be more naturally left to women. If the truth were known, we might very likely find that it was man rather than woman who has been the interloper in the domain of literature. Nausicaa was more probably a survival than an interloper, but most probably of all she was in the height of the fashion.

---

* " Iliad," iii. 126.

Chapter II

IT will help the reader to follow the arguments by which I
shall sustain the female authorship of the " Odyssey," the fact
of its being written at Trapani on the west coast of Sicily, and
its development in the hands of the writer, if I lay before him
an abridgement of the complete translation that I have made,
but not yet published. If space permitted I should print my
translation in full, but this is obviously impossible, for what I
give here is only about a fourth of the whole poem. I have,
therefore, selected those parts that throw most light upon the
subjects above referred to, with just so much connecting matter
as may serve to make the whole readable and intelligible. I
am aware that the beauty of the poem is thus fatally marred,
for it is often the loveliest passages that serve my purpose
least. The abridgement, therefore, that I here give is not to
be regarded otherwise than as the key-sketch which we so
often see under an engraving of a picture that contains many
portraits. It is intended not as a work of art, but as an eluci-
datory diagram.

As regards its closeness to the text, the references to the
poem which will be found at the beginning of each paragraph
will show where the abridgement has been greatest, and will
also enable the reader to verify the fidelity of the rendering
either with the Greek or with Messrs. Butcher and Lang's
translation. I affirm with confidence that if the reader is
good enough to thus verify any passages that may strike him as
impossibly modern, he will find that I have adhered as severely
to the intention of the original as it was possible for me to do
while telling the story in my own words and abridging it.

One of my critics, a very friendly one, has hold me that I
have " distorted the simplicity of the ' Odyssey ' in order to put

it in a ludicrous light." I do not think this. I have revealed, but I have not distorted. I should be shocked to believe for one moment that I had done so. True, I have nothing extenuated, but neither have I set down aught in malice. Where the writer is trying to make us believe impossibilities, I have shown that she is doing so, and have also shown why she wanted us to believe them ; but until a single passage is pointed out to me in which I have altered the intention of the original, I shall continue to hold that the conception of the poem which I lay before the reader in the following pages is a juster one than any that, so far as I know, has been made public hitherto ; and, moreover, that it makes both the work and the writer a hundred times more interesting than any other conception can do.

I preface my abridgement with a plan of Ulysses' house, so far as I have been able to make it out from the poem. The reader will find that he understands the story much better if he will study the plan of the house here given with some attention.

I have read what Prof. Jebb has written on this subject,* as also Mr. Andrew Lang's Note 18 at the end of Messrs. Butcher and Lang's translation of the "Odyssey." I have also read Mr. Arthur Platt's article on the slaying of the suitors,† and find myself in far closer agreement with Mr. Lang than with either of the other writers whom I have named. The only points on which I differ from Mr. Lang are in respect of the inner court, which he sees as a roofed hall, but which I hold to have been open to the sky, except the covered cloister or μέγαρα σκιόεντα, an arrangement which is still very common in Sicilian houses, especially at Trapani and Palermo. I also differ from him in so far as I see no reason to think that the "stone pavement" was raised, and as believing the ὀρσοθύρα to have been at the top of Telemachus's tower, and called "in the wall" because the tower abutted on the wall.

---

* *Journal of Hellenic Studies*, Vol. VII. 170–88, and *Introduction to Homer*, 3rd ed. 1888, pp. 57–62, and Appendix, note 1.

† *Journal of Philology*, Vol. XXIV. p. 39, &c.

These are details : substantially my view of the action and scene during the killing of the suitors agrees with Mr. Lang's. I will not give the reasons which compel me to differ from Prof. Jebb and Mr. Platt, but will leave my plan of the house and the abridged translation to the judgement of the reader.

A was the body of the house, containing the women's apartments and other rooms. It had an upper story, in which was Penelope's room overlooking the court where the suitors passed the greater part of their time.

It also contained the store-room, which seems to have been placed at the far end of the house, perhaps in a basement. The store-room could be reached by a passage from a doorway *A'*, and also by back-passages from a side-entrance *A''*, which I suppose to have been the back door of the house. The women's apartments opened on to the passage leading from *A'* to the store-room.

B and *B'* were the Megaron or Megara, that is to say inner court, of which *B'* was a covered cloister with a roof supported by bearing-posts with cross-beams and rafters. The open part of the court had no flooring but the natural soil. Animals seem to have been flayed and dressed here, for Medon, who was certainly in the inner court while the suitors were being killed, concealed himself under a freshly-flayed ox (or heifer's) hide (xxii. 363).

B' was called the μέγαρα σκιόεντα or " shaded " part of the court, to distinguish it from that which was open to the sun. The end nearest the house was paved with stone, while that nearest the outer court (and probably the other two sides) were floored with ash. The part of the cloister that was paved with stone does not appear to have been raised above the level of the rest ; at one end of the stone pavement there was a door *a*, opening on to a narrow passage ; this door, though mentioned immediately after the ὀρσοθύρα or trap door (xxii. 126), which we shall come to presently, has no connection with it. About the middle of the pavement, during the trial of the axes, there was a seat *b*, from which Ulysses shot through the axes, and from which he sprang when he began to shoot the suitors ;

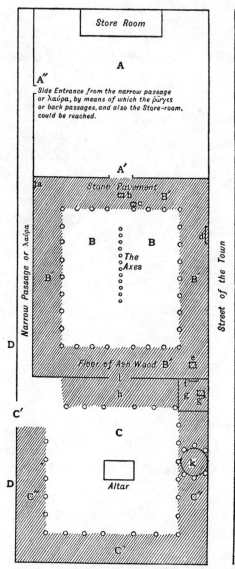

THE HOUSE OF ULYSSES

against one of the bearing-posts that supported the roof of the cloister, there was *c*, a spear-stand.

All the four sides of the cloisters were filled with small tables at which the suitors dined. A man could hold one of these tables before him as a shield (xxii. 74, 75).

In the cloisters there were also

d, an open hearth or fire-place in the wall at right angles to the one which abutted on the house. So, at least, I read τοίχου τοῦ ἑτέρου (xxiii. 90).

e, the table at which the wine was mixed in the mixing-bowl—as well, of course, as the other tables above mentioned.

f, a door leading into *g*, the tower in which Telemachus used to sleep [translating ἄγχι παρ' ὀρσοθύρην (xxii. 333) not " near the ὀρσοθύρα," but " near towards the ὀρσοθύρα "].

At the top of this tower there was a trap-door *g'* (ὀρσοθύρα), through which it was possible to get out on to the roof of the tower and raise an alarm, but which afforded neither ingress nor egress—or the ὀρσοθύρα may have been a window.

C was the outer court or αὐλή, approached by *C'*, the main entrance, or πρῶται θύραι, a covered gateway with a room over it. This covered gateway was the αἰθούση ἐρίδουπος, or reverberating portico which we meet with in other Odyssean houses, and are so familiar with in Italian and Sicilian houses at the present day. It was surrounded by *C"*, covered sheds or barns in which carts, farm implements, and probably some farm produce would be stored. It contained

h, the prodomus, or vestibule in front of the inner court, into which the visitor would pass through

i, the πρόθυρον or inner gateway (the word, πρόθυρον, how-ever, is used also for the outer gateway), and

k, the tholus or vaulted room, above the exact position of which all we know is that it is described in xxii. 459, 460, as close up against the wall of the outer court. I suspect, but cannot prove it, that this was the room in which Ulysses built his bed (xxiii. 181–204).

D was the τυκτὸν δάπεδον or level ground in front of Ulysses' house, on which the suitors amused themselves playing at quoits and aiming a spear at a mark (iv. 625–627).

The only part of the foregoing plan and explanatory notes that forces the text is in respect of the main gateway, which I place too far from the mouth of the λαύρα for one man to be able to keep out all who would bring help to the suitors ; but considering how much other impossibility we have to accept, I think this may be allowed to go with the rest. A young woman, such as I suppose the writer of the " Odyssey " to have been, would not stick at such a trifle as shifting the gates a little nearer the λαύρα if it suited her purpose.

In passing, I may say that Agamemnon appears to have been killed (" Od." iv. 530, 531) in much such a cloistered court as above supposed for the house of Ulysses. A banquet seems to have been prepared in the cloister on one side the court, while men were ambuscaded in the one on the opposite side.

Lastly, for what it may be worth, I would remind the reader that there is not a hint of windows in the part of Ulysses' house frequented by the suitors.

The Story of the Odyssey
Book I

THE COUNCIL OF THE GODS—TELEMACHUS AND THE SUITORS IN
THE HOUSE OF ULYSSES.

Tell me, O Muse, of that ingenious hero who met with many adventures while trying to bring his men home after the Sack of Troy. He failed in this, for the men perished through their own sheer folly in eating the cattle of the Sun, and he himself, though he was longing to get back to his wife, was now languishing in a lonely island, the abode of the nymph Calypso. Calypso wanted him to marry her, and kept him with her for many years, till at last all the gods took pity upon him except Neptune, whose son Polyphemus he had blinded.

21   Now it so fell out that Neptune had gone to pay a visit to the Ethiopians, who lie in two halves, one half looking on to the Atlantic and the other on to the Indian Ocean. The other gods, therefore, held a council, and Jove made them a speech
35 about the folly of Ægisthus in wooing Clytemnestra and

murdering Agamemnon ; finally, yielding to Minerva, he consented that Ulysses should return to Ithaca.

"In that case," said Minerva, "we should send Mercury to 80 Calypso to tell her what we have settled. I will also go to Ithaca and embolden Ulysses' son Telemachus to dismiss the suitors of his mother Penelope, who are ruining him by their extravagance. Furthermore, I will send him to Sparta and Pylos to seek news of his father, for this will get him a good name."

The goddess then winged her way to the gates of Ulysses' 96 house, disguised as an old family friend, and found the suitors playing draughts in front of the house and lording it in great style. Telemachus, seeing her standing at the gate, went up to her, led her within, placed her spear in the spear-stand against a strong bearing-post, brought her a seat, and set refreshments before her.

Meanwhile the suitors came trooping into the sheltered 144 cloisters that ran round the inner court ; here, according to their wont, they feasted ; and when they had done eating they compelled Phemius, a famous bard, to sing to them. On this Telemachus began talking quietly to Minerva ; he told her how his father's return seemed now quite hopeless, and concluded by asking her name and country.

Minerva said she was Mentes, chief of the Taphians, and 178 was on her way to Temesa* with a cargo of iron, which she should exchange for copper. She told Telemachus that her ship was lying outside the town, under Mt. Neritum,† in the 186 harbour that was called Rheithron.‡ "Go," she added, "and ask old Laertes, who I hear is now living but poorly in the 189 country and never comes into the town ; he will tell you that I am an old friend of your father's."

She then said, "But who are all these people whom I see 224

---

* Temesa was on the West side of the toe of Italy and was once famous for its copper mines, which, however, were worked out in Strabo's time. See *Smith's Dictionary of Ancient Geography*.

† Reading Νηρίτῳ instead of Νηίῳ, cf. Book xiii, 96, &c., and 351, where the same harbour is obviously intended.

‡ i.e. " flowing," or with a current in it.

behaving so atrociously about your house ? What is it all about ? Their conduct is enough to disgust any right-minded person."

230   "They are my mother's suitors," answered Telemachus, "and come from the neighbouring islands of Dulichium, Same, and Zacynthus, as well as from Ithaca itself. My mother does not say she will not marry again and cannot bring her courtship to an end. So they are ruining me."

252   Minerva was very indignant, and advised him to fit out a ship and go to Pylos and Sparta, seeking news of his father. "If," she said, "you hear of his being alive, you can put up with all this extravagance for yet another twelve months. If on the other hand you hear of his death, return at once, send your 296 mother to her father's, and by fair means or foul kill the suitors."

306   Telemachus thanked her for her advice, promised to take it, and pressed her to prolong her visit. She explained that she could not possibly do so, and then flew off into the air, like an eagle.

325   Phemius was still singing : he had chosen for his subject the disastrous return of the Achæans from Troy. Penelope could hear him from her room upstairs, and came down into the presence of the suitors holding a veil before her face, and waited upon by two of her handmaids, one of whom stood on either side of her. She stood by one of the bearing-posts that supported the roof of the cloisters, and bade Phemius change his theme, which she found too painful as reminding her of her lost husband.

345   Telemachus reasoned with her, and ended by desiring her to go upstairs again. " Go back," he said, " within the house and see to your daily duties, your loom, your distaff, and the ordering of your servants ; for speech is man's matter, and mine above all others, for it is I who am master here."

360   On this Penelope went back, with her women, wondering into the house, and as soon as she was gone Telemachus challenged the suitors to meet him next day in full assembly, that he might formally and publicly warn them to leave his house.

Antinous and Eurymachus, their two leaders, both rejoined ; 383 but presently night fell, and the whole body of suitors left the house for their own several abodes. When they were gone his old nurse Euryclea conducted Telemachus by torch light to his bedroom, in a lofty tower, which overlooked the outer courtyard and could be seen from far and near.

Euryclea had been bought by Laertes when she was quite 430 young ; he had given the worth of twenty oxen for her, and she was made as much of in the house as his own wife was, but he did not take her to his bed, for he respected his wife's displeasure. The good old woman showed Telemachus to his room, and waited while he undressed. She took his shirt from him, folded it carefully up, and hung it on a peg by his bed side. This done, she left him to dream all night of his intended voyage.

Book II

ASSEMBLY OF THE PEOPLE OF ITHACA—TELEMACHUS STARTS
FOR PYLOS.

Next morning, as soon as he was up and dressed, Telemachus sent the criers round the town to call the people in assembly. When they came together he told them of his misfortune in the death of his father, and of the still greater one that the suitors were making havoc of his estate. " If 46 anybody," he concluded, " is to eat me out of house and home I had rather you did it yourselves ; for you are men of substance, so that if I sued you household by household I should recover from you ; whereas there is nothing to be got by suing a number of young men who have no means of their own."   85

To this Antinous rejoined that it was Penelope's own fault. She had been encouraging the suitors all the time by sending flattering messages to every single one of them. He explained how for nearly four years she had tricked them about the web, which she said was to be a pall for Laertes. " The answer, therefore," said he, " that we make you is this : ' Send your mother away, and let her marry the man of her own and of her father's choice ; ' for we shall not go till she has married some one or other of us."

129   Telemachus answered that he could not force his mother to leave against her will. If he did so he should have to refund to his grandfather Icarius the dowry that Ulysses had received on marrying Penelope, and this would bear hardly on him. Besides it would not be a creditable thing to do.

146   On this Jove sent two eagles from the top of a mountain,* who flew and flew in their own lordly flight till they reached the assembly, over which they screamed and fought, glaring death into the faces of those who were below. The people wondered what it might all mean, till the old Soothsayer Halitherses told them that it foreshadowed the immediate return of Ulysses to take his revenge upon the suitors.

177   Eurymachus made him an angry answer. " As long," he concluded, " as Penelope delays her choice, we can marry no one else, and shall continue to waste Telemachus's estate."

208   Telemachus replied that there was nothing more to be said, and asked the suitors to let him have a ship with a crew of twenty men, that he might follow the advice given him by Minerva.

224   Mentor now upbraided his countrymen for standing idly by when they could easily coerce the suitors into good behaviour, and after a few insolent words from Leocritus the meeting dispersed. The suitors then returned to the house of Ulysses.

260   But Telemachus went away all alone by the sea side to pray. He washed his hands in the grey waves, and implored Minerva to assist him ; whereon the goddess came up to him in the form of Mentor. She discoursed to him about his conduct generally, and wound up by saying that she would not only find him a ship, but would come with him herself. He was therefore to go home and get the necessary provisions ready.

296   He did as she directed him and went home, where, after an angry scene with the suitors, in which he again published his intention of going on his voyage, he went down into the store

---

* The mountain is singular, as though it were an isolated mountain rather than a range that was in the mind of the writer. It is also singular, not plural, in the parallel cases of xv. 175 and xix. 538.

room and told Euryclea to get the provisions ready ; at the same time he made her take a solemn oath of secrecy for ten or twelve days, so as not to alarm Penelope. Meanwhile Minerva, still disguised as Mentor, borrowed a ship from a neighbour, Noëmon, and at nightfall, after the suitors had left as usual, she and Telemachus with his crew of twenty volunteers got the provisions on board and set sail, with a fair wind that whistled over the waters.

Book III

TELEMACHUS AT THE HOUSE OF NESTOR.

They reached Pylos on the following morning, and found Nestor, his sons, and all the Pylians celebrating the feast of Neptune. They were cordially received, especially by Nestor's son Pisistratus, and were at once invited to join the festivities. After dinner Nestor asked them who they were, and Telemachus, emboldened by Minerva, explained that they came from Ithaca under Neritum,* and that he was seeking news of the death of his father Ulysses.

When he heard this, Nestor told him all about his own 102 adventures on his way home from Troy, but could give him no news of Ulysses. He touched, however, on the murder of Agamemnon by Ægisthus, and the revenge taken by Orestes.†

Telemachus said he wished he might be able to take a like 201 revenge on the suitors of his mother, who were ruining him ; " but this," he exclaimed, " could not happen, not even if the gods wished it. It is too much even to think of."

Minerva reproved him sharply. "The hand of heaven," 229 she said, " can reach far when it has a mind to save a man." Telemachus then changed the conversation, and asked Nestor how Ægisthus managed to kill Agamemnon, who was so much the better man of the two. What was Menelaus doing ?

---

* Reading ὑπονηρίτου for ὑπονηίου, cf. i. 186 and also xiii. 351.

† The reader will note that the fact of Orestes having also killed his mother is not expressly stated here, nor in any of the three other passages in which the revenge taken by Orestes is referred to— doubtless as being too horrible. The other passages are " Od." i. 40 and 299 (not given in this summary), and xi. 408, &c.

253   "Menelaus," answered Nestor, "had not yet returned from
266 his long wanderings. As for Clytemnestra, she was naturally
of a good disposition, but was beguiled by Ægisthus, who
reigned seven years in Mycene after he had killed Agamemnon.
In the eighth year, however, Orestes came from Athens and
311 killed him, and on the very day when Orestes was celebrating
the funeral feast of Ægisthus and Clytemnestra, Menelaus
returned. Go then to Sparta, and see if he can tell you anything."

329   By this time the sun had set, and Minerva proposed that
she and Telemachus should return to their ship, but Nestor
would not hear of their doing so. Minerva therefore consented that Telemachus should stay on shore, and explained
that she could not remain with him inasmuch as she must
start on the following morning for the Cauconians, to recover a
large debt that had been long owing to her.

371   Having said this, to the astonishment of all present she
flew away in the form of an eagle. Whereon Nestor grasped
Telemachus's hand and said he could see that he must be a
very important person. He also at once vowed to gild the
horns of a heifer and sacrifice her to the goddess. He then took
Telemachus home with him and lodged him in his own house.

404   Next day Nestor fulfilled his vow ; the heifer was brought
in from the plains, her horns were gilded, and Nestor's wife
Eurydice and her daughters shouted with delight at seeing her
killed.

477   After the banquet that ensued Nestor sent Telemachus and
his son Pisistratus off in a chariot and pair for Lacedæmon,
which they reached on the following morning, after passing a
night in the house of Diocles at Pheræ.

Book IV

TELEMACHUS AT THE HOUSE OF MENELAUS—THE SUITORS
RESOLVE TO LIE IN WAIT FOR HIM AS HE RETURNS, AND
MURDER HIM.

When the two young men reached Lacedæmon they drove
straight to Menelaus's house [and found him celebrating

the double marriage of his daughter Hermione and his son Megapenthes.]*

Menelaus (after a little demur on the part of his *major* 22 *domo* Eteoneus, for which he was severely reprimanded by his master) entertained his guests very hospitably, and overhearing Telemachus call his friend's attention to the splendour of the house, he explained to them how much toil and sorrow he had endured, especially through the murder of his brother Agamemnon, the plundering of his house by Paris when he carried off Helen, and the death of so many of his brave comrades at Troy. " There is one man, however," he added, " of whom I cannot even think without loathing both food and sleep. I mean Ulysses."

When Telemachus heard his father thus mentioned he could 112 not restrain his tears, and while Menelaus was in doubt what to say or not say, Helen came down (dinner being now half through) with her three attendant maidens, Adraste, Alcippe, and Phylo, who set a seat for her and brought her her famous work box which ran on wheels, that she might begin to spin.

" And who pray," said she to her husband, " may these two 138 gentlemen be who are honouring us with their presence ? Shall I guess right or wrong, but I really must say what I think. I never saw such a likeness—neither in man nor woman. This young man can only be Telemachus, whom Ulysses left behind him a baby in arms when he set out for Troy."

" I too," answered Menelaus, " have observed the likeness.147 It is unmistakeable."

On this Pisistratus explained that they were quite right, 155 whereon Menelaus told him all he had meant doing for Ulysses, and this was so affecting that all the four who were at table burst into tears. After a little while Pisistratus complimented Menelaus on his great sagacity (of which indeed his father Nestor had often told him), and said that he did not like weeping when he was getting his dinner ; he therefore

---

* For fuller translation and explanation why I have bracketed the passage, see Chapter vi.

proposed that the remainder of their lamentation should be deferred until next morning. Menelaus assented to this, and 220 dinner was allowed to proceed. Helen mixed some Nepenthe with the wine, and cheerfulness was thus restored.

235   Helen then told how she had met Ulysses when he entered Troy as a spy, and explained that by that time she was already anxious to return home, and was lamenting the cruel calamity 261 which Venus had inflicted on her in separating her from her little girl and from her husband, who was really not deficient either in person or understanding.

265   Menelaus capped her story with an account of the adventures of the Achæans inside the wooden horse. " Do you not remember," said he, " how you walked all round it when we were inside, and patted it ? You had Deiphobus with you, and 279 you kept on calling out our names and mimicking our wives, till Minerva came and took you away. It was Ulysses' presence of mind that then saved us."

290   When he had told this, Telemachus said it was time to go to rest, so he and Pisistratus were shown to their room in the vestibule, while Menelaus and Helen retired to the interior of the house.*

306   When morning came Telemachus told Menelaus about the suitors, and asked for any information he could give him concerning the death of his father. Menelaus was greatly shocked, but could only tell him what he had heard from Proteus. He said that as he was coming from Egypt he had been detained some weeks, through the displeasure of the gods, in the island of Pharos, where he and his men would have been starved but for the assistance given him by a goddess Idothea, daughter to Proteus, who taught him how to ensnare her father, and compel him to say why heaven was detaining him.

440   " Idothea," said Menelaus, " disguised me and my three chosen comrades as seals ; to this end she had brought four

---

* It is curious that the sleeping arrangements made by Helen for Telemachus and Pisistratus, as also those made for Ulysses by Queen Arête (vii. 336, &c.), though taken almost verbatim from those made by Achilles for Priam and Idæus (" Il." xxiv. 643–47 and 673–76), should do so well for a building of such a different character as the house of Menelaus must have been from the quarters of Achilles before Troy.

fresh-flayed seal-skins, under which she hid us. The strong
smell of these skins was most distressing to us—Who would
go to bed with a sea monster if he could help it ? but Idothea 443
put some ambrosia under each man's nostrils, and this afforded
us great relief. Other seals (Halosydne's chickens as they call
them) now kept coming up by hundreds, and lay down to bask
upon the beach.

" Towards noon Proteus himself came up. First he counted 450
all his seals to see that he had the right number, and he
counted us in with the others ; when he had so done he lay
down in the midst of them, as a shepherd with his sheep, and
as soon as he was asleep we pounced upon him and gripped
him tight ; at one moment he became a lion, the next he was
running water, and then again he was a tree ; but we never
loosed hold, and in the end he grew weary, and told us what
we would know.

" He told me also of the fate of Ajax, son of Oïleus, and of 499
my brother Agamemnon. Lastly he told me about Ulysses,
who he said was in the island of the nymph Calypso, unable to
get away inasmuch as he had neither ship nor crew.

" Then he disappeared under the sea, and I, after appeasing 570
heaven's anger as he had instructed me, returned quickly and
safely to my own country."

Having finished his story Menelaus pressed Telemachus to 587
remain with him some ten or twelve days longer, and promised
to give him a chariot and a pair of horses as a keepsake, but
Telemachus said that he could not stay. " I could listen to
you," said he, " for a whole twelve months, and never once
think about my home and my parents ; but my men, whom I
have left at Pylos, are already impatient for me to return. As
for any present you may make me, let it be a piece of plate.
I cannot take horses to Ithaca ; it contains no plains nor
meadow lands, and is more fit for breeding goats than horses.
None of our islands are suited for chariot races, and Ithaca
least among them all."

Menelaus smiled, and said he could see that Telemachus 609
came of good family. He had a piece of plate, of very great
value, which was just the thing, and Telemachus should have it.

621   [Guests now kept coming to the king's house, bringing both wine and sheep, and their wives had put them up a provision of bread. Thus, then, did they set about cooking their dinner in the courts.]*

625   Meanwhile, the suitors in Ithaca were playing at quoits, aiming spears at a mark, and behaving with all their old insolence on the level ground in front of Ulysses' house. While they were thus engaged Noëmon came up and asked Antinous if he could say when Telemachus was likely to be back from Pylos, for he wanted his ship. On this everything came out, and the suitors, who had no idea that Telemachus had really gone (for they thought he was only away on one of his farms in Ithaca), were very angry. They therefore determined to lie in wait for him on his return, and made ready to start.

675   Medon, a servant, overheard their plot, and told all to Penelope, who, like the suitors, learned for the first time that her son had left home and gone to Pylos. She bitterly upbraided her women for not having given her a call out of her bed when Telemachus was leaving, for she said she was sure they knew all about it. Presently, however, on being calmed by Euryclea, she went upstairs and offered sacrifice to Minerva. After a time she fell into a deep slumber, during which she was comforted by a vision of her sister Ipthime, which Minerva had sent to her bedside.

842   When night fell the suitors set sail, intending to way-lay Telemachus in the Strait between Same and Ithaca.

Book V

ULYSSES IN THE ISLAND OF CALYPSO—HE LEAVES THE ISLAND ON A RAFT, AND AFTER GREAT SUFFERING REACHES THE LAND OF THE PHÆACIANS.

The gods now held a second council, at which Minerva and Jove both spoke.

28   When Jove had done speaking he sent Mercury to Calypso

---

* For explanation why I bracket this passage see Chapter vi.

to tell her that Ulysses was to return home, reaching the land of the Phæacians in twenty days. The Phæacians would load him with presents and send him on to Ithaca.

Mercury, therefore, flew over the sea like a cormorant that fishes every hole and corner of the deep. In the course of time he reached Calypso's cave and told his story. Calypso was very angry, but seeing there was no help for it promised obedience. As soon as Mercury was gone she went to look for Ulysses, whom she found weeping as usual and looking out ever sadly upon the sea ; she told him to build himself a raft and sail home upon it, but Ulysses was deeply suspicious and would not be reassured till she had sworn a very solemn oath that she meant him no harm, and was advising him in all good faith.

The pair then returned to Calypso's cave. " I cannot understand," she said, " why you will not stay quietly here with me, instead of all the time thinking about this wife of yours. I cannot believe that I am any worse looking than she is. If you only knew how much hardship you will have to undergo before you get back, you would stay where you are and let me make you immortal."

" Do not be angry with me," answered Ulysses, " you are infinitely better looking than Penelope. You are a goddess, and she is but a mortal woman. There can be no comparison. Nevertheless, come what may, I have a craving to get back to my own home."

The next four days were spent in making the raft. Calypso lent him her axe and auger and shewed him where the trees grew which would be driest and whose timber would be the best seasoned, and Ulysses cut them down. He made the raft about as broad in the beam as people generally make a good big ship, and he gave it a rudder—that he might be able to steer it.

Calypso then washed him, gave him clean clothes, and he set out, steering his ship skilfully by means of the rudder. He steered towards the Great Bear, which is also called the Wain, keeping it on his left hand, for so Calypso had advised him.

278   All went well with him for seventeen days, and on the eighteenth he caught sight of the faint outlines of the Phæacian coast lying long and low upon the horizon.

282   Here, however, Neptune, who was on his way home from the Ethiopians, caught sight of him and saw the march that the other gods had stolen upon him during his absence. He therefore stirred the sea round with his trident, and raised a frightful hurricane, so that Ulysses could see nothing more, 294 everything being dark as night; presently he was washed overboard, but managed to regain his raft.

333   He was giving himself up for lost when Ino, also named Leucothea, took pity on him and flew on to his raft like a sea gull; she reassured him and gave him her veil, at the same time telling him to throw it back into the sea as soon as he reached land, and to turn his face away from the sea as he did so.

351   The storm still raged, and the raft went to pieces under its fury, whereon Ulysses bound Ino's veil under his arms and began to swim. Neptune on seeing this was satisfied and went away.

382   As soon as he was gone Minerva calmed all the winds except the North, which blew strong for two days and two nights, so that Ulysses was carried to the South again. On the morning of the third day he saw land quite close, but was nearly dashed to pieces against the rocks on trying to leave the 451 water. At last he found the mouth of a river, who, in answer to Ulysses's prayer, stayed his flow, so that Ulysses was able to swim inland and get on shore.

456   Nearly dead with exhaustion and in great doubt what to do, he first threw Ino's veil into the salt waters of the river, and then took shelter on the rising ground, inland. Here he covered himself with a thick bed of leaves and fell fast asleep.

Book VI

THE MEETING BETWEEN ULYSSES AND NAUSICAA.

While Ulysses was thus slumbering, Minerva went to the land of the Phæacians, on which Ulysses had been cast.

Now the Phæacians used to live in Hypereia near the law- 4
less Cyclopes, who were stronger than they were and plundered
them ; so their king Nausithous removed them to Scheria,*
where they were secure.   Nausithous was now dead, and his
son Alcinous was reigning.

Alcinous had an only daughter, Nausicaa, who was in her 15
bedroom fast asleep.   Minerva went to her bedside and
appeared to her in a dream, having assumed the form of one
Captain Dymas's daughter, who was a bosom friend of Nausicaa's.   She reminded her of her approaching marriage (for
which, however, the bridegroom had not yet been decided
upon), and upbraided her for not making due preparation by
the washing of her own and of the family linen.   She proposed,
therefore, that on the following morning Nausicaa should
take all the unwashed clothes to the washing cisterns, and said
that she would come and help her : the cisterns being some
distance from the town, she advised Nausicaa to ask her father
to let her have a waggon and mules.

Nausicaa, on waking, told her father and mother about her 50
dream, " Papa, dear,"† said she, " could you manage to let me
have a good big waggon ?   I want to take all our dirty clothes
to the river and wash them.   You are the chief man here, so
it is only proper that you should have a clean shirt when you 60
attend meetings of the Council.   Moreover you have five sons,
two of them married, while the other three are good looking
young bachelors ; you know they always like to have clean
linen when they go out to a dance."

Her father promised her all she wanted.   The waggon was 71
made ready, her mother put her up a basket of provisions, and
Nausicaa drove her maids to the bank of the river, where were
the cisterns, through which there flowed enough clear water to
wash clothes however dirty they might be.   They washed their
clothes in the pits by treading upon them, laid them out to dry
upon the sea-beach, had their dinner as the clothes were drying,
and then began to play at ball while Nausicaa sang to them.

In the course of time, when they were thinking about 110

---

* Scheria means " Jutland "—a piece of land jutting out into
the sea.   † Gr. πάππα φίλ', line 57.

starting home, Minerva woke Ulysses, who was in the wood just above them. He sat up, heard the voices and laughter of the women, and wondered where he was.

127   He resolved on going to see, but remembering that he had no clothes on, he held a bough of olive before him, and then, all grim, naked, and unkempt as he was, he came out and drew near to the women, who all of them ran away along the beach and the points that jutted into the sea. Nausicaa, however, stood firm, and Ulysses set himself to consider whether he should go boldly up to her and embrace her knees, or speak to her from a respectful distance.

145   On the whole he concluded that this would be the most prudent course; and having adopted it, he began by asking Nausicaa to inform him whether she was a goddess or no. If she was a goddess, it was obvious from her beauty that she could only be Diana. If on the other hand she was a mortal, how happy would he be whose proposals in the way of settlements had seemed most advantageous, and who should take her to his own home. Finally he asked her to be kind enough to give him any old wrapper which she might have brought with her to wrap the clothes in, and to show him the way to the town.

186   Nausicaa replied that he seemed really to be a very sensible person, but that people must put up with their luck whatever it might happen to be. She then explained that he had come to the land of the Phæacians, and promised to conduct him to their city.

198   Having so said, she told her maids not to be such cowards. "The man," she said, "is quite harmless; we live away from all neighbours on a land's end, with the sea roaring on either side of us, and no one can hurt us. See to this poor fellow, therefore, and give him something to eat."

211   When they heard this the maids came back and gave Ulysses a shirt and cloak; they also gave him a bottle of oil and told him to go and wash in the river, but he said, "I will not wash myself while you keep standing there. I cannot bring myself to strip before a number of good-looking young women." So they went and told their mistress.

When Ulysses had done washing, Minerva made him look 224 much grander and more imposing, and gave him a thick head of hair which flowed down in hyacinthine curls about his shoulders. Nausicaa was very much struck with the change in his appearance. " At first," she said, " I thought him quite plain, but now he is of godlike beauty. I wish I might have such a man as that for my husband, if he would only stay here. But never mind this ; girls, give him something to eat and drink."

The maids then set meat and drink before Ulysses, who 247 was ravenously hungry. While he was eating, Nausicaa got the clothes folded up and put on to the cart ; after which she gave him his instructions. " Follow after the cart," she said, " along with the maids, till you get near the houses. As for the town, you will find it lying between two good harbours, 263 and approached by a narrow neck of land, on either side of which you will see the ships drawn up—for every man has a place where he can let his boat lie. You will also see the walls, and the temple of Neptune standing in the middle of the paved market-place, with the ship-brokers' shops all round it.

" When you get near the town drop behind, for the people 273 here are very ill-natured, and they would talk about me. They would say, ' Who is this fine looking stranger that is going about with Nausicaa ? Where did she find him ? I suppose she is going to marry him. Is he a sailor whom she has picked up from some foreign vessel, or has a god come down from heaven in answer to her prayers and he is going to marry her ? It would be a good thing if she would go and find a husband somewhere else, for she will have nothing to say to any of the many excellent Phæacians who are in love with her.' This is what people would say, and I could not blame them, for I should be scandalised myself if I saw any girl going about with a stranger, while her father and mother were yet alive, without being married to him in the face of all the world.

" Do then as I say. When you come to the grove of 289 Minerva a little outside the town, wait till you think I and the

maids must have got home. Then come after us, ask which is
Alcinous's house, and when you reach it go straight through
the outer and inner courts till you come to my mother. You
will see her sitting with her back to a bearing-post, and
spinning her purple yarn by the fire. My father will be sitting
close by her ; never mind about him, but go and embrace my
mother's knees, for if she looks favourably on your suit you
will probably get what you want."

316   Nausicaa then drove on, and as the sun was about setting
they came to the grove of Minerva, where Ulysses sat down
and waited. He prayed Minerva to assist him, and she heard
his prayer, but she would not manifest herself to him, for she
did not want to offend her uncle Neptune.

Book VII

THE SPLENDOURS OF THE HOUSE OF KING ALCINOUS—QUEEN
ARĒTE WANTS TO KNOW WHERE ULYSSES GOT HIS SHIRT AND
CLOAK, FOR SHE KNOWS THEM AS HER OWN WORK—ULYSSES
EXPLAINS.

WHEN Nausicaa reached home her brothers attended to the
waggon and mules, and her waiting-woman Eurymedusa lit
the fire and brought her supper for her into her own room.

14   Presently Ulysses considered it safe to come on, and entered
the town enveloped in a thick mist which Minerva shed round
him for his protection from any rudeness that the Phæacians
might offer him. She also met him outside the town disguised
as a little girl carrying a pitcher.

21   Ulysses saw her in spite of the mist, and asked her to show
him the way to the house of Alcinous ; this, she said, she could
easily do, and when they reached the house she told Ulysses
all about the king's family history, and advised him how he
should behave himself.

50   "Be bold," she said ; "boldness always tells, no matter
where a man comes from. First find the mistress of the
house. She is of the same family as her husband, and her
descent is in this wise. Eurymedon was king of the giants,
but he and his people were overthrown, and he lost his own

life. His youngest daughter was Peribœa, a woman of sur-
passing beauty, who gave birth by Neptune to Nausithous,
king of the Phæacians. He had two sons, Rhexenor and 62
Alcinous ; Rhexenor died young, leaving an only daughter,
Arēte, whom her uncle Alcinous married, and whom he
honours as no other woman in the whole world is honoured by
her husband. All her family and all her neighbours adore her
as a friend and peacemaker, for she is a thoroughly good
woman. If you can gain her good offices all will go well with
you."

Minerva then left him and went to Marathon and Athens, 78
where she visited the house of Erechtheus, but Ulysses went
on to the house of Alcinous, and he pondered much as he paused
awhile before he reached the threshold of bronze, for the
splendour of the palace was like that of the sun and moon.
The walls on either side were of bronze from end to end, and
the cornice was of blue enamel. The doors were of gold and
hung on pillars of silver that rose from a floor of bronze, while
the lintel was of silver and the hook of the door was of gold.

On either side there were gold and silver mastiffs which 91
Vulcan with his consummate skill had fashioned expressly to
keep watch over the palace of King Alcinous, so they were
immortal and could never grow old. Seats were ranged here
and there all along the wall, from one end to the other, with
coverings of fine woven work, which the women of the house
had made. Here the chief persons of the Phæacians used to
sit and eat and drink, for there was abundance at all seasons ;
and there were golden figures of young men with lighted
torches in their hands, raised on pedestals to give light to them
that sat at meat.

There are fifty women servants in the house, some of whom 103
are always grinding rich yellow grain at the mill, while others
work at the loom and sit and spin, and their shuttles go back-
wards and forwards like the fluttering of aspen leaves,
while the linen is so closely woven that it will turn oil. As
the Phæacians are the best sailors in the world, so their
women excel all others in weaving, for Minerva has taught
them all manner of useful arts, and they are very intelligent.

Outside the gate of the outer court there is a large garden* of about four acres, with a wall all round it. It is full of beautiful trees—pears, pomegranates, and the most delicious apples. There are luscious figs also, and olives in full growth. The fruits never rot nor fail all the year round, neither winter nor summer, for the air is so soft that a new crop ripens before the old has dropped. Pear grows on pear, apple on apple, and fig on fig, and so also with the grapes, for there is an excellent vineyard ; on the level ground of a part of this, the grapes are being made into raisins ; on another part they are being gathered ; some are being trodden in the wine-tubs ; others, further on, have shed their blossom and are beginning to show fruit ; others, again, are just changing colour. In the furthest part of the ground there are beautifully arranged beds of flowers that are in bloom all the year round. Two streams go through it, the one turned in ducts throughout the whole garden, while the other is carried under the ground of the outer court to the house itself, and the townspeople drew water from it. Such, then, were the splendours with which heaven had endowed the house of King Alcinous.

133   So here Ulysses stood for a while and looked about him, but when he had looked long enough he crossed the threshold and went within the precincts of the house. He passed through the crowd of guests who were nightly visitors at the table of King Alcinous, and who were then making
137 their usual drink offering to Mercury before going for the night. He was still shrouded in the mist of invisibility with which Minerva had invested him, and going up to Arēte he embraced her knees, whereon he suddenly became visible. Everyone was greatly surprised at seeing a man there, but Ulysses paid no attention to this, and at once implored the queen's assistance ; he then sat down among the ashes on the hearth.

154   Alcinous did not know what to do or say, nor yet did any one else till one of the guests Echeneüs told him it was not

---

* Penelope and Calypso also had gardens : so had Laertes (xxiv. 247). I remember no allusion to them in the " Iliad."

creditable to him that a suppliant should be left thus grovelling among the ashes. Alcinous ought to give him a seat and set food before him. This was accordingly done, and after Ulysses had finished eating Alcinous made a speech, in which he proposed that they should have a great banquet next day in their guest's honour, and then provide him an escort to take him to his own home. This was agreed to, and after a while the other guests went home to bed.

When they were gone Ulysses was left alone with Alcinous 230 and Arēte sitting over the fire, while the servants were taking the things away after supper. Then Arēte said, " Stranger, before we go any further there is a question I should like to put to you. Who are you ? and who gave you those clothes ? " for she recognised the shirt and cloak Ulysses was wearing as her own work, and that of her maids.

Ulysses did not give his name, but told her how he had 240 come from Calypso's island, and been wrecked on the Phæacian coast. " Next day," he said, " I fell in with your daughter, who treated me with much greater kindness than one could have expected from so young a person—for young people are apt to be thoughtless. It was she who gave me the clothes."

Alcinous then said he wished the stranger would stay with 308 them for good and all and marry Nausicaa. They would not, however, press this, and if he insisted on going they would send him, no matter where. " Even though it be further than Eubœa, which they say is further off than any other place, we will send you, and you shall be taken so easily that you may sleep the whole way if you like."   318

To this Ulysses only replied by praying that the king 329 might be as good as his word. A bed was then made for him in the gate-house and they all retired for the night.

Book VIII

THE PHÆACIAN GAMES AND BANQUET IN HONOUR OF ULYSSES.

When morning came Alcinous called an assembly of the Phæacians, and Minerva went about urging every one to come and see the wonderful stranger. She also gave Ulysses a more imposing presence that he might impress the people favourably. When the Phæacians were assembled Alcinous said :—

28   " I do not know who this stranger is, nor where he comes from ; but he wants us to send him to his own home, and no guest of mine was ever yet able to complain that I did not send him home quickly enough. Let us therefore fit out a new ship with a crew of fifty-two men, and send him. The crew shall come to my house and I will find them in food which they can cook for themselves. The aldermen and councillors shall be feasted inside the house. I can take no denial, and we will have Demodocus to sing to us."

46   The ship and crew were immediately found, and the sailors with all the male part of the population swarmed to the house of Alcinous till the yards and barns and buildings were crowded. The king provided them with twelve sheep, eight pigs and two bullocks, which they killed and cooked.

62   The leading men of the town went inside the inner court-yard ; Pontonous, the *major domo*, conducted the blind bard Demodocus to a seat which he set near one of the bearing-posts that supported the roof of the cloisters, hung his lyre on a peg over his head, and shewed him how to feel for it with his hands. He also set a table close by him with refreshments on it, to which he could help himself whenever he liked.

72   As soon as the guests had done eating Demodocus began to sing the quarrel between Ulysses and Achilles before Troy, a lay which at the time was famous. This so affected Ulysses that he kept on weeping as long as the bard sang, and though he was able to conceal his tears from the company generally, Alcinous perceived his distress and proposed that they should all now adjourn to the athletic sports—which were to consist mainly of boxing, wrestling, jumping, and foot racing.

105   Demodocus, therefore, hung the lyre on its peg and was led out to the place where the sports were to be held. The whole town flocked to see them. Clytoneüs won the foot race, Euryalus took the prize for wrestling, Amphialus was the best jumper, Elatreus the best disc-thrower, and Alcinous' son **Laodamas** the best boxer.

Laodamas and Euryalus then proposed that Ulysses should 131
enter himself for one of the prizes. Ulysses replied that he
was a stranger and a suppliant ; moreover, he had lately gone
through great hardships, and would rather be excused.

Euryalus on this insulted Ulysses, and said that he sup- 158
posed he was some grasping merchant who thought of nothing
but his freights. " You have none of the look," said he, " of
an athlete about you."

Ulysses was furious, and told Euryalus that he was a good- 164
looking young fool. He then took up a disc far heavier than
those which the Phæacians were in the habit of throwing.*
The disc made a hurtling sound as it passed through the air,
and easily surpassed any throw that had been made yet. Thus
encouraged he made another long and very angry speech, in
which he said he would compete with any Phæacian in any
contest they chose to name, except in running, for he was still
so much pulled down that he thought they might beat him
here. " Also," he said, " I will not compete in anything with
Laodamas. He is my host's son, and it is a most unwise thing
for a guest to challenge any member of his host's family. A
man must be an idiot to think of such a thing."

" Sir," said Alcinous, " I understand that you are displeased 236
at some remarks that have fallen from one of our athletes, who
has thrown doubt upon your prowess in a way that no gentleman would do. I hear that you have also given us a general
challenge. I should explain that we are not famous for our
skill in boxing or wrestling, but are singularly fleet runners
and bold mariners. We are also much given to song and
dance, and we like warm baths and frequent changes of linen.
So now come forward some of you who are the nimblest
dancers, and show the stranger how much we surpass other
nations in all graceful accomplishments. Let some one
also bring Demodocus's lyre from my house where he has
left it."

---

* It is a little odd that this disc should have been brought,
considering that none such were used by the Phæacians. We must
suppose that Minerva put it in along with the others, and then shed
a thick darkness over it, which prevented the attendants from
noticing it.

256   The lyre was immediately brought, the dancers began to dance, and Ulysses admired the merry twinkling of their feet.

266   While they were dancing Demodocus sang the intrigue between Mars and Venus in the house of Vulcan, and told how Vulcan took the pair prisoners.   All the gods came to see

324 them ; but the goddesses were modest and would not come.

370   Alcinous then made Halius and Laodamas have a game at ball, after which Ulysses expressed the utmost admiration of their skill.   Charmed with the compliment Ulysses had paid his sons, the king said that the twelve aldermen (with himself, which would make thirteen) must at once give Ulysses a shirt and cloak and a talent of gold, so that he might eat his supper with a light heart.   As for Euryalus, he must not only make a present, but apologise as well, for he had been rude.

398   Euryalus admitted his fault, and gave Ulysses his sword with its scabbard, which was of new ivory.   He said Ulysses would find it worth a great deal of money to him.

412   Ulysses thanked him, wished him all manner of good fortune, and said he hoped Euryalus would not feel the want of the sword which he had just given him along with his apology.

417   Night was now falling, they therefore adjourned to the house of Alcinous.   Here the presents began to arrive, whereon the king desired Arēte to find Ulysses a chest in which to stow them, and to put a shirt and clean cloak in it as his own contribution ; he also declared his intention of giving him a gold cup.*   Meanwhile, he said that Ulysses had better have a warm bath.

433   The bath was made ready.   Arēte packed all the gold and presents which the Phæacian aldermen had sent, as also the shirt and tunic from Alcinous.   Arēte told Ulysses to see to the fastening, lest some one should rob him while he was

445 asleep on the ship ; Ulysses therefore fastened the lid on to

---

* Alcinous never seems to have got beyond saying that he was going to give the cup ; he never gives it, nor yet the talent—the familiar ὡς εἰπὼν ἐν χερσὶ τίθει κ.τ.λ. is noticeably absent.   He found the chest, and he took a great deal of pains about stowing the presents in the ship that was to take Ulysses to Ithaca (see xiii. 18, &c.), but here his contributions seem to have ended.

the chest with a knot which Circe had taught him. He then went into the bath room—very gladly, for he had not had a bath since he left Calypso, who as long as he was with her had taken as good care of him as though he had been a god.

As he came from the bath room Nausicaa was standing by 457 one of the bearing-posts that supported the roof of the cloisters and bade him farewell, reminding him at the same time that it was she who had been the saving of him—a fact which Ulysses in a few words gracefully acknowledged.

He then took his seat at table, and after dinner, at his 469 request, Demodocus sang the Sack of Troy and the Sally of the Achæans from the Wooden Horse. This again so affected him that he could not restrain his tears, which, however, Alcinous again alone perceived.

The king, therefore, made a speech in which he said that 536 the stranger ought to tell them his name. He must have one, for people always gave their children names as soon as they were born. He need not be uneasy about his escort. All he had to do was to say where he wanted to go, and the Phæacian ships were so clever that they would take him there of their own accord. Nevertheless he remembered hearing his father Nausithous say, that one day Neptune would be angry with the Phæacians for giving people escorts so readily, and had said he would wreck one of their ships as it was returning, and would also bury their city under a high mountain.

Book IX

THE VOYAGES OF ULYSSES—THE CICONS, LOTUS EATERS, AND THE CYCLOPS POLYPHEMUS.

Then Ulysses rose. " King Alcinous," said he, " you ask my name and I will tell you. I am Ulysses, and dwell in Ithaca, an island which contains a high mountain called Neritum. In its neighbourhood there are other islands near to one another, Dulichium, Same, and Zacynthus. It lies on the horizon all highest up in the sea towards the West, while 25 the other islands lie away from it to the East. This is the island which I would reach, for however fine a house a man may have in a land where his parents are not, there will still be nothing sweeter to him than his home and his own father and mother.

37   " I will now tell you of my adventures. On leaving Troy we first made a descent on the land of the Cicons, and sacked their city but were eventually beaten off, though we took our booty with us.

62   " Thence we sailed South with a strong North wind behind us, till we reached the island of Cythera, where we were driven off our course by a continuance of North wind which prevented my doubling Cape Malea.

82   " Nine days was I driven by foul winds, and on the tenth we reached the land of the Lotus eaters, where the people were good to my men but gave them to eat of the lotus, which made them lose all desire to return home, so that I had a great work to get those who had tasted it on board again.

105   " Thence we were carried further, till we came to the land of the savage Cyclopes. Off their coast, but not very far, there is a wooded island abounding with wild goats. It is untrodden by the foot of man ; even the huntsmen, who as a 120 general rule will suffer any hardship in forest or on mountain top, never go there ; it is neither tilled nor fed down, but remains year after year uninhabited save by goats only. For the Cyclopes have no ships, and cannot therefore go from place to place as those who have ships can do. If they had ships they would have colonised the island, for it is not at all a bad one and would bring forth all things in their season. There is meadow land, well watered and of good quality, that stretches down to the water's edge. Grapes would do wonderfully well there ; it contains good arable land, which would yield heavy crops, for the soil is rich ; moreover it has a convenient port— into which some god must have taken us, for the night was so dark that we could see nothing. There was a thick darkness all round the ships, neither was there any moon, for the sky was covered with clouds. No one could see the island, nor yet waves breaking upon the shore till we found ourselves in the harbour. Here, then, we moored our ships and camped down upon the beach.

THE CAVE OF POLYPHEMUS

SIG. SUGAMELI AND THE AUTHOR, IN THE CAVE OF POLYPHEMUS

" When morning came we hunted the wild goats, of which 152 we killed over a hundred,* and all day long to the going down of the sun we feasted on them and the store of wine we had taken from the Cicons. We kept looking also on the land of the Cyclopes over against us, which was so near that we could see the smoke of their stubble fires, and almost fancy we heard the bleating of their sheep and goats.

" We camped a second night upon the beach, and at day 169 break, having called a council, I said I would take my own ship and reconnoitre the country, but would leave the other ships at the island. Thereon I started, but when we got near the main land we saw a great cave in the cliff, not far from the sea, and there were large sheep yards in front of it. On landing I chose twelve men and went inland, taking with me a goat skin full of a very wondrous wine that Maron, priest of Apollo, had given me when I spared his life and that of his family at the time that we were sacking the city of the Cicons. The rest of my crew were to wait my return by the sea side.

" We soon reached the cave, and finding that the owner 216 was not at home we examined all that it contained ; we saw vessels brimful of whey, and racks loaded with cheeses : the yards also were full of lambs and kids. My men implored me to let them steal some cheeses, drive off some of the lambs and kids, and sail away, but I would not, for I hoped the owner might give me something.

" We lit a fire in the cave, sacrificed some of the cheeses to 231 the gods, and ate others ourselves, waiting till the owner should return. When he came we found him to be a huge monster, more like a peak standing out against the sky on

---

* Dwellers on the East coast of Sicily believe the island here referred to to be Acitrezza, between Acireale and Catania. I have been all over it and do not believe that it contains more than two acres of land on which any goat could ever have fed. The idea that the writer of the " Odyssey " would make Ulysses and his large body of men spend half a day in killing over a hundred goats on such a site need not be discussed seriously, I shall therefore pass it over without notice when I come to discuss the voyage of Ulysses. That it should be so confidently believed to be the island off the land of the Cyclopes serves as a warning to myself, inasmuch as it shows how easily people can bring themselves to accept any site for any scene if they make up their minds to do so.

some high mountain than a human being. He brought in with
233 him a great bundle of firewood, which he flung down upon the
floor with such a noise that we were scared and hid ourselves.
He drove all his female goats and ewes into the cave, but left
the males outside; and then he closed the door with a huge
stone which not even two and twenty waggons could carry.
245 He milked his goats and ewes all orderly, and gave each one
her own young [for these had been left in the yard all day];
then he drank some of the milk, and put part by for his supper.
Presently he lit his fire and caught sight of us, whereon he
asked us who we were.

256 "I told him we were on our way home from Troy, and
begged him in heaven's name to do us no hurt; but as soon as
I had answered his question he gripped up two of my men,
dashed them on the ground, and ate them raw, blood, bones,
and bowels, like a savage lion of the wilderness. Then he lay
down on the ground of the cave and went to sleep: on which
I should have crept up to him and plunged my sword into his
heart while he was sleeping had I not known that if I did we
should never be able to shift the stone. So we waited till
dawn should come.

307 "When day broke the monster again lit his fire, milked his
ewes all orderly, and gave each one her own young. Then
he gripped up two more of my men, and as soon as he had
eaten them he rolled the stone from the mouth of the cave,
drove out his sheep, and put the stone back again. He had,
however, left a large and long piece of olive wood in the cave,
and when he had gone I and my men sharpened this at one
end, and hid it in the sheep dung of which there was much
in the cave. In the evening he returned, milked his ewes, and
ate two more men; whereon I went up to him with the skin of
wondrous wine that Maron had given me and gave him a bowl
full of it. He asked for another, and then another, so I gave
them to him, and he was so much delighted that he enquired
my name and I said it was Noman.

371 "The wine now began to take effect, and in a short time he
fell dead drunk upon the ground. Then my men and I put
the sharp end of the piece of olive wood in the fire till it was

well burning, and drove it into the wretch's eye, turning it
round and round as though it were an auger. After a while
he plucked it out, flung if from him, and began crying to his
neighbours for help. When they came, they said, 'What ails
you ? Who is harming you ? ' and he answered, ' No man is
harming me.' They then said that he must be ill, and had
better pray to his father Neptune ; so they went away, and I
laughed at the success of my stratagem.

"Then I hid my men by binding them under the sheep's 424
bellies. The Cyclops, whose name was Polyphemus, groped
his way to the stone, rolled it away, and sat at the mouth of
the cave feeling the sheep's backs as they went out ; but the
men were under their bellies so he did not find one of them.
Nor yet did he discover me, for I was ensconced in the thick
belly-fleece of a ram which by some chance he had brought in
with the ewes. But he was near finding me, for the ram went
last, and he kept it for a while and talked to it.

"When we were outside, I dropped from under the ram and
unbound my companions. We drove the ewes down to my 462
ship, got them on board, and rowed out to sea. When we
were a little way out I jeered at the Cyclops, whereon he tore
up a great rock and hurled it after us ; it fell in front of the
ship and all but hit the rudder ; the wash, moreover, that it 483
made nearly carried us back to the land, but I kept the ship
off it with a pole.

"When we had got about twice as far off as we were before, 491
I was for speaking to the Cyclops again, and though my men
tried to stay me, I shouted out to him ' Cyclops, if you would
know who it is that has blinded you, learn that it is I, Ulysses,
son of Laertes, who live in Ithaca.'

"'Alas,' he cried in answer, ' then the old prophecy about 506
me is coming true. I knew that I was to lose my sight by the
hand of Ulysses, but I was looking for some man of great
stature and noble mien, whereas he has proved to be a mere
whippersnapper. Come here, then, Ulysses that I may offer
you gifts of hospitality and pray my father Neptune, who shall
heal my eye, to escort you safely home.'

"'I wish,' said I, 'that I could be as sure of killing you 521 body and soul as I am that not even Neptune will be able to cure your eye.'

526   " Then he prayed to Neptune saying ' Hear me Neptune, if I am indeed your son, and vouchsafe me that Ulysses son of Laertes may never reach his home.   Still, if he must do so, and get back to his friends, let him lose all his men, and though he get home after all, let it be late, on another man's ship, and let him find trouble in his house.'

537   " So saying he tore up a still larger rock and flung it this time a little behind the ship, but so close that it all but hit the rudder : the wash, however, that it made carried us forward to the island from which we had set out.

556   " There we feasted on the sheep that we had taken, and mourned the loss of our comrades whom Polyphemus had eaten.

Book X

ÆOLUS—THE LÆSTRYGONIANS—CIRCE.

" So we sailed on and reached the island where dwells Æolus with his wife and family of six sons and six daughters, who live together amid great and continuous plenty.   I staid with him a whole month, and when I would go, he tied all the winds up (for he was their keeper) in a leather sack, which he gave me ; but he left the West wind free, for this was the one I wanted.

28   " Nine days did we sail, and on the tenth we could see our native land with the stubble fires burning thereon.   I had never let the rudder out of my hands till then, but being now close in shore I fell asleep.   My men, thinking I had treasure in the sack, opened it to see, on which the winds came howling out and took us straight back to the Æolian island.   So I went to the house of Æolus and prayed him to help me, but he said, ' Get you gone, abhorred of heaven : him whom heaven hates will I in no wise help.'   So I went full sadly away.

77   " Six days thence did we sail onward, worn out in body and mind, and on the seventh we reached the stronghold of king Lamus, the Læstrygonian city Telepylus, where the shepherd who drives his flock into the town salutes another who is

driving them out, and the other returns his salute. A man in that country could earn double wages if he could do without sleep, for they work much the same by night as they do by day.* Here we landed, and I climbed a high rock to look round, but could see no signs of man or beast, save only smoke rising from the ground.

"Then I sent two of my crew with an attendant, to see what 100 manner of men the people might be, and they met a young woman who was coming down to fetch water from the spring Artacia, whence the people drew their water. This young woman took my men to the house of her father Antiphates, whereon they discovered the people to be giants and ogres like Polyphemus. One of my men was gripped up and eaten, but the other two escaped and reached the ships. The Læstrygonians raised a hue and cry after them, and rushing to the harbour, within which all my ships were moored except my own, they dashed my whole fleet in pieces with the rocks that they threw. I and my own ship alone escaped them, for we were outside, and I bade the men row for their lives.

"On and on did we sail, till we reached the island of Circe, 133 where heaven guided us into a harbour. Here I again climbed a rock and could see the smoke from Circe's house rising out of a thick wood ; I then went back to the ship, and while on my way had the good fortune to kill a noble stag, which gave us a supply of meat on which we feasted all the rest of the day. Next morning I held a council and told my men of the smoke that I had seen.

"Eurylochus and twenty-two men then went inland to 210 reconnoitre, and found Circe's house made of squared stones and standing on high ground in the middle of the forest. This forest was full of wild beasts, poor dazed creatures whom Circe had bewitched, but they fawned upon my men and did not harm them. When the men got to the door of her house they could hear her singing inside most beautifully, so they called her down, and when she came she asked them in, gave them a drugged drink, and then turned them into pigs—all except Eurylochus who had remained outside.

---

* [See Butler's footnote on this passage in his Translation of the "Odyssey."]

244   "Eurylochus made all haste back to tell me, and I started for Circe's house. When I was in the wood where the wild
277   beasts were, Mercury met me and gave me an herb called
305   Moly, which would protect me from Circe's spells ; he also told me how I should treat her. Then I went to her house, and called her to come down.

312   "She asked me in, and tried to bewitch me as she had the others, but the herb which Mercury had given me protected me ; so I rushed at her with my drawn sword. When she saw this, she said she knew I must be Ulysses, and that I must marry her at once. But I said, ' Circe, you have just turned my men into pigs, and have done your best to bewitch me into the bargain ; how can you expect me to be friendly with you ? Still, if you will swear to take no unfair advantage of me, I will consent.' So she swore, and I consented at once.

348   "Then she set the four maid servants of her house to wash me and feast me, but I was still moody and would not eat till Circe removed her spells from off my men, and brought them back safe and sound in human form. When she had done this she bade me go back to my ship and bring the rest of my men—which I presently did, and we staid with her for a whole twelve months, feasting continually and drinking an untold quantity of wine. At last, however, my men said that if I meant going home at all it was time I began to think of starting.

480   "That night, therefore, when I was in bed with Circe, I told her how my men were murmuring, and asked her to let me go. This she said she would do ; but I must first go down into the house of Hades, and consult the blind Theban prophet Tiresias. And she directed me what I should do.

551   "On the following morning I told my men, and we began to get ready ; but we had an accident before we started, for there was a foolish and not very valiant young man in my ship named Elpenor, who had got drunk and had gone on to the roof of Circe's house to sleep off his liquor in the cool. The bustle my men made woke him, and in his flurry he forgot all about coming down by the staircase, and fell right off the roof ; whereby he broke his neck and was killed. We started,

however, all the same, and Circe brought us a lamb and a black sheep to offer to the Shades below. She passed in and out among us, but we could not see her ; who, indeed, can see the gods, when they are in no mind to be seen ?

Book XI

ULYSSES IN THE HOUSE OF HADES.

" When we were at the water side we got the lamb and the ewe on board and put out to sea, running all that day before a fair wind which Circe had sent us, and at nightfall entering the deep waters of the river Oceanus. Here is the land of the Cimmerians, who dwell in darkness which the sun's rays never pierce ; we therefore made our ship fast to the shore and came out of her, going along the beach till we reached the place of which Circe had told us.

" Perimedes and Eurylochus then held the victims, while I 23 followed the instructions of Circe and slaughtered them, letting their blood flow into a trench which I had dug for it. On this, the ghosts came up in crowds from Erebus, brides, young bachelors, old men, maids who had been crossed in love, and warriors with their armour still smirched with blood. They cried with a strange screaming sound that made me turn pale with fear, but I would let none of them taste of the blood till Tiresias should have come and answered my questions.

" The first ghost I saw was that of Elpenor whose body was 51 still lying unburied at Circe's house. Then I said, ' How now, Elpenor ? you have got here sooner by land than I have done by water.' The poor fellow told me how he had forgotten about the stairs, and begged me to give him all due rites when I returned to Circe's island—which I promised faithfully that I would do.

" Then I saw the ghost of my mother Anticlea, but in all 81 sadness I would not let her taste of the blood till Tiresias should have come and answered my questions.

" Presently Tiresias came with his golden sceptre in his 90 hand, bade me let him taste of the blood, and asked me why I had come.

97   " I told him I would learn how I was to get home to Ithaca,
and he said I should have much difficulty : ' Still,' he continued,
' you will reach your home if you can restrain your men when
you come to the Thrinacian island, where you will find the
cattle of the Sun. If you leave these unharmed, after much
trouble you will yet reach Ithaca ; but if you harm them, you
will lose your men, and though you may get home after all, it
115 will be late, [on another man's ship,* and you will find your
house full of riotous men who are wasting your substance and
wooing your wife.

118   " ' When you have got back you will indeed kill these men
either by treachery or in fair fight, and you must then take an
oar, which you must carry till you have reached a people who
know nothing about the sea and do not mix salt with their
bread. These people have never heard of ships, nor of oars
that are the wings with which ships fly ; I will tell you how you
may know them ; you will meet a man by the way who will
ask you whether it is a winnowing shovel that you have got
upon your shoulder ; when you hear this you must fix your oar
in the ground, and offer sacrifice to Neptune, a ram, a bull, and
a boar ; then go home again, and offer hecatombs to the gods
that dwell in heaven.† As for your own end, death shall come
to you very gently from the sea, and shall take you when you are
137 full of years and peace of mind, and your people shall bless you.']
150   " Having thus said he went back within the house of Hades.
Then I let my mother's ghost draw near and taste of the blood,
whereon she knew me, and asked me what it was that had
brought me though still alive into the abode of death. So I
told her, and asked her how she had come by her end. ' Tell
me, also,' I continued, ' about my father, and the son whom I
left behind me. Is my property still safe in their hands, or
does another hold it who thinks that I shall not return ? Of
177 what mind, again, is my wife ? Does she still live with her
son and keep watch over his estate, or is she already married
to the best man among the Achæans ? '

* See Chapter xv. for reasons why I have bracketed lines 115–137.

† Ulysses was to appease Neptune's anger by going as a missionary
to preach his name among a people that did not know him.

" ' Your wife,' answered my mother, ' is still at home, but 180 she spends her life in tears both night and day.   Telemachus holds your estate, and sees much company, for he is a magistrate and all men invite him.   Your father lives a poor hard life in the country and never goes near the town.   As for me, I died of nothing but sheer grief on your account.   And now, return to the upper world as fast as you can, that you may tell all that you have seen to your wife.'

" Then Proserpine sent up the ghosts of the wives and 225 daughters of great kings and heroes of old time, and I made each of them tell me about herself.   There were Tyro, Antiope, Alcmena, Epicaste the mother of Œdipus, Chloris, Leda, Iphimedea, Phædra, Procris, Ariadne, and hateful Eriphyle ; with all these did I discourse, nor can I tell you with how many more noble women, for it is now late, and time to go to rest."

Here Ulysses ceased, and from one end of the covered 333 cloisters to the other his listeners sat entranced with the charm of his story.

Then Arête said, " What think you of this man now, 336 Phæacians, both as regards his personal appearance and his abilities ?   True he is my guest, but his presence is an honour to you all.   Be not niggardly, therefore, in the presents that you will make him, for heaven has endowed you all with great abundance."   Alcinous also spoke urging Ulysses to tell still more of his adventures, and to say whether he met any of the heroes who had fought together with him at Troy.   Thus pressed Ulysses resumed his story.

" When Proserpine," said he, " had dismissed the female 385 ghosts, the ghost of Agamemnon drew near, surrounded by those of the men who had fallen with him in the house of Ægisthus.   He was weeping bitterly, and I asked him how he met his end ; whereon he detailed to me the treachery of Clytemnestra, which he said threw disgrace upon all women, even on the good ones.   ' Be sure,' he continued, ' that you 433 never be too open with your wife ; tell her a part only, and keep the rest to yourself.   Not that you need have any fear about Penelope for she is an admirable woman.   You will

449 meet your son, too, who by this time must be a grown man. Nevertheless, do not let people know when you are coming home, but steal a march upon them. And now give me what news you can about my son Orestes.' To which I answered that I could tell him nothing.

465 "While we were thus holding sad talk with one another, the ghost of Achilles came up and asked me for news of his father Peleus, and of his son. I said I could tell him nothing about Peleus, but his son Neoptolemus was with me in the wooden horse, and though all the others were trembling in every limb and wiping the tears from their cheeks, Neoptolemus did not even turn pale, nor shed a single tear. Whereon Achilles strode away over a meadow full of asphodel, exulting in the prowess of his son.

541 "Other ghosts then came up and spoke with me but that of Ajax alone held aloof, for he was still brooding over the armour of Achilles which had been awarded to me and not to him. I spoke to him but he would not answer ; nevertheless I should have gone on talking to him till he did, had I not been anxious to see yet other ghosts.

568 "I saw Minos with his golden sceptre passing sentence on the dead ; Orion also, driving before him over a meadow full of asphodel the ghosts of the wild beasts whom he had slain upon the mountains. I saw Tityus with the vulture ever digging its beak into his liver, Tantalus also, in a lake whose waters reached his neck but fled him when he would drink, and Sisyphus rolling his mighty stone uphill till the sweat ran off him and the steam rose from him.

601 "Then I saw mighty Hercules. The ghosts were screaming round him like scared birds, flying all whithers. He looked black as night with his bare bow in his hand and his arrow on the string, glaring round as though ever on the point of taking aim. About his breast there was a wondrous golden belt marvellously enriched with bears, wild boars, and lions with gleaming eyes ; there were also war, battle, and death.

630 "And I should have seen yet others of the great dead had not the ghosts come about me in so many thousands that I feared Proserpine might send up the Gorgon's head. I there-

fore bade my men make all speed back to their ship ; so they hastened on board and we rowed out on to the waters of Oceanus, where before long we fell in with a fair wind.

Book XII

THE SIRENS—SCYLLA AND CHARYBDIS—THE CATTLE OF THE SUN.

" As soon as we were clear of the river Oceanus, we got out into the open and reached the Ææan island, where there is dawn and sunrise. There we landed, camped down upon the beach, and waited till morning came. At daybreak I sent my men to fetch the body of Elpenor, which we burned and buried. We built a barrow over him, and in it we fixed the oar with which he had been used to row.

" When Circe heard that we had returned, she came down 16 with her maids, bringing bread and wine. ' To-day,' she said, ' eat and drink, and to-morrow go on your way.'

" We agreed to this, and feasted the live-long day to the 28 going down of the sun, but at nightfall Circe took me aside, and told me of the voyage that was before us. ' You will first,' said she, ' come to the island of the two Sirens, who sit in a field of flowers, and warble all who draw near them to death with the sweetness of their song. Dead men's bones are lying strewn all round them ; still, if you would hear them, you can stop your men's ears with wax and bid them bind you to a cross-plank on the mast.

" ' As regards the next point that you will reach I can give 55 you no definite instructions as to which of two courses you must take. You must do the best you can. I can only put the alternatives before you. I refer to the cliffs which the gods call " the wanderers," and which close in on anything that would pass through them—even upon the doves that are bringing ambrosia to Father Jove. The sea moreover is strewn with wreckage from ships which the waves and hurricanes of fire have destroyed.

73   " ' Of the two rocks,* the one rises in a peak to heaven, and
is overhung at all times with a dark cloud that never leaves it.
It looks towards the West, and there is a cave in it, higher
than an arrow can reach. In this sits Scylla yelping with a
squeaky voice like that of a young hound, but she is an awful
monster with six long necks and six heads with three rows of
teeth in each ; whenever a ship passes, she springs out and
snatches up a man in each mouth.

101   " ' The other rock is lower, but they are so close that you
can shoot an arrow from the one to the other. [On it there is
103 a fig-tree in full leaf].† Underneath it is the terrible whirlpool of Charybdis, which sucks the water down and vomits it
out again three times a day. If you are there when she is
sucking, not even Neptune can save you ; so hug the Scylla
side, for you had better lose six men than your whole crew.

127   " ' You will then arrive at the Thrinacian island, where you
will see the cattle of the sun (and also his sheep) in charge of
132 the two nymphs Lampetie and Phaëthusa. If you leave these
flocks unharmed, after much trouble you will yet reach Ithaca ;
but if you harm them, you will lose your men, and though you
may get home after all, it will be late.'

142   " Here she ended, and at break of day we set out, with a
fair wind which Circe sent us. I then told my men about the
two Sirens, but had hardly done so before we were at the island
itself, whereon it fell a dead calm. I kneaded wax and stopped
the men's ears ; they bound me to a cross-plank on the
mast ; I heard the Sirens sing, and when I struggled to
free myself they bound me still tighter. So we passed the
island by.

201   " Shortly after this I saw smoke and a great wave ahead,
and heard a dull thumping sound. The sea was in an uproar,
and my men were so frightened that they loosed hold of their

---

* The want of coherence here is obvious, but as it is repeated
when Ulysses ought to come to the wandering cliffs (which he never
does) it must be referred to a *lacuna* not in the text, but in the
writer's sources of information—of which she seems fully aware.

† I suppose this line to have been added when lines 426–446 of
this book were added.

oars, till I put heart into them, bade them row their hardest, and told the steersman to hug the Scylla side. But I said nothing about Scylla, though I kept straining my eyes all over her rock to see if I could espy her.

" So there we were, with Scylla on the one hand and dread 234 Charybdis on the other. We could see the sea seething as in a cauldron, and the black ooze at the bottom with a wall of whirling waters careering round it. While my men were pale with fear at this awful sight, Scylla shot out her long necks and swooped down on six of them. I could see their poor hands and feet struggling in the air as she bore them aloft, and hear them call out my name in one last despairing cry. This was the most horrid sight that I saw in all my voyages.

" Having passed the cliffs,* and Scylla and Charybdis, we 260 came to the Thrinacian island, and from my ship I could hear the cattle lowing, and the sheep bleating. Then, remembering the warning that Tiresias and Circe had given me, I bade my men give the island a wide berth. But Eurylochus was insolent, and sowed disaffection among them, so that I was forced to yield and let them land for the night, after making them swear most solemnly that they would do the cattle no harm. We camped, therefore, on the beach near a stream.

" But in the third watch of the night there came up a great 312 gale, and in the morning we drew our ship ashore and left her in a large cave wherein the sea nymphs meet and hold their dances. I then called my men together, and again warned them.

" It blew a gale from the South for a whole month, except 325 when the wind shifted to the East, and there was no other wind save only South and East. As long as the corn and wine which Circe had given us held out, my men kept their word, but after a time they began to feel the pangs of hunger, and I went apart to pray heaven to take compassion upon us. I washed my hands and prayed, and when I had done so, I fell asleep.

* The wandering cliffs are certainly intended, for when Ulysses is recapitulating his adventures in Book xxiii. he expressly mentions having reached the πλαγκτὰς πέτρας, just after the Sirens, and before Scylla and Charybdis (xxiii. 327). The writer is determined to have them in her story however little she may know about them.

339   " Meanwhile Eurylochus set my men on to disobey me, and they drove in some of the cattle and killed them. When I woke, and had got nearly back to the ship, I began to smell roast meat and knew full well what had happened.

374   " The nymph Lampetie went immediately and told the Sun what my men had done. He was furious, and threatened Jove that if he was not revenged he would never shine in heaven again but would go down and give his light among the dead. ' All day long,' said he. ' whether I was going up heaven or down, there was nothing I so dearly loved to look upon as those cattle.'

385   " Jove told him he would wreck our ship as soon as it was well away from land, and the Sun said no more. I know all this because Calypso told me, and she had it from Mercury.

397   " My men feasted six days—alarmed by the most awful prodigies : for the skins of the cattle kept walking about, and the joints of meat lowed while they were being roasted. On the seventh day the wind dropped and we got away from the island, but as soon as we were out of sight of land a sudden squall sprang up, during which Jove struck our ship with his thunderbolts and broke it up. All my men were drowned, and so too should I have been, had I not made myself a raft by lashing the mast (which I found floating about) and the ship's keel together.

426 [" The wind, which during the squall came from the West, now changed to the South, and blew all night, so that by morning I was back between Scylla and Charybdis again. My raft got carried down the whirlpool, but I clung on to the boughs of the fig tree, for a weary weary while, during which I felt as impatient as a magistrate who is detained in court by troublesome cases when he wants to get home to dinner. But in the course of time my raft worked its way out again, and when it was underneath me I dropped on to it and was carried out of the pool. Happily for me Jove did not let Scylla see me.]*

447   " Thence I was borne along for nine days in the sea, and was

---

* I incline to think that these lines are an after thought, added by the writer herself.

taken to the Ogygian island of Calypso. I told you about this yesterday and will not repeat it, for I hate saying the same thing twice over."

Book XIII

ULYSSES IS TAKEN BACK TO ITHACA BY THE PHÆACIANS.

Thus did Ulysses speak, and Alcinous immediately proposed that they should make him still further presents. The expense, however, of these, he said, should be borne by a levy or rate upon the public at large. The guests assented, and then went home to bed.

Next morning they brought their presents of hardware 18 down to the ship, and Alcinous saw them so stowed that they should not incommode the rowers. There was then a second banquet at Alcinous's house, but Ulysses kept looking at the sun all the time, longing for it to set that he might start on his way. At last he rose and addressed the Phæacians ; after thanking them, he concluded by saying that he hoped he should find his wife on his return living among her friends in peace 43 and quietness,* and that the Phæacians would continue to give satisfaction to their wives and children. He also bade farewell to Arête, and wished her all happiness with her children, her people, and with King Alcinous.

When Ulysses reached the ship, a rug and sail were spread 73 for him, on which he lay down, and immediately fell into a deep sleep—so deep as to resemble death itself. The ship sped 80 on her way faster than a falcon's flight and with the break of day they reached Ithaca.

Now in Ithaca there is a sheltered harbour in which a ship 96 can ride without being even moored. At the head of this there is a large olive tree, near which there is a cave sacred to the Naiads, where you may find their cups and amphoræ of stone, and the stone looms whereon they weave their robes of sea-purple—very curious. The wild bees, too, build their nests in it. There is water in it all the year round, and it has two entrances, one looking North, by which mortals can go down

---

* σὺν ἀρτεμέεσσι φίλοισιν.

into the cave, and the other towards the South, but men cannot enter by it—it is the way taken by gods.

112   The sailors knew this harbour, and took the ship into it. They were rowing so hard that they ran half her length on to the shore, and when they had got out of her they took Ulysses off, still fast asleep on his rug and sail, and laid him down on the ground.   Hard by him they also laid all the presents the Phæacians had made him ; they left them by the roots of the olive tree, a little out of the path, that no passer by might steal them, and then went back to Scheria.

125   Neptune now saw what the Phæacians had done, and went to consult Jove how he should be revenged.   It was arranged that he should go to Scheria, turn the ship into stone just as it

163   was coming into port, and root it in the sea.   So he did this, and the Phæacians said, " Alack, who has rooted the ship in the sea just as it was coming in ?   We could see all of it a minute ago."

171   Then Alcinous told them how Neptune had long ago threatened to do this to some Phæacian ship on its return from giving an escort, and also to bury their city under a high mountain as a punishment for giving escorts so freely.   The Phæacians, therefore, made ready great sacrifices to Neptune, that he might have mercy upon them.

185   While they were thus standing round the altar of the god, Ulysses woke in his own land, but he had been away so long that he did not know it.   Minerva, too, had shed a thick mist round him so that he might remain unseen while she told him how things were going on ; for she did not want his wife or anyone else to know of his return until he had taken his revenge upon the suitors.   Therefore she made everything look strange to him—the long straight paths, the harbours with their shipping, the steep precipices, and the trees.

197   Ulysses now stood up and wondered where he was.   He did not believe he was in Ithaca and complained bitterly of the Phæacians for having brought him wrong.   Then he counted all the tripods, cauldrons, gold, and raiment, that they had given him, to see if he had been robbed ; but everything was there, and he was in dismay as to what he should do with them.

As he was thus in doubt Minerva came up to him disguised as a young shepherd, so he asked her what country he was in, and she answered that he was in Ithaca.

Ulysses said he had heard that there was such a place ; he 256 told Minerva a long lying story as to how he had come to be where she saw him, and on this the goddess assumed the form of a woman, fair, stately, and wise, and laughed at him for not knowing her. Ulysses answered that she was not an easy person to recognise for she was continually changing her appearance. Moreover, though she had been very good to him at Troy, she had left him in the lurch ever since, until she had taken him into the city of the Phæacians. " Do not," he said, " deceive me any further, but tell me whether or no this is really Ithaca."

" You are always cunning and suspicious," replied the 329 goddess, " and that is why I cannot find it in my heart to leave you. Any one else on returning from a long voyage would have at once gone up to his house to see his wife and children, but you do not seem to care about knowing anything about them, and only think of testing your wife's fidelity. As for my having left you in the lurch, I knew all the time that 339 you would get home safely in the end, and I did not want to quarrel with my uncle Neptune. I will now prove to you that you are in Ithaca—Here is the harbour of the old merman 345 Phorcys, with the large olive tree at the head of it ; near it is the cave which is sacred to the Naiads ; here, again, is the 347 overarching cavern in which you have sacrificed many a 349 hecatomb to the nymphs, and this is the wooded mountain of Neritum."   351

The goddess then dispersed the mist and let the prospect 352 be seen. Ulysses was thus convinced, and Minerva helped him to hide the treasure which the Phæacians had given him, by concealing it in the cave. Having done this she bade Ulysses consider how he should kill the wicked suitors. " They have been lording it," she said, " in your house this three years,*

---

* Minerva, in her desire to minimise the time during which the suitors had been at Ulysses' house, seems to have forgotten that they had been there ever since Telemachus was quite a child (" Od." ii. 312–314).

paying court to your wife and making her gifts of wooing,
380 while she, poor woman, though she flatters them, and holds out
hopes to every man of them by sending him messages, is really
plunged in the deepest grief on your account, and does not
mean a word of what she says."

382   "Great heavens," replied Ulysses, "what a narrow escape
I have had from meeting the fate of Agamemnon. Stand by
me, goddess, and advise me how I shall be revenged."

397   "I will disguise you," said Minerva, "as a miserable old
beggar so that no one shall know you. When I have done so,
go to your swineherd, who has been always loyal to you and
yours. You will find him with his pigs by the fountain
Arethusa near the rock that is called Raven. Meantime I will
go to Sparta and fetch Telemachus, who is gone thither to try
and get news of you."

416   "But why," Ulysses answered, "did you not tell him, for
you knew all about it ? "

420   "Do not be uneasy about him," she answered, "he is in
the midst of great abundance. I sent him, that he might get
himself a good name by having gone."

429   Minerva then disguised Ulysses beyond all possible recog-
nition, and the two separated—she going to Sparta, and
Ulysses to the abode of his swineherd.

Book XIV

ULYSSES IN THE HUT OF EUMÆUS.

Ulysses followed a steep path that led from the harbour
through the forest and over the top of the mountain, till he
reached the hut of Eumæus, who was the most thrifty servant
he had, and had built a number of fine yards and pigstyes
during his master's absence.

5   Ulysses found him sitting at the door of his hut, which had
been built high up in a place that could been seen from far ;
he had his four fierce dogs about him, and was cutting himself
out a pair of sandal shoes.

29   The dogs flew at Ulysses, and it was all Eumæus could do
to check them ; "They were like," said he, "to have made an

end of you, which would have got me into a scrape, and I am
in sorrow enough already through the loss, which I deplore
without ceasing, of the best of masters. But come in, have
something to eat, and then tell me your story."

On this he brought him inside, threw some brushwood on 48
the floor, and spread a goat's skin over it for Ulysses to lie on.
"I cannot do much for you," he said ; "servants go in fear
when they have young lords over them, as I now have, for my
good old master went to Troy with Agamemnon and I shall
never see him again."

He then went out and killed two sucking pigs, singed them, 72
cut them up, put the pieces of meat on skewers to roast on the
embers, and brought them smoking hot, skewers and all, to
Ulysses, who floured them. "Eat," said the swineherd, "a
dish of servant's pork ; the fuller grown meat has to go down
to the suitors." He then explained how rich Ulysses was.

"And who, pray," said Ulysses, "was this noble master of 115
yours ? You say that he fell at Troy, and in that case I might
be able to give you news of him."

"That," answered Eumæus, "may not be : people are 121
always coming and flattering my poor mistress with false
hopes, but they are all liars. My master Ulysses is dead and
gone, and I shall never see another like him. I cannot bear
even to mention his name."

"My friend," replied Ulysses, "do not be too hard of belief. 148
I swear by this hearth to which I am now come, that Ulysses
will return before the present month is over. If he comes you
shall give me a shirt and cloak, but I will take nothing till
then."

"My friend," said Eumæus, "say not another word. You 165
will never get your shirt and cloak. Now, moreover, I am as
anxious about his son Telemachus as I have been about Ulysses
himself ; for he is gone to Pylos, and the suitors are lying in
wait for him on his return. Let us, however, say no more
about him now ; tell me, rather, about yourself, who you are
and how you came here."

Then Ulysses told him a long lying story about his adven- 191
tures in Crete : how he was compelled to go to Troy in joint

command with Idomeneus over the Cretan forces ; how he made a descent on Egypt, got taken prisoner, acquired wealth, and afterwards was inveigled into going to Libya ; how on the voyage thither, after leaving Crete, the ship was wrecked and he was cast on the coast of Thesprotia. " Here it was," he continued, " that I heard of Ulysses from King Pheidon, who was expecting him back daily from Dodona, where he had been to consult the oracle ; he told me Ulysses was to return to Ithaca immediately, but there was a ship bound for Dulichium, and the king sent me on board it before Ulysses returned from Dodona. The sailors on this ship resolved to sell me as a slave, and bound me ; but they landed on the coast of Ithaca, where I gave them the slip, and found my way to your hut."

360   " Poor man," answered the swineherd, " but you will never get me to believe about Ulysses. Why should you tell me such lies ? I have heard these stories too often, and will never believe them again."

390   Ulysses tried still further to convince him, but it was no use, and presently the under swineherds came back with the pigs that had been out feeding, and Eumæus told them to kill the best pig they had, and get supper ready, which they accordingly did. He was a good man and mindful of his duties to the gods, so when the pig was killed he threw some of its bristles into the fire and prayed heaven for the return of Ulysses. Then they supped and went to bed.

457   Now it was a wild rough night, and after they had lain down, Ulysses, fearing that he might be cold, told another lying story of an adventure he had had at Troy in company with Ulysses, by means of which Eumæus was induced to cover him over with a spare cloak of his own. Then the swineherd went out to pass the night with the pigs—and Ulysses was pleased at seeing how well he looked after his property, though he believed his master to be absent. First he slung his sword over his shoulders, and put on a thick cloak to keep out the wind ; he also took the skin of a well-fed goat, and a javelin in case of attack from men or dogs. Thus equipped he went to his rest where the pigs were camped under an overhanging rock that sheltered them from the North Wind.

Book XV

TELEMACHUS RETURNS FROM PYLOS, AND ON LANDING GOES TO
THE HUT OF EUMÆUS.

Minerva now went to Lacedæmon and found Telemachus
and Pisistratus fast asleep. She appeared to Telemachus in a
dream, and told him that he was to return at once to Ithaca,
for his mother was about to marry Eurymachus, and would 17
probably go off with some of his property. She also told him
how the suitors were lying in wait for him in the straits
between Ithaca and Samos. She said that as soon as he 29
reached Ithaca he was to leave the ship before sending it on
to the town, and go to the swineherd's hut. "Sleep there,"
she said, "and in the morning send the swineherd to tell
Penelope that you have returned safely."

Then she went away and Telemachus woke up. He kicked 43
Pisistratus to wake him, and said that they must start at
once. Pisistratus answered that this was impossible ; it was
still dark, and they must say good bye to Menelaus, who, if
Telemachus would only wait, would be sure to give him a
present.

At break of day, seeing Menelaus up and about, Telemachus 56
flung on his shirt and cloak, and told him that they must go.

Menelaus said he would not detain them, but on the score 67
alike of propriety and economy, they must have something to
eat before starting, and also receive the presents that were
waiting Telemachus's acceptance. "I will tell the servants,"
said he, "to get something ready for you of what there may be
in the house, and if you would like to make a tour of the
principal cities of the Peloponnese, I will conduct you. No one
will send us away empty handed. Every one will give us
something."

But Telemachus said he must start at once, for he had left 86
property behind him that was insecurely guarded.

When Menelaus heard this he told his wife and servants to 92
get dinner ready at once. Eteoneus, who lived at no great
distance, now came up, and Menelaus told him to light the fire
and begin cooking ; and he did as he was told.

99   Menelaus then went down into his store room together with Megapenthes, and brought up a double cup and a silver mixing bowl, while Helen fetched a dress of wondrous beauty, the work of her own hands.   Menelaus presented the cup and 125 mixing bowl, and then Helen said, " Take this, my son, as a keepsake from the hand of Helen, and let your bride wear it on her wedding day. Till then let your dear mother keep it for you. Thus may you go on your way with a light heart."

130   Telemachus thanked her ; Pisistratus stowed the presents in the chariot, and they all sat down to dinner. Eteoneus carved, and Megapenthes served round the wine. When they had done eating the two young men prepared to set out.

160   As they were on the point of starting, an eagle flew upon their right hand, with a goose in its talons which it had carried off from the farm yard. This omen was so good that every one was delighted to see it, and Pisistratus said, " Say, king Menelaus, is the omen for us or for yourself ? "

169   Menelaus was in doubt how to answer, but Helen said that as the eagle had come from a mountain and seized the goose, so Ulysses should return and take vengeance on the suitors. Telemachus said he only hoped it might prove so, and the pair then drove on. They reached Pylos on the following day, and 199 Telemachus urged Pisistratus to drive him straight to his ship, for fear Nestor should detain him if he went to his house.

211   " I know," said Pisistratus, " how obstinate he is. He would come down to your ship, if he knew you were there, and would never go back without you. But he will be very angry." He then drove to the ship, and Telemachus told the crew to get her under way as fast as they could.

222   Now as he was attending to every thing and sacrificing to Minerva, there came to him a man of the race of Melampus who was flying from Argos because he had killed a man. His name was Theoclymenus and he came of an old and highly honourable family, his father and grandfather having been celebrated prophets and divines. He besought Telemachus to take him to Ithaca and thus save him from enemies who were in pursuit. Telemachus consented, took Theoclymenus on board, and laid his spear down on the deck.

Then they sailed away, and next day they got among the 287
flying islands,* whereon Telemachus wondered whether he
should be taken or should escape.

All this time Ulysses was in the hut with Eumæus, and 301
after supper Ulysses said he should like to go down to the
town next day, and see if the suitors would take him into their
service. Eumæus at once explained to him that any such idea
was out of the question. " You do not know," he said, " what
men these suitors are ; their insolence reaches heaven ; the
young men who wait on them have good looking faces and
well kempt heads ; the tables are always clean and loaded
with abundance. The suitors would be the death of you ; stay
here, then, where you are in nobody's way, till Telemachus
returns from Pylos."

Ulysses thanked Eumæus for his information, and then 340
began to ask whether his father and mother were still living ;
he was told that Anticlea was dead,† and that Laertes, though
still alive, would be glad to follow her. Eumæus said he had
been brought up in their service, and was better off formerly,
for there was no getting a good word out of his mistress now,
inasmuch as the suitors had turned the house upside down.
" Servants," he said, " like to have a talk with their mistress
and hear things from her own lips ; they like being told to eat
and drink, and being allowed to take something back with
them into the country. This is what will keep servants cheerful
and contented."

On being further questioned by Ulysses, Eumæus told how 380
he had been kidnapped as a child by some Phœnician traders
who had seduced his nurse (also a Phœnician) and persuaded
her to go away with them, and bring him with her.

" I was born," he said, " in the island of Syra over against 403
Ortygia, where the sun turns.‡ It is not populous, but contains two cities which occupy the whole land between them,
and my father was king over them both. A few days after my

* *i.e.* which seemed to fly past them.

† According to tradition, she had hanged herself on hearing a
report of the death of her son.

‡ See Chapter xii. near the beginning.

nurse had kidnapped me, and while we were on our voyage, Diana killed her, and she was flung overboard, but I was taken to Ithaca where Laertes bought me."

493 Ulysses and Eumæus spent the greater part of the night talking with one another, and at dawn Telemachus's crew drew near to land, furled their sails and rowed into the harbour. There they threw out their mooring stones, made their ship fast, landed, and ate their dinner on the shore. When they had done, Telemachus said, " Now take the ship on to the city ; I will go to look after my farm and will come down in the evening. Tomorrow morning I will give you all a hearty meal to reward you for your trouble."

508 " But what," said Theoclymenus, " is to become of me ? To whose house am I to go ? "

512 " At any other time," answered Telemachus, " I should take you to my own house, but you would not find it convenient now, for I shall not be there, and my mother will not see you. I shall therefore send you to the house of Eurymachus, who is one of the first men we have, and is most eager in his suit for my mother's hand."

525 As he spoke a hawk flew on Telemachus's right hand, with a dove whose feathers it was plucking while it flew. Theoclymenus assured Telemachus that this was an omen which boded most happily for the prosperity of his house. It was then settled that Theoclymenus should go to the house of Piræus the son of Clytius.

547 The crew now loosed the ship from her moorings and went on as they had been told to do, while Telemachus wended his way in all haste to the pig farm where Eumæus lived.

Book XVI

ULYSSES AND TELEMACHUS BECOME KNOWN TO ONE ANOTHER.

Ulysses and Eumæus prepared their meal at daybreak. When Telemachus was reaching the hut, Ulysses observed that the dogs did not bark, though he heard footsteps, and 7 enquired whether the visitor was some acquaintance of the swineherd's. He had hardly done speaking when Telemachus entered, and was welcomed by Eumæus.

"Is my mother still at the house," said he, "or has she 33 left it with another husband, so that the bed of Ulysses is festooned with cobwebs ? "

"She is still there," answered Eumæus, "spending her 36 time in tears both night and day."

Eumæus set refreshments before him and when he had done 49 eating he asked who the stranger might be.

When Telemachus heard that Ulysses was a ship-wrecked 68 suppliant he was much displeased. "I am as yet too young," he said, "to be able to hold my own in the house ; what sufficient support, then, can I give this man ? Still, as he has come to you I will send him clothes and all necessary food ; and let him stay with you ; I will not have him go near the suitors, for harm would be sure to come of it."

Ulysses expressed his surprise and indignation about the 90 suitors, whereon Telemachus explained still further, and wound up by telling Eumæus to go at once and inform Penelope of his return. Eumæus asked if he should turn a little out of his way and tell Laertes, but Telemachus said he was not to do so. Penelope would send him word all in due course.

As soon as Eumæus was gone Minerva came to the hut. 157 Ulysses knew her, and so did the dogs, for they went whining away to the other end of the yards, but Telemachus did not see her. She made a sign to Ulysses that he was to come outside, and when he had done so she told him he was to reveal himself to his son—whereon she struck him with her wand, endowed him with a noble presence, and clothed him in goodly raiment.

Then he went back into the hut and told his son who 178 he was ; but for a long while Telemachus would not believe. At last, however, when he was convinced, the pair flung their arms about each other's neck, and wept like eagles or vultures who had been robbed of their young. Indeed they would have wept till sundown had it not occurred to Telemachus to ask his father in what ship he had come to Ithaca, and whose crew it was that had brought him.

225   Ulysses told him about the Phæacians, and how he had hidden the presents they had given him. " I am now come," he said, " by Minerva's advice, to consult with you as to how we shall take vengeance on the suitors. I would therefore learn how many there are of them, and consider whether we two can kill them, or whether we must get help from outside."

240   Telemachus said it was hopeless to think of attacking the suitors without assistance. There were fifty-two from Dulichium, with six followers, twenty-four from Same, twenty from Zacynthus, and twelve from Ithaca.

258   Ulysses explained that he could rely on help from Jove and from Minerva, and thought that this would be enough. " They will not be long in joining us," said he, " when the fight has begun in good earnest. Go, then, tomorrow to the town, and join the suitors ; let the swineherd bring me later, disguised as a poor miserable beggar. Never mind how much violence you may see the suitors do me. Look on and say nothing, beyond asking them in a friendly way to leave me alone. Also, find some pretext for removing the armour from the walls. Say it is taking harm with the smoke, and that the sight of armour sometimes sets men fighting, so that it is better away—but
295 leave two swords, shields and spears for you and me to snatch up."

321   As they were thus conversing, the ship that had brought Telemachus from Pylos reached the harbour of Ithaca, and the crew took the presents which Menelaus had given him to the house of Clytius. They sent a man to tell Penelope that Telemachus was at the farm, and had sent the ship on to allay her anxiety. This man and the swineherd met at the house of Ulysses, and the man said, in the presence of the maids, " Madam, your son is returned from Pylos ;" but Eumæus stood by her, and told her all that her son had bidden him. Then he went back to his pig farm.

342   The suitors were very angry, and were about sending a ship to fetch those who had been lying in wait for Telemachus, when Amphinomus, a suitor, happened to turn round and saw their ship coming into harbour. So he laughed and said, " We have no need to send, for the men are here." On this they all

went to meet the ship, and Antinous said that as Telemachus
had escaped them in spite of their great vigilance, they must
kill him, either at the farm or as he was coming thence.
Otherwise he would expose their plot, and they would have the
people rise against them.   " If," he concluded, " this does not
please you, and you would let him live, we cannot eat up his
estate any longer, but must go home, urge our suit each from
his own house, and let the one among us take Penelope who
will give most for her, or whose lot it may happen to be."

Amphinomus, who came from the well-grassed and grain- 394
growing island of Dulichium, then spoke.   He was a man of
good natural disposition, and his conversation was more
pleasing to Penelope than that of any of the other suitors ;
" I will only consent to kill Telemachus," said he, " if the gods
give us their approval.   It is a serious thing to kill a man who
is of royal race.   If they sanction it, I will be with you ; otherwise I am for letting it alone."

The rest assented, and they went back to the house.   But 406
Medon told Penelope of this new plot, so she went attended by
her gentlewomen, stood by one of the bearing-posts that supported the roof of the cloister, and bitterly rebuked Antinous
for his ingratitude in forgetting how Ulysses in old days had
saved the life of his father Eupeithes.

Eurymachus then made a fair but false speech vowing 434
eternal friendship to Telemachus, and Penelope returned to
her own room to mourn her husband till Minerva closed her
eyes in slumber.

In the evening Eumæus got back to his hut just as the 452
others had killed a yearling pig and were getting supper ready.
Meanwhile Minerva had again disguised Ulysses as an old
beggar.

" What news from the town, Eumæus ? " said Telemachus. 460
" Have the suitors got back with their ship ? "

" I did not ask," answered Eumæus, " for when I had given 464
my message I turned straight home ; but I met the messenger
from your own crew, who told your mother of your return
before I could do so.   As I was coming here, and was on the
hill of Mercury above the town, I saw a ship with many men

and much armour coming into port ; so I suppose it was the suitors, but I cannot be sure."

476 Telemachus gave his father a look, but so that the swineherd could not see him. Then they all got their supper and went to bed.

Book XVII

TELEMACHUS GOES TO THE TOWN, AND IS FOLLOWED BY EUMÆUS
AND ULYSSES, WHO IS MALTREATED BY THE SUITORS.

When morning came Telemachus told Eumæus that he would now go to the town and show himself to his mother, who would never be comforted till she saw him with her own eyes. "As for this miserable stranger," he continued, "take him to the town, that he may beg there and get what he can ; if this does not please him, so much the worse for him, but I like to say what I mean."

16 Ulysses said he should be glad to go, for a beggar could do much better in town than country ; but he must warm himself first, and wait till the sun had got some heat in it ; his clothes were very bad, and he should perish with cold, for the town was some way off.

26 Telemachus then left, and when he reached the house he set his spear against a strong bearing post, crossed the stone pavement and went inside. He found Euryclea putting the sheep skins on to the seats. She and all the other maids ran up to him as soon as they saw him, and kissed him on the head and shoulders. Then Penelope came weeping from her room, embraced him, and told him to tell her all that he had seen.

45 Telemachus bade her go back to her room and pray to Minerva that they might be revenged on the suitors. "I must go," said he, "to the place of assembly, to look after a guest whom I have brought with me, and whom I have left with Piræus."

61 Penelope did as her son had said, while Telemachus went to the place of assembly, and his two dogs with him. The suitors, who had not yet gone to the house of Ulysses for the day, gathered round him, and made him fair speeches, but

he knew their falsehood and went to sit with his old friends
Mentor, Antiphus and Halitherses. Presently Piræus came
up, bringing Theoclymenus with him, and said, " I wish you
would send some of your women to my house to take away the
presents that Menelaus gave you."

Telemachus said he did not know what might happen ; if 77
the suitors killed him, he had rather Piræus kept the presents
than that the suitors should have them. If, on the other hand,
he killed the suitors he should be much obliged if Piræus
would let him have the presents.

Then he took Theoclymenus to his own house, where they 84
had a bath, and refreshments were set before them. Penelope
sat near them, spinning, while they were at table, and then
said she should go up stairs and lie down on that couch which
she had never ceased to water with her tears from the day her
husband left her. " But you had not the patience," she added,
" to tell me, before the suitors came, whether you had been
able to hear anything about your father."

Telemachus told her how good Nestor had been to him, and 107
how he had sent him on to Menelaus, who had assured him
that Ulysses was still alive, but was detained by Calypso, from
whom he could not get away for want of a ship. Penelope was
very much agitated, but Theoclymenus reassured her by telling
her about the omen which had greeted Telemachus on his
return to Ithaca.

While they were thus conversing, the suitors were playing 166
at quoits and aiming javelins at a mark on the level ground in
front of Ulysses' house. But when it was near dinner time
and the flocks were coming in from all the country round with
their shepherds as usual [to be milked], Medon, who was a
great favourite with the suitors, called them to come in and set
about getting their dinner ready. They therefore came in and
began to butcher some sheep, goats, pigs, and a heifer.

Meanwhile Eumæus told Ulysses that it was time to make 182
a start, for the day was well up and if he waited till afternoon
he would find the cold more severe. " At any rate," said
Ulysses, " let me have a staff if you have one, for the path is
rugged." Eumæus gave him one, and they set out along the

steep path leading to the town. When they were nearly there
they came to the fountain which Ithacus, Neritus, and Polyctor
had made, and from which the people drew their water ; here
they fell in with Melantheus* son of Dolius, who was bringing
goats for the suitors' dinner, he and his two under shepherds.

215   Melanthius heaped all kinds of insult on Ulysses and
Eumæus, and tried to kick Ulysses off the path, but could not
do so. Ulysses restrained himself, and prayed to the nymphs,
whereon Melanthius said he would put him on board ship and
sell him in some foreign country. He then hurried on, leaving
the swineherd and his master to follow at their own pace.

260   When they got near the house they could hear the sound of
Phemius's lyre, and his voice as he sang to the suitors. They
could also smell the savour of roast meats.† Eumæus said
that he would go in first, but that Ulysses had better follow
him soon, for if he was seen standing about in the outer court
people might throw things at him.

290   As they were thus talking the old hound Argus who was
lying on the dunghill, very full of fleas, caught sight of
Ulysses, recognised him, wagged his tail, and tried to come to
him, but could not do so. Thereon Ulysses wiped a tear from
his eyes, and asked Eumæus whether the dog was of any
use, or whether he was kept only for his good looks. Eumæus
said what a noble hound Argus had been, but the dog, having
seen his master, died just as Eumæus went inside the house.

328   Telemachus saw him enter and beckoned him to a seat at
his own table. Ulysses followed him shortly, and sat down on
the floor of ash wood inside the door way, leaning against a
bearing-post of well-squared cypress wood. Telemachus noted
him and said to Eumæus, "Take the stranger this handful of
bread and meat, tell him also to go round and beg from the
others, for a beggar must not be shamefaced." Eumæus gave
him both the message and the bread and meat.

360   Then Ulysses began to go round begging, for he wanted to
exploit the suitors. He went from left to right, and some took

---

* In almost all other places he is called Melanthius.

† All this might very well be, if the scene is laid in an open court,
but hardly if it was in a hall inside a house.

compassion on him while others began asking who he might be ; Melanthius then said that he had come with the swine-herd. Antinous, therefore, asked Eumæus what he meant by bringing such a man to plague them.

"I did not ask him to come," answered Eumæus. "Who 380 was likely to ask a man of that sort ? One would ask a divine, a physician, a carpenter, or a bard. You are always hardest of all the suitors on Ulysses' servants, and especially upon me, but I do not care so long as I have Penelope and Telemachus on my side."

"Hush," said Telemachus, "Antinous has the bitterest 392 tongue of them all, and he makes the others worse." Then he turned towards Antinous and said, "Give him something : I do not grudge it. Never mind my mother or any of the servants —not you—but you are fonder of eating than of giving."

Antinous said, "You are a swaggering upstart ; if all the 405 suitors will give him as much as I will, he will not come near the house again this three months."

As he spoke he menaced Ulysses with the footstool from 409 under his table. The other suitors all gave him something ; and he was about to leave, when he determined to again beg from Antinous and trumped him up a story of the misfortunes that had befallen him in Egypt.

"Get out," said Antinous, "into the open part of the court,* 445 and away from my table, or I will give you Egypt over again."

Ulysses drew back, and said, "Your looks are better than 453 your understanding. I can see that if you were in your own house you would not spare a poor man so much as a pinch of salt."

Antinous scowled at him. "Take that," he cried, "and be 458 off out of the court." As he spoke he threw a footstool at him which hit him on the right shoulder, but Ulysses stood firm as a rock, and prayed that if there was a god, or an avenger of beggars Antinous might be a corpse before he was a bridegroom.

"Have a care," replied Antinous, "and hold your peace, or 477 we will flay you alive."

---

* ἐς μέσσον (line 447).

481   The others reproved Antinous. " You did ill," they said, " to strike the man. Who knows but he may be one of the gods who go about the world in disguise to redress wrong, and chastise the insolence of mankind ? "

492   Penelope from her room upstairs heard what had been going on, and spoke with her women bitterly about the suitors. The housekeeper Eurynome answered that if her prayers were heard, not a single one of them would live till morning. " Nurse," replied Penelope, " I hate them all, but Antinous is the worst." Then she sent for Eumæus and said, " Tell the stranger that I want to see him ; he looks like a man who has travelled, and he may have seen or heard something of Ulysses."

515   " He has been three days and three nights at my hut, Madam," replied Eumæus, " and the most accomplished bard could not have given me better entertainment. He told me that Ulysses was among the Thesprotians and would return shortly, bringing much treasure with him."

528   " Then call him to me," said Penelope, " and as for the others, let them dine at their own expense for the future or how they best may, so long as they leave off coming here."

541   Telemachus, who was down below, gave a great sneeze as she spoke, which echoed over the whole house. Penelope explained to Eumæus that this was a most favourable omen, and added that if she was satisfied of the truth of what the stranger told her she would give him a shirt and cloak.

551   Eumæus gave Penelope's message to Ulysses, but he feared the violence of the suitors, and told him to say that she must wait till nightfall, when the suitors would be gone. " Then," he said, " let her set me down in a warm seat by the fire, and I will tell her about her husband ; for my clothes are in a very bad state ; you know they are, for yours was the first house I came to."

574   Penelope was displeased at his delay, and asked Eumæus whether his fears were reasonable, or whether it was only that he was shamefaced. Eumæus explained that he was quite reasonable, whereon Penelope was satisfied ; he then went back to where the suitors were, and told Telemachus that he would return to his pigs.

Telemachus said that he had better get something to eat 598
first, and was to come back to the town on the following
morning, bringing the pigs that were to be killed for dinner.
It was now afternoon, and the suitors had turned to their
singing and dancing.

Book XVIII

THE FIGHT BETWEEN ULYSSES AND IRUS—THE SUITORS MAKE PRESENTS TO PENELOPE—AND ILL-TREAT ULYSSES.

Now there came a common tramp to Ulysses' house,
begging—a great hulking fellow with no stay in him—whose
name was Arnæus ; but people called him Irus, because he
would run errands for any one who would send him on them.
This man began to threaten Ulysses, and said the suitors had
urged him to turn him away from the house.

Ulysses said there was room enough for both of them, and 14
that it should be a case of live-and-let-live between them.
" If, however," he continued, " it comes to blows, I will deluge
your mouth and chest with blood, and I shall have the place
to myself, for you will not come back again."

Irus retorted angrily, and Antinous, hearing them wrangle, 34
told the other suitors that Irus and the stranger were about to
have a fight.　" It is the finest piece of sport," he said, " that
heaven ever sent into this house.　We are to have goat's
paunches stuffed with blood and fat for supper ; whichever of
the two beats in this fight shall have his pick of the lot of
them."

The preliminaries being arranged, and fair play bargained 58
for by Ulysses, he began to strip.　When Irus saw his muscles
his heart misgave him ; but Antinous kept him up to it, and
the fight began.*　Ulysses forthwith nearly killed Irus and
dragged him by the heels into the outer court, where he put
his staff in his hand and propped him up against the wall
more dead than alive.　Antinous then gave Ulysses a great
goat's paunch, and Amphinomus drank his health.

---

* They might very well fight in the middle of an open court, but
hardly in a covered hall.　They would go outside.

124   Ulysses made Amphinomus a very grave and impressive speech, warning him to leave the house, inasmuch as Ulysses would return shortly. "You seem," said he, "to be a man of good understanding, as indeed you may well be, seeing whose son you are. I have heard your father well spoken of; he is Nisus of Dulichium, a man both brave and wealthy. They tell me you are his son and you seem to be a considerable person; listen, therefore, and take heed to what I am saying. Man is the vainest of all creatures that live and move upon the earth: as long as heaven vouchsafes him health and strength he thinks that he shall come to no harm hereafter, and even when the blessed gods bring sorrow upon him, he bears it as he needs must and makes the best of it, for God Almighty gives men their daily minds day by day. I know all about it, for I was a rich man once, and did much wrong in the stubbornness of my pride and in the confidence that my father and my brothers would support me; therefore let a man fear God in all things always, and take the good that heaven may see fit to send him without vainglory." But Amphinomus, though his heart boded ill, would not be persuaded.

158   Minerva then put it in Penelope's mind to get some presents out of the suitors. "I hate them," said she to Eurynome, "but still for once in a way I will see them; I want to warn my son against them."

169   "Certainly, my dear child," answered Eurynome, "but you must wash your face first. You cannot be seen with the stain of tears upon your cheeks."

177   "Eurynome," replied her mistress, "do not try to persuade me. Heaven robbed me of all my beauty on the day when my husband sailed for Troy; but send Autonoë and Hippodamia to attend me, for I cannot think of seeing the suitors unattended." The old woman then went through the house to fetch the women; and as soon as she was gone, Minerva sent Penelope into a deep sleep during which she endowed her with the most dazzling beauty, washing her face with the ambrosial loveliness which Venus wears when she goes out dancing with the Graces, and giving her a statelier and more imposing presence. When the two maids came, the noise of their

coming woke her. "What a delicious sleep," she exclaimed, "has overshadowed me. Would that it had been the sleep of death, which had thus ended all my sorrows."

She then went down stairs, and the suitors were dazzled 206 with her beauty. She began by upbraiding Telemachus for having allowed the fight to take place. Telemachus admitted his fault, but pleaded the extreme difficulty of his situation and the fact that after all Ulysses had thrashed Irus.

Eurymachus broke in upon their conversation by telling 243 Penelope how very beautiful she was ; and Penelope answered that heaven had robbed her of all her beauty on the day when her husband sailed for Troy. "Moreover," she added, "I have another great sorrow—you suitors are not wooing me in the 275 usual way. When men are suing for the hand of one who they think will make them a good wife, they generally bring oxen and sheep for her relations to feast upon, and make rich presents to the lady herself, instead of sponging upon other people's property."

When Ulysses heard her say this, he was delighted at 281 seeing his wife trying to get presents out of the suitors, and hoodwinking them.

Then Antinous said, "Penelope, take all the presents you 284 can get, but we will not go till you have married the best man among us." On this they all made Penelope magnificent presents, and she went back to her own room, followed by the women, who carried the presents for her.

The suitors now turned to singing and dancing, lighted by 304 large braziers that were placed in the court,* and also by 307 torches, which the maids held up by turns. Ulysses after a while told them to go inside, saying that he would hold the 317 torches himself. The maids laughed at this, and Melantho, who was one of them, began to gibe at him. She was daughter to Dolius but Penelope had brought her up from childhood, and used to give her toys ; she showed no considera-tion, however, for Penelope's sorrows, but misconducted herself with Eurymachus. "Are you drunk ?" she said to Ulysses, "or are you always like this ?"

---

* ἐν μεγάροισιν, but not ἐν μεγάροισι σκιόεσσι.

337　Ulysses scowled at her, and said he would tell Telemachus, who would have her cut up into mincemeat. The women, therefore, were frightened and went away, so Ulysses was left holding up the flaming torches—looking upon all the suitors and brooding over his revenge.

346　Presently Eurymachus began to jeer at him, and taunt him by saying he preferred begging to working. Ulysses answered, "If you and I, Eurymachus, were matched one against the other in early summer, when the days are at their longest—give us each a good scythe, and see whether you or I will mow the stronger or fast the longer, from dawn till dark when the mowing grass is about. Or let us be in a four acre field with a couple of tawny full fed oxen each, and see which of us can drive the straighter furrow. Again, let war break out this day—give me armour and you will find me fighting among the foremost. You are insolent and cruel, and think yourself a great man because you live in a little world, and that a bad one."

394　Eurymachus was furious, and seized a stool ; but Ulysses sat down by the knees of Amphinomus of Dulichium, for he was afraid ; the stool hit the cupbearer and knocked him down, whereon there was a general uproar, amid which Telemachus said that he would compel no man, but he thought it would be better if they would all go home to bed. To this they assented, and shortly afterwards left the house.

Book XIX

ULYSSES CONVERSES WITH PENELOPE, AND IS RECOGNISED BY EURYCLEA.

Ulysses and Telemachus were left alone in the cloister, and Ulysses said, " We must take the armour down from the walls ; if the suitors are surprised, say what I told you when we were in Eumæus's hut."

15　Telemachus called Euryclea, and bade her shut the women up in their room, for he was going to take the armour down into the store room. " Who," asked Euryclea, " will show you

a light if the women are all shut up ? " " The stranger,"
answered Telemachus ; " I will not have people doing nothing
about my premises."

He and Ulysses then began removing the armour, and 31
Minerva went before them, shedding a strange lambent light
that played on walls and rafters. Telemachus was lost in
wonder, but Ulysses said, " Hush, this is the manner of the
gods. Get you to bed, and leave me to talk with your mother
and the maids." So Telemachus crossed the court and went
to the room in which he always slept, leaving Ulysses in the
cloister.

Penelope now came down, and they set a seat for her by 53
the fire ; the maids also were let out, and came to take away
the meats on which the suitors had been feasting, and to heap
fresh wood upon the braziers after they had emptied the ashes
on to the ground.* Melantho again began scolding at Ulysses
for stopping in the house to spy on the women. Penelope
heard her and said, " Bold hussy, I hear you, and you shall
smart for it ; I have already told you that I wish to see the
stranger and enquire from him about my husband. Eurynome,
bring a seat for him, and spread a fleece on it."

Eurynome did as she was told, and when Ulysses had sat 100
down Penelope wanted to know who he was. Ulysses implored
her not to ask this, for it would make him weep, and she or
the servants might then think he had been drinking.

" Stranger," answered Penelope, " heaven robbed me of all 123
my beauty when the Argives set out for Troy and Ulysses with
them." She then told about the suitors, and her web, and
said that she was now at the very end of her resources. Her
parents were urging her to marry again, and so also was her
son, who chafed under the heavy burden of expense which her
long courtship had caused him. " In spite of all this, however," she continued, " I want to know who you are ; for you
cannot be the son of a rock or of an oak."

Thus pressed, Ulysses said that his name was Æthon and 164

---

* There is no indication as though they went out to do this ; they
seem to have emptied the ashes on to the open part of the court.

that he came from Crete, where he had entertained Ulysses and his men for many days when they were on their way to Troy. Penelope wept bitterly as she listened, and it was all Ulysses could do to restrain his own tears—but he succeeded. "I will now prove you," said she ; "tell me how my husband was dressed. Tell me also what manner of man he was, and about the men who were with him."

220   "I will tell you," replied Ulysses, "as nearly as I can remember after so long a time. He wore a mantle of purple wool, double lined, and it was fastened by a gold brooch with two catches for the pin. On the face of this there was a device that shewed a dog holding a spotted fawn between its fore paws, and watching it as it lay panting on the ground. Every one marvelled at the way in which these things had been done in gold—the dog looking at the fawn and strangling

231   it, while the fawn was struggling convulsively to escape. As for his shirt, it fitted him like the skin of an onion, and glistened in the sunlight to the admiration of all the women who beheld it. He had a servant with him, a little older than

246   himself, whose shoulders were hunched ; he was dark, and had thick curly hair. His name was Eurybates."

249   Penelope was deeply moved. "You shall want for nothing," she said, "It was I who gave him the clothes and the brooch you speak of, but I shall never see him again."

261   "Be not too dejected, Madam," answered Ulysses ; "when I was with the Thesprotians I heard for certain that he was alive and well. Indeed he would have been here ere now, had he not deemed it better to amass great wealth before returning. Before this month is out I swear most solemnly that he will be here."

308   "If you say truly," replied Penelope, "you shall indeed be rewarded richly, but he will not come. Still, you women, take the stranger and wash him ; make him a comfortable bed, and in the morning wash him again and anoint him, that he may sit at the same table with Telemachus ; if any of the suitors

322   molest him, he shall rue it, for fume as he may, he shall have no more to do in this house. How indeed, Sir, can you know how much I surpass all other women in goodness and discretion unless I see that you are well clothed and fed ? "

"Make me no bed, Madam," said Ulysses, "I will lie on the 336 bare ground as I am wont to do. Nor do I like having my feet washed. I will not allow any of your serving women to touch my feet ; but if you have any respectable old woman who has gone through as much as I have, I will let her wash them."

"Stranger," answered Penelope, "your sense of propriety 349 exceeds that of any foreigner who has ever come here. I have exactly the kind of person you describe ; she was Ulysses' nurse from the day of his birth, and is now very old and feeble, but she shall wash your feet. Euryclea, come and wash the stranger's feet. He is about the same age as your master would be."

Euryclea spoke compassionately to Ulysses, and ended by 361 saying that he was very like her master. To which Ulysses replied that many other people had observed the likeness.

Then the old woman got a large foot bath and put some 386 cold water into it, adding hot water until it was the right heat. As soon, however, as she got Ulysses' leg in her hands, she recognised a scar on it as one which her master had got from being ripped by a boar when he was hunting on Mt. Parnassus with his mother's father Autolycus, whom 394 Mercury had endowed with the gift of being the most accomplished thief and perjurer in the whole world, for he was very fond of him. She immediately dropped the leg, which 468 made a loud noise against the side of the bath and upset all the water. Her eyes filled with tears, and she caught Ulysses by the beard and told him that she knew him.

She looked towards Penelope to tell her ; but Minerva 476 had directed Penelope's attention elsewhere, so that she had observed nothing of what had been going on. Ulysses gripped Euryclea's throat, and swore he would kill her, nurse to him though she had been, unless she kept his return secret—which she promised to do. She also said that if heaven delivered the suitors into his hands, she would give him a list of all the women in the house who had misconducted themselves.

"You have no need," said Ulysses, "I shall find that out 499 for myself. See that you keep my counsel and leave the rest to heaven."

503 Euryclea now went to fetch some more water, for the first had been all spilt. When she had brought it, and had washed Ulysses, he turned his seat round to the fire to dry himself, and drew his rags over the scar that Penelope might not see it.

508 Then Penelope detailed her sorrows to Ulysses. Others, she said, could sleep, but she could not do so, neither night nor day. She could not rest for thinking what her duty might be. Ought she to stay where she was and stand guard over her son's estate, or ought she to marry one of the suitors and
530 go elsewhere? Her son, while he was a boy, would not hear of her doing this, but now that he was grown up and realised the havoc that the suitors were making of his property, he was continually urging her to go. Besides, she had had a strange
538 dream about an eagle that had come from a mountain and swooped down on her favourite geese as they were eating mash out of a tub,* and had killed them all. Then the eagle came back and told her he was Ulysses, while the geese were the suitors; but when she woke the geese were still feeding at the mash tub. Now, what did all this mean?

554 Ulysses said it could only mean the immediate return of her husband, and his revenge upon the suitors.

559 But Penelope would not believe him. "Dreams," she said, "are very curious things. They come through two gates, one of horn, and the other of ivory. Those that come through the gate of ivory have no significance. It is the others that alone are true, and my dream came through the gate of ivory. To-morrow, therefore, I shall set Ulysses' bow before the suitors, and I will leave this house with him who can draw it most easily and send an arrow through the twelve holes whereby twelve axeheads are fitted into their handles."

582 "You need not defer this competition," said Ulysses, "for your husband will be here before any one of them can draw the bow and shoot through the axes."

588 "Stranger," replied Penelope, "I could stay talking with you the whole night through, but there is a time for every-

---

* I have repeatedly seen geese so feeding at Trapani and in the neighbourhood. In summer the grass is all burned up so that they cannot graze as in England.

thing, and I will now go to lie down upon that couch which I have never ceased to water with my tears from the day my husband set out for the city with an ill-omened name. You can sleep within the house, either on the ground or on a bedstead, whichever you may prefer."

Then she went upstairs and mourned her dear husband till 600 Minerva shed sweet sleep over her eyes.

Book XX

ULYSSES CONVERSES WITH EUMÆUS, AND WITH HIS HERDSMAN PHILŒTIUS—THE SUITORS AGAIN MALTREAT HIM—THEO-CLYMENUS FORETELLS THEIR DOOM AND LEAVES THE HOUSE.

Ulysses made himself a bed of an untanned ox-hide in the vestibule and covered himself with sheep skins ; then Eurynome threw a cloak over him. He saw the women who misbehaved themselves with the suitors go giggling out of the house, and 6 was sorely tempted to kill them then and there, but he restrained himself. He kept turning round and round, as a man turns a paunch full of blood and fat before a hot fire to cook it, and could get no rest till Minerva came to him and comforted him, by reminding him that he was now in Ithaca.

" That is all very well," replied Ulysses, " but suppose I do 36 kill these suitors, pray consider what is to become of me then ? Where am I to fly to from the revenge their friends will take upon me ? "

" One would think," answered Minerva, " that you might 44 trust even a feebler aid than mine ; go to sleep ; your troubles shall end shortly."

Ulysses then slept, but Penelope was still wakeful, and 54 lamented her impending marriage, and her inability to sleep, in such loud tones that Ulysses heard her, and thought she was close by him.

It was now morning and Ulysses rose, praying the while to 91 Jove. " Grant me," he cried, " a sign from one of the people who are now waking in the house, and another sign from outside it."

102   Forthwith Jove thundered from a clear sky. There came also a miller woman from the mill-room, who, being weakly,
110 had not finished her appointed task as soon as the others had done ; as she passed Ulysses he heard her curse the suitors and pray for their immediate death. Ulysses was thus assured that he should kill them.

122   The other women of the house now lit the fire, and Telemachus came down from his room.

129   " Nurse," said he, " I hope you have seen that the stranger has been duly fed and lodged. My mother, in spite of her many virtues, is apt to be too much impressed by inferior people, and to neglect those who are more deserving."

134   " Do not find fault, child," said Euryclea, " when there is no one to find fault with. The stranger sat and drank as much wine as he liked. Your mother asked him if he would take any more bread, but he said he did not want any. As for his bed, he would not have one, but slept in the vestibule on an untanned hide, and I threw a cloak over him myself."

144   Telemachus then went out to the place of assembly, and his two dogs with him. " Now, you women," said Euryclea, " be quick and clean the house down. Put the cloths on the seats, sponge down the tables ; wash the cups and mixing bowls, and go at once, some of you, to fetch water from the fountain. It is a feast day, and the suitors will be here directly." So twenty of them went for water, and others busied themselves setting things straight about the house.

160   The men servants then came and chopped wood. The women came back from the fountain, and Eumæus with them, bringing three fine pigs, which he let feed about the yards. When he saw Ulysses he asked him how he was getting on, and Ulysses prayed that heaven might avenge him upon the suitors.

172   Then Melanthius came with the best goats he had, and made them fast in the gate-house. When he had done this he gibed at Ulysses, but Ulysses made him no answer.

185   Thirdly came Philœtius with a barren heifer and some fat goats for the suitors. These had been brought over for him by the boatman who plied for all comers. When he saw

Ulysses, he asked Eumæus who he was, and said he was very like his lost master. Then he told Ulysses how well his old master had treated him, and how well also he had served his old master. Alas! that he was no longer living. "We are fallen," said he, "on evil times, and I often think that though it would not be right of me to drive my cattle off, and put both myself and them under some other master while Telemachus is still alive, yet even this would be better than leading the life I have to lead at present. Indeed I should have gone off with them long ago, if I did not cling to the hope that Ulysses may still return."

"I can see," said Ulysses, "that you are a very honest and 226 sensible person. Therefore I will swear you a solemn oath that Ulysses will be here immediately, and if you like you shall see him with you own eyes kill the suitors."

While they were thus conversing the suitors were again 240 plotting the murder of Telemachus, but there appeared an unfavourable omen, so Amphinomus said they had better go to the house and get dinner ready, which they accordingly did. When they were at table, Eumæus gave them their cups, Philœtius handed round the bread and Melantheus poured them out their wine. Telemachus purposely set Ulysses at a little table on the part of the cloister that was paved with stone, and told the suitors that it should be worse for any of them who molested him. "This," he said, "is not a public house, but it is mine, for it has come to me from Ulysses."

The suitors were very angry but Antinous checked them. 268 "Let us put up with it," said he; "if Jove had permitted, we should have been the death of him ere now." Meanwhile, it being the festival of Apollo, the people of the town were bearing his holy hecatomb about the streets.

The servants gave Ulysses an equal portion with what they 279 gave the others, for Telemachus had so bidden them. Presently one of the suitors named Ctesippus observed this and said, "I see the stranger has as good a portion as any one else. I will give him a better, that he may have something to give 296 the bath-woman or some other of the servants in the house"—and with this he flung a cow's heel at Ulysses' head.

302   Ulysses smiled with a grim Sardinian* smile, and bowed his head so that the heel passed over it and hit the wall. Telemachus rebuked Ctesippus very fiercely, and all were silent till Agelaus tried to calm them saying, "What Telemachus has said is just : let us not answer. Nevertheless I would urge him to talk quietly with his mother and tell her that as long as there was any chance of Ulysses coming back there was nothing unreasonable in her deferring a second marriage ; but there is now no hope of his return, and if you would enjoy your own in peace, tell her to marry the best man among us and the one who will make her the most advantageous offer."

338   "Nay," answered Telemachus, "it is not I that delay her marriage. I urge her to it, but I cannot and will not force her."

345   Then Minerva made the suitors break out into a forced hysterical laughter, and the meats which they were eating became all smirched with blood. Their eyes were filled with tears and their hearts were oppressed with terrible forebodings. Theoclymenus saw that all was wrong, and said, "Unhappy men, what is it that ails you ? There is a shroud of darkness drawn over you from head to foot, your cheeks are wet with tears ; the air is alive with wailing voices ; the walls and roof beams drip blood ; the gate of the cloisters, and the yard beyond them are full of ghosts trooping down into the night of hell ; the sun is blotted out from heaven, and a blighting gloom is over all the land."

358   The suitors laughed at him, and Eurymachus said, "If you find it so dark here, we had better send a man with you to take you out into the open."

363   "I have eyes," he answered, "that can guide, and feet that can take me from the doom that I see overhanging every single one of you." On this he left them and went back to the house of Piræus.

375   Then one of the suitors said, "Telemachus, you are very unfortunate in your guests. You had better ship both the

---

* This is the only reference to Sardinia in either "Iliad" or "Odyssey."

stranger and this man off to the Sicels and sell them." Telemachus made no answer, but kept his eye on his father for any signal that he might make him.

Penelope had had a seat placed for her overlooking the 387 cloister, and heard all that had passed. The dinner had been good and plentiful and there had been much laughter, for they had slaughtered many victims, but little did they guess the terrible supper which the goddess and a strong man were preparing for them.

Book XXI

THE TRIAL OF THE BOW AND OF THE AXES.

Then Minerva put it in Penelope's mind to let the suitors compete for the bow and for a prize of iron. So she went upstairs and got the key of the store room, where Ulysses' treasures of gold, copper, and iron were kept, as also the mighty bow which Iphitus son of Eurytus had given him, and which had been in common use by Eurytus as long as he was alive. Hither she went attended by her women, and when she had unlocked the door she took the bow down from its peg and carried it, with its quiverfull of deadly arrows, to the suitors, while her maids brought the chest in which were the many prizes of iron that Ulysses had won. Then, still attended by her two maidens, she stood by one of the bearing posts that supported the roof of the cloister, and told the suitors she would marry the man among them who could string Ulysses' bow most easily, and send an arrow through the twelve holes by which twelve axe-heads were fastened on to their handles.

So saying she gave the bow into the hands of Eumæus and 80 bade him let the suitors compete as she had said. Eumæus wept as he took it, and so did Philœtius who was looking on, whereon Antinous scolded them for a couple of country bumpkins.

Telemachus said that he too should compete, and that if he 113 was successful he should certainly not allow his mother to leave her home with a second husband, while he remained alone. So saying he dug a long trench quite straight, set the axes in a line within it, and stamped the earth about them to keep them steady ; every one was surprised to see how accurately he fixed them, considering that he had never seen anything of the kind before.* Having set the axes duly, he stood on the stone pavement, and tried to string the bow, but failed three times. He would, however, have succeeded the fourth time, if Ulysses had not made him a sign that he was not to try any more. So he laid both bow and arrow down and took his seat.

140   "Then," said Antinous, "begin at the place where the cup-bearer begins, and let each take his turn, going from left to right." On this Leiodes came forward. He was their sacrificial priest, and sat in the angle of the wall hard by the mixing bowl ; but he had always set his face against the wicked conduct of the suitors. When he had failed to string the bow he said it was so hard to string that it would rob many a man among them of life and heart—for which saying Antinous rebuked him bitterly.

175   "Bring some fire, Melantheus, and a wheel of fat from inside the house," said he to Melanthius, [sic] "that we may warm the bow and grease it." So they did this, but though many tried they could none of them string it. There remained only Antinous and Eurymachus who were their ring leaders.

188   The swineherd and the stockman Philœtius then went outside the forecourt, and Ulysses followed them ; when they had got beyond the outer yard Ulysses sounded them, and having satisfied himself that they were loyal he revealed himself and shewed them the scar on his leg. They were overjoyed, and Ulysses said, "Go back one by one after me, and follow these instructions. The other suitors will not be for letting me have the bow, but do you, Eumæus, when you have got it in your hands, bring it to me, and tell the women to shut themselves

---

* If Telemachus had never seen anything of the kind before, so probably, neither had the writer of the " Odyssey "—at any rate no commentator has yet been able to understand her description, and I doubt whether she understood it herself. It looks as though the axe heads must have been wedged into the handles or so bound on to them as to let the hole be visible through which the handle would go when the axe was in use. The trial is evidently a double one, of strength as regards the bending of the bow, and accuracy of aim as regards shooting through a row of rings.

into their room. If the sound of groaning or uproar reaches any of them when they are inside, tell them to stick to their work and not come out. I leave it to you, Philœtius, to fasten the gate of the outer court securely." He then went inside, and resumed the seat that he had left.

Eurymachus now tried to string the bow but failed. "I do 245 not so much mind," he said, "about not marrying Penelope, for there are plenty of other women in Ithaca and elsewhere. What grieves me is the fact of our being such a feeble folk as compared with our forefathers."

Antinous reminded him that it was the festival of Apollo. 256 "Who," said he, "can shoot on such a day as this ? Let us leave the axes where they are—no one will take them ; let us also sacrifice to Apollo the best goats Melanthius can bring us, and resume the contest tomorrow."

Ulysses then cunningly urged that he might be allowed to 274 try whether he was as strong a man as he used to be, and that the bow should be placed in his hands for this purpose. The suitors were very angry, but Penelope insisted that Ulysses should have the bow ; if he succeeded in stringing it she said it was absurd to suppose that she would marry him ; but she would give him a shirt and cloak, a javelin, sword, and a pair of sandals, and she would send him wherever he might want to go.

"The bow, mother, is mine," said Telemachus, "and if I 343 choose to give it this man out and out I shall give it him. Go within the house and mind your own proper duties."

Penelope went back, with her women, wondering into the 354 house, and going upstairs into her room she wept for her dear husband till Minerva shed sweet sleep over her eyes.

Eumæus was about to take the bow to Ulysses, but the 359 suitors frightened him and he was for putting it down, till Telemachus threatened to stone him back to his farm if he did not bring it on at once ; he therefore gave the bow to Ulysses. Then he called Euryclea aside and told her to shut the women up, and not to let them out if they heard any groans or uproar. She therefore shut them up.

At this point Philœtius slipped out and secured the main 388

gate of the outer court with a ship's cable of Byblus fibre
that happened to be lying beside it. This done, he returned
to his seat and kept his eye on Ulysses, who was examining
the bow with great care to see whether it was sound in all its
parts.

397   "This man," said the suitors, "is some old bow-fancier ;
perhaps he has got one like it at home, or wants to make one,
so cunningly does the old rascal handle it."

404   Ulysses, having finished his scrutiny, strung the bow as
easily as a bard puts a new string on to his lyre. He tried the
string and it sang under his hand like the cry of a swallow.
He took an arrow that was lying out of its quiver by his table,
placed the notch on the string, and from his seat sent the
arrow through the handle-holes of all the axes and outside into
the yard.

424   "Telemachus," said he, " your guest has not disgraced you.
It is now time for the suitors to have their supper, and to take
their pleasure afterwards with song and playing on the lyre."
So saying he made a sign to Telemachus, who girded on his
sword, grasped his spear, and stood armed beside his father's
seat.

Book XXII

THE KILLING OF THE SUITORS.

Ulysses tore off his rags, and sprang on the broad pavement,* with his bow and his quiver full of arrows. He shed
the arrows on to the ground at his feet and said, " The contest
is at an end. I will now see whether Apollo will vouchsafe
me to hit another mark which no man has yet aimed at."

8   He took aim at Antinous as he spoke. The arrow struck
him in the throat, so that he fell over and a thick stream of
blood gushed from his nostrils. He kicked his table from him
and upset the things on it, whereby the bread and meats were

---

* It is not expressly stated that the " stone pavement " is here
intended. The Greek has simply ἇλτο δ' ἐπὶ μέγαν οὐδόν, but I do
not doubt that the stone pavement is intended.

all soiled as they fell over on to the ground. The suitors were instantly in an uproar, and looked towards the walls for armour, but there was none. "Stranger," they cried, "you shall pay dearly for shooting people down in this way. You are a doomed man." But they did not yet understand that Ulysses had killed Antinous on purpose.

Ulysses glared at them and said, "Dogs, did you think that 34 I should not return from Troy? You have wasted my substance, you have violated the women of my house, you have wooed my wife while I was still alive, you have feared neither god nor man, and now you shall die."

Eurymachus alone answered. "If you are Ulysses," said 44 he, "we have done you great wrong. It was all Antinous's doing. He never really wanted to marry Penelope : he wanted to kill your son and to be chief man in Ithaca. He is no more ; then spare the lives of your people and we will pay you all."

Ulysses again glared at him and said, "I will not stay my 60 hand till I have slain one and all of you. You must fight, or fly as you can, or die—and fly you neither can nor shall."

Eurymachus then said, "My friends, this man will give us 68 no quarter. Let us show fight. Draw your swords and hold the tables up in front of you as shields. Have at him with a rush, and drive him from the pavement and from the door. We could then get through into the town and call for help."

While he spoke and was springing forward, Ulysses sent an 79 arrow into his heart and he fell doubled up over his table. The cup and all the meats went over on to the ground as he smote the earth with his forehead in the agonies of death.

Amphinomus then made for Ulysses to try and dislodge 89 him from the door, but Telemachus got behind him, and struck him through. He left his spear in the body and flew back to his father's side ; "Father," said he, "let me bring armour for you and me, as well as for Eumæus and Philœtius." "Run and fetch it," answered Ulysses, "while my arrows hold out ; be quick, or they may get me away from the door when I am single-handed."

Telemachus went to the store-room and brought four 108 shields, eight spears, and four helmets. He armed himself, as did also Eumæus and Philœtius, who then placed themselves beside Ulysses. As long as his arrows held out Ulysses shot the suitors down thick and threefold, but when they failed him he stood the bow against the end wall of the house hard by the door way, and armed himself.

126   Now there was a trap-door (see plan, and *f* on p. 17) on the wall, while at one end of the pavement there was an exit, closed by a good strong door and leading out into a narrow passage ; Ulysses told Philœtius to stand by this door and keep it, for only one person could attack it at a time. Then Agelaus shouted out, " Go up, somebody, to the trap-door and tell the people what is going on ; they would come in and help us."

135   " This may not be," answered Melanthius, " the mouth of the narrow passage is dangerously near the entrance from the street into the outer court. One brave man could prevent any number from getting in, but I will bring you arms from the store-room, for I am sure it is there that they have put them."

143 As he spoke he went back by passages to the store-room, and brought the suitors twelve shields and the same number of helmets ; when Ulysses saw the suitors arming his heart began to fail him, and he said to Telemachus, " Some of the women inside are helping the suitors—or else it is Melanthius."

153   Telemachus said that it was his fault, for he had left the store-room door open. " Go, Eumæus," he added, " and close it ; see whether it is one of the women, or Melanthius, son of Dolius."

160   Melanthius was now going back for more armour when Eumæus saw him and told Ulysses, who said, " Follow him, you and Philœtius ; bind his hands and feet behind him, and throw him into the store-room ; then string him up to a bearing-post till he is close to the rafters, that he may linger on in agony."

178   The men went to the store-room and caught Melanthius. They bound him in a painful bond and strung him up as Ulysses had told them. Eumæus wished him a good night and the two men returned to the side of Ulysses. Minerva 205 also joined them, having assumed the form of Mentor ; but

Ulysses felt sure it was Minerva. The suitors were very angry when they saw her ; " Mentor," they cried, " you shall pay for this with your life, and we will confiscate all you have in the world."

This made Minerva furious, and she rated Ulysses roundly. 224 " Your prowess," said she, " is no longer what it was at Troy. How comes it that you are less valiant now that you are on your own ground ? Come on, my good fellow, and see how Mentor will fight for you and requite you for your many kindnesses." But she did not mean to give him the victory just yet, so she flew up to one of the rafters and sat there in the form of a swallow.*

The struggle still continued. " My friends," said Agelaus, 241 " he will soon have to leave off. See how Mentor has left him after doing nothing for him except brag. Do not aim at him all at once, but six of you throw your spears first."

They did so, but Minerva made all their spears take no 265 effect. Ulysses and the other three then threw, and each killed his man. The suitors drew back in fear into a corner, whereon the four sprang forward and regained their weapons. The suitors again threw, and this time Amphimedon really did take a piece of the top skin from Telemachus's wrist, and Ctesippus just grazed Eumæus's shoulder above his shield. It was now the turn of Ulysses and his men, and each of their spears killed a man.

Then Minerva from high on the roof held up her deadly 297 ægis, and struck the suitors with panic, whereon Ulysses and his men fell upon them and smote them on every side. They made a horrible groaning as their brains were being battered in, and the ground seethed with their blood. Leiodes implored Ulysses to spare his life, but Ulysses would give him no quarter.

The minstrel Phemius now begged for mercy. He was 330

---

* This again suggests, though it does not prove, that we are in an open court surrounded by a cloister, on the rafters of which swallows would often perch. Line 297 suggests this even more strongly, " the roof " being, no doubt, the roof of the cloister, on to which Minerva flew from the rafter, that her ægis might better command the whole court.

standing near towards the trap-door, and resolving to embrace Ulysses' knees, he laid his lyre on the ground between the mixing-bowl and the high silver-studded seat. " Spare me," he cried, " you will be sorry for it afterwards if you kill such a bard as I am. I am an original composer, and heaven visits me with every kind of inspiration. Do not be in such a hurry to cut my head off. Telemachus will tell you that I only sang to the suitors because they forced me."

354 " Hold," cried Telemachus to his father, " do him no hurt, he is guiltless ; and we will spare Medon, too, who was always good to me when I was a boy, unless Eumæus or Philœtius has already killed him, or you happened to fall in with him yourself."

361 " Here I am, my dear Sir," said Medon, coming out from under a freshly flayed heifer's hide* which had concealed him ; " tell your father, or he will kill me in his rage against the suitors for having wasted his substance and been so disrespectful to yourself." Ulysses smiled, and told them to go outside into the outer court till the killing should be over. So they went, but they were still very much frightened. Ulysses then went all over the court to see if there were any who had concealed themselves, or were not yet killed, but there was no one ; they were all as dead as fish lying in a hot sun upon the beach.

390 Then he told Telemachus to call Euryclea, who came at once, and found him all covered with blood. When she saw the corpses she was beginning to raise a shout of triumph, but

411 Ulysses checked her : " Old woman," said he, " rejoice in silence ; it is an unholy thing to vaunt over dead men. And now tell me which of the women of the house are innocent and which guilty."

419 " There are fifty women in the house," said Euryclea ; " twelve of these have misbehaved, and have been wanting in respect to me and to Penelope. They showed no disrespect to Telemachus, for he has only lately grown up, and his mother

---

* Probably the hide of the heifer that Philœtius had brought in that morning (xx. 186).

never permitted him to give orders to the female servants. And now let me go upstairs and tell your wife."

" Do not wake her yet," answered Ulysses, " but send the 430 guilty women to me."

Then he called Telemachus, Eumæus, and Philœtius. 435 " Begin," he said, " to remove the dead bodies, and make the women help you. Also get sponges and clean water to swill down the tables and the seats. When you have thoroughly cleansed the cloisters take the women outside and run them through with your swords."

The women came down weeping and wailing bitterly. 446 First they carried the dead bodies out, and propped them against one another in the gatehouse of the outer court. Ulysses ordered them about and saw that they lost no time. When they had carried the bodies out they cleaned all the tables and seats with sponges and water, while Telemachus and the two others shovelled up the blood and dirt from the ground and the women carried it all outside. When they had thus thoroughly cleaned the whole court, they took the women out and hemmed them up in the narrow space between the vaulted room and the wall of the outer yard. Here Telemachus determined to hang them, as a more dishonourable death than 462 stabbing. He therefore made a ship's rope fast to a strong bearing-post supporting the roof of the vaulted room, and threw it round, making the women put their heads in the nooses one after another. He then drew the rope high up, so that none of their feet might touch the ground. They kicked convulsively for a while, but not for very long.

As for Melanthius they took him through the cloisters into 474 the outer court. There they cut off his nose and ears ; they drew out his vitals and gave them to the dogs, raw ; then they cut off his hands and feet. When they had done this they washed their hands and feet, and went back into the house. " Go," said Ulysses, to Euryclea, " and bring me sulphur that I may burn it and purify the cloisters. Go, moreover, and bid Penelope come here with her gentlewomen and the women of the house."

" Let me first bring you a clean shirt and cloak," said 485

Euryclea, " do not keep those rags on any longer, it is not right."

490 " Light me a fire," answered Ulysses, and she obeyed and brought him sulphur, wherewith he thoroughly purified both the inner and outer court, as well as the cloisters. Then Euryclea brought the women from their apartment, and they pressed round Ulysses, kissing his head and shoulders, and taking hold of his hands. It made him feel as if he should like to weep, for he remembered every one of them.

Book XXIII

PENELOPE COMES DOWN TO SEE ULYSSES, AND BEING AT LAST
CONVINCED THAT HE IS HER HUSBAND, RETIRES WITH HIM TO
THEIR OWN OLD ROOM—IN THE MORNING ULYSSES, TELE-
MACHUS, PHILŒTIUS, AND EUMÆUS GO TO THE HOUSE OF
LAERTES.

Euryclea now went upstairs and told Penelope what had happened. " Wake up, my dear child," said she, " Ulysses is come home at last and has killed the suitors who were giving so much trouble in the house, eating up his estate and ill-treating his son."

10 " My good nurse," answered Penelope, " you must be mad. The gods sometimes send very sensible people out of their minds, and make foolish people sensible. This is what they must have been doing to you. Moreover, you have waked me from the soundest sleep that I have enjoyed since my husband left me. Go back into the women's room ; if it had been any one but you, I should have given her a severe scolding."

25 Euryclea still maintained that what she had said was true, and in answer to Penelope's further questions told her as much as she knew about the killing of the suitors. " When I came down," she said, " I found Ulysses standing over the corpses ; you would have enjoyed it, if you had seen him all bespattered with blood and filth, and looking just like a lion. But the corpses are now piled up in the gatehouse, and he has sent me to bring you to him."

Penelope said that it could not be Ulysses, but must be 58
some god who had resolved to punish the suitors for their great
wickedness. Then Euryclea told her about the scar.

" My dear nurse," answered Penelope, " however wise you 80
may be, you can hardly fathom the counsels of the gods. Still
I will go and find my son that I may see the corpses of the
suitors, and the man who has killed them."

On this she came down into the cloister and took her seat 85
opposite Ulysses, in the fire-light, by the wall at right angles
to that by which she had entered, while her husband sat by
one of the bearing-posts of the cloister, looking down and
waiting to hear what she would say. For a long time she sat
as one lost in amazement and said nothing, till Telemachus
upbraided her for her coldness. " Your heart," he said, " was
always hard as a stone."

" My son," said his mother, " I am stupefied ; nevertheless 104
if this man is really Ulysses, I shall find it out ; for there are
tokens which we two alone know of."

Ulysses smiled at this, and said to Telemachus, " Let your 111
mother prove me as she will, she will make up her mind about
it presently. Meanwhile let us think what we shall do, for we
have been killing all the picked youth of Ithaca."

" We will do," answered Telemachus, " whatever you may 123
think best."

" Then," said Ulysses, " wash, and put your shirts on. Bid 129
the maids also go to their own room and dress. Phemius shall
strike up a dance tune, so that any who are passing in the
street may think there is a wedding in the house, and we can
get away into the woods before the death of the suitors is
noised abroad. Once there, we will do as heaven shall direct."

They did as he had said. The house echoed with the sound of 141
men and women dancing, and the people outside said, " So the
queen has been getting married at last. She ought to be
ashamed of herself, for not staying to protect her husband's
property."

Eurynome washed and anointed Ulysses ; Minerva also 152
beautified him, making the hair grow thick on the top of his
head and flow down in hyacinthine curls. He came from the

bath looking like an immortal god, and sat down opposite his wife. Finding, however, that he could not move her, he said to Euryclea, " Nurse, get a bed ready for me. I will sleep alone, for this woman has a heart as hard as iron."

173   " My dear," said Penelope, " I have no wish to set myself up, nor to depreciate you, but I am not struck by your appearance, for I well remember what kind of a man you were when you left Ithaca. Nevertheless, Euryclea, take his bed out of the room he built for it, and make it ready for him."

181   Ulysses knew that the bed could not be moved without cutting down the stem of a growing olive tree on the stump of which he had built it. He was very angry, and desired to know who had ventured on doing this, at the same time describing the bed fully to Penelope.

205   Then Penelope was convinced that he really was Ulysses, and fairly broke down. She flung her arms about his neck, and said she had only held aloof so long because she had been shuddering at the bare thought of any one deceiving her. Ulysses in his turn melted and embraced her, and they would have gone on indulging their sorrow till morning came, had not Minerva miraculously prolonged the night.

247   Ulysses then began to tell her of the voyages which Tiresias had told him he must now undertake, but soon broke off by saying that they had better go to bed. To which Penelope rejoined that as she should certainly have to be told about it sooner or later, she had perhaps better hear it at once.

263   Thus pressed Ulysses told her. " In the end," said he, " Tiresias told me that death should come to me from the sea. He said my life should ebb away very gently when I was full of years and peace of mind, and that my people should bless me."

288   Meanwhile Eurynome and Euryclea made the room ready,*

---

* This room was apparently not within the body of the house. It was certainly on the ground floor, for the bed was fixed on the stump of a tree ; I strongly suspect it to be the vaulted room, round the outside of which the bodies of the guilty maids were still hanging, and I also suspect it was in order to thus festoon the room that Telemachus hanged the women instead of stabbing them, but this is treading on that perilous kind of speculation which I so strongly deprecate in others. If it were not for the gruesome horror of the dance, in lines 129 –151, I should not have entertained it.

and Euryclea went inside the house, leaving Eurynome to light Penelope and Ulysses to their bed-room.   Telemachus, Philœtius, and Eumæus now left off dancing, and made the women leave off also.   Then they laid themselves down to sleep in the cloisters.

When they were in bed together, Penelope told Ulysses how 300 much she had had to bear in seeing the house filled with wicked suitors who had killed so many oxen and sheep on her account, and had drunk so many casks of wine.   Ulysses in his turn told her the whole story of his adventures, touching 310 briefly upon every point, and detailing not only his own sufferings but those he had inflicted upon other people.   She was delighted to listen, and never went to sleep till he ended his story and dropped off into a profound slumber.

When Minerva thought that Ulysses had slept long enough 344 she permitted Dawn to rise from the waters of Oceanus, and Ulysses got up.   " Wife," said he to Penelope, " now that we have at last come together again, take care of the property that is in my house.   As for the sheep and goats that the wicked suitors have eaten, I will take many by force from other people, and will compel the men of the place to make good the rest.   I will now go out to my father's house in the country.   At sunrise it will get noised about that I have been killing the suitors.   Go upstairs, therefore, and stay there with your waiting women.   See nobody, and ask no questions."

As he spoke he girded on his armour ; he roused the others 366 also and bade them arm.   He then undid the gate, and they all sallied forth.   It was now daylight, but Minerva enshrouded them in darkness, and led them quickly out of the town.

Book XXIV

THE GHOSTS OF THE SUITORS IN HADES—ULYSSES SEES HIS FATHER—IS ATTACKED BY THE FRIENDS OF THE SUITORS—LAERTES KILLS EUPEITHES—PEACE IS MADE BETWEEN HIM AND THE PEOPLE OF ITHACA.

Then Mercury took the fair golden wand with which he seals men's eyes in sleep or wakes them just as he pleases, and led the ghosts of the suitors to the house of Hades whining and gibbering as they followed. As bats fly squealing about the hollow of a great cave when one of them has fallen from the cluster in which they hang—even so did they whine and squeal as Mercury the healer of sorrow led them down into the dark abode of death. When they had passed the waters of Oceanus and the rock Leucas, they came to the gates of the Sun and the land of dreams, whereon they reached the meadow of asphodel where dwell the souls and shadows of men that can labour no more.

15 Here they came upon the ghosts of Achilles, Patroclus, Antilochus, and Ajax, and that of Agamemnon joined them. As these were conversing, Mercury came up with the ghosts of the suitors, and Agamemnon's ghost recognised that of Amphimedon who had been his host when he was in Ithaca ; so he asked him what this sudden arrival of fine young men—all of an age too—might mean, and Amphimedon told him the whole story from first to last.

203 Thus did they converse in the house of Hades deep within the bowels of the earth. Meanwhile Ulysses and the others passed out of the city and soon reached the farm of Laertes, which he had reclaimed with infinite labour. Here was his house with a lean-to running all round it, where the slaves who worked for him ate and slept, while inside the house there was an old Sicel woman, who looked after him in this his country farm.

214 " Go," said Ulysses to the others, " to the house, and kill the best pig you have for dinner ; I wish to make trial of my father and see whether he will know me."

219 So saying he gave his armour to Eumæus and Philœtius, and turned off into the vineyard, where he found his father alone, hoeing a vine. He had on a dirty old shirt, patched and very shabby ; his legs were bound round with thongs of oxhide to keep out the brambles, and he wore sleeves of leather against the thorns. He had a goatskin cap on his head and was looking very woebegone.

232 When Ulysses saw him so worn, so old and full of sorrow, he stood still under a tall pear tree and began to weep. He

doubted whether to embrace him, kiss him, and tell him all about his having come home, or whether he should first question him and see what he would say. On the whole he decided that he would be crafty with him, so he went up to his father who was bending down and digging about a plant.

"I see, Sir," said Ulysses, "that you are an excellent 244 gardener—what pains you take with it to be sure. There is not a single plant, not a fig-tree, vine, olive, pear, nor flower-bed, but bears the traces of your attention. I trust, however, that you will not be offended if I say that you take better care of your garden than of yourself. You are old, unsavoury, and very meanly clad. It cannot be because you are idle that your master takes such poor care of you ; indeed, your face and figure have nothing of the slave about them, but proclaim you of noble birth. I should have said you were one of those who should wash well, eat well, and lie soft at night as old men have a right to do. But tell me, and tell me true, whose bondsman are you, and in whose garden are you working ? Tell me also about another matter—is this place that I have come to really Ithaca ? I met a man just now who said so, but he was a dull fellow, and had not the patience to hear my story out when I was asking whether an old friend of mine who used to live here was still alive. My friend said he was the son of Laertes son of Arceisius, and I made him large presents on his leaving me."

Laertes wept and answered that in this case he would never 280 see his presents back again, though he would have been amply requited if Ulysses had been alive. "But tell me," he said, "who and whence are you ? Where is your ship ? or did you come as passenger on some other man's vessel ? "

"I will tell you every thing," answered Ulysses, "quite 302 truly. I come from Alybas, and am son to king Apheides. My name is Eperitus ; heaven drove me off my course as I was leaving Sicania, and I have been carried here against my will. 307 As for my ship, it is lying over yonder off the open country outside the town. It is five years since Ulysses left me— 308 Poor fellow ! we had every hope that we should meet again and exchange presents."

315 Laertes was overcome with grief, and Ulysses was so much touched that he revealed himself. When his father asked for proof, he shewed him the scar on his leg. " Furthermore," he added, " I will point out to you the trees in the vineyard which you gave me, and I asked you all about them as I followed you round the garden. We went over them all, and you told me their names and what they all were. You gave me thirteen pear trees, ten apple trees, and forty fig trees, and you also said you would give me fifty rows of vines ; there was corn planted between each row, and the vines yield grapes of every kind when the heat of heaven has beaten upon them." He also told his father that he had killed the suitors.

345 Laertes was now convinced, but said he feared he should have all the people of Ithaca coming to attack them. Ulysses answered that he need not trouble about this, and that they had better go and get their dinner, which would be ready by the time they got to the house.

361 When they reached the house the old Sicel woman took Laertes inside, washed him, and anointed him. Minerva also gave him a more imposing presence and made him look taller and stronger than before. When he came back, Ulysses said, " My dear father, some god has been making you much taller and better looking." To which Laertes answered that if he was as young and hearty as when he took the stronghold Nericum on the foreland, he should have been a great help to him on the preceding day, and would have killed many suitors.

383 Dolius and his sons, who had been working hard by, now came up, for the old Sicel woman, who was Dolius's wife, had been to fetch them. When they were satisfied that Ulysses was really there, they were overjoyed and embraced him one after the other. " But tell me," said Dolius, " does Penelope know, or shall we send and tell her ? " " Old man," answered Ulysses, " she knows already. What business is that of yours ? " Then they all took their seats at table.

412 Meanwhile the news of the slaughter of the suitors had got noised abroad, and the people gathered hooting and groaning before the house of Ulysses. They took their dead, buried every man his own, and put the bodies of those who came

from elsewhere on board the fishing vessels, for the fishermen to take them every man to his own place. Then they met in assembly and Eupeithes urged them to pursue Ulysses and the others before they could escape over to the main land.

Medon, however, and Phemius had now woke up, and came 439 to the assembly. Medon dissuaded the people from doing as Eupeithes advised, inasmuch as he had seen a god going about killing the suitors, and it would be dangerous to oppose the will of heaven. Halitherses also spoke in the same sense, and half the people were persuaded by him. The other half armed themselves and followed Eupeithes in pursuit of Ulysses.

Minerva then consulted Jove as to the course events should 472 take. Jove told her that she had had everything her own way so far, and might continue to do as she pleased. He should, however, advise that both sides should now be reconciled under the continued rule of Ulysses. Minerva approved of this and darted down to Ithaca.

Laertes and his household had now done dinner, and 489 Eupeithes with his band of men were seen to be near at hand. Ulysses and the others put on their armour, and Minerva joined them. "Telemachus," said Ulysses, "now that you are about to fight in a decisive engagement, see that you do no discredit to your ancestors, who were eminent all the world over for their strength and valour."

"You shall see, my dear father," replied Telemachus, "if 510 you choose, that I am in no mind, as you say, to disgrace your family."

"Good heavens," exclaimed Laertes, "what a day I am 513 enjoying. My son and grandson are vying with one another in the matter of valour." Minerva then came up to him, and bade him pray to her. She infused fresh vigour into him, and when he had prayed to her he aimed his spear at Eupeithes and killed him. Ulysses and his men fell upon the others, routed them, and would have killed one and all of them had not Minerva raised her voice and made every one pause. "Men of Ithaca," she cried, "cease this dreadful war, and settle the matter without further bloodshed."

On this they turned pale with fear, dropped their armour, 533 and fled every man towards the city. Ulysses was swooping down upon them like an eagle, but Jove sent a thunderbolt of fire that fell just in front of Minerva. Whereon she said, "Ulysses, stay this strife, or Jove will be angry with you."

545 Ulysses obeyed her gladly. Minerva then assumed the voice and form of Mentor, and presently made a covenant of peace between the two contending parties.

Chapter III

HAVING in my first chapter met the only *à priori* objections to my views concerning the sex of the writer which have yet been presented to me, I now turn to the evidence of female authorship which is furnished by the story which I have just laid before the reader.

What, let me ask, is the most unerring test of female authorship ? Surely a preponderance of female interest, and a fuller knowledge of those things which a woman generally has to deal with, than of those that fall more commonly within the province of man. People always write by preference of what they know best, and they know best what they most are, and have most to do with. This extends to ways of thought and to character, even more than to action. If man thinks the noblest study for mankind to be man, woman not less certainly believes it to be woman.

Hence if in any work the women are found to be well and sympathetically drawn, while the men are mechanical and by comparison perfunctorily treated, it is, I imagine, safe to infer that the writer is a woman ; and the converse holds good with man. Man and woman never fully understand one another save, perhaps, during courtship and honeymoon, and as a man understands man more fully than a woman can do, so does a woman, woman. Granted, it is the delight of either sex to understand the other as fully as it can, and those who succeed most in this respect are the best and happiest whether men or women ; but do what we may the barriers can never be broken down completely, and each sex will dwell mainly, though not, of course, exclusively, within its own separate world. When, moreover, we come to think of it, it is not desirable that they should be broken down, for it is on their existence that much of the attraction of either sex to the other depends.

Men seem unable to draw women at all without either laughing at them or caricaturing them ; and so, perhaps, a woman never draws a man so felicitously as when she is making him ridiculous. If she means to make him so she is certain to succeed ; if she does not mean it she will succeed more surely still. Either sex, in fact, can caricature the other delightfully, and certainly no writer has ever shown more completely than the writer of the " Odyssey " has done that, next to the glorification of woman, she considers man's little ways and weaknesses to be the fittest theme on which her genius can be displayed. But I doubt whether any writer in the whole range of literature (excepting, I suppose, Shakespeare) has succeeded in drawing a full length, life-sized, serious portrait of a member of the sex opposite to the writer's own.

It is admitted on all hands that the preponderance of interest in the " Iliad " is on the side of man, and in the " Odyssey " on that of woman. Women in the " Iliad " are few in number and rarely occupy the stage. True, the goddesses play important parts, but they are never taken seriously.

Shelley, again, speaking of the " perpetually increasing magnificence of the last seven books " of the " Iliad," says, " The ' Odyssey ' is sweet, but there is nothing like this."* The writer of the " Odyssey " is fierce as a tigress at times, but the feeling of the poem is on the whole exactly what Shelley says it is. Strength is felt everywhere, even in the tenderest passages of the " Iliad," but it is sweetness rather than strength that fascinates us throughout the " Odyssey." It is the charm of a woman not of a man.

So, again, to quote a more recent authority, Mr. Gladstone in his work on Homer already referred to, says (p. 28) :—

It is rarely in the " Iliad " that grandeur or force give way to allow the exhibition of domestic affection. Conversely, in the " Odyssey " the family life supplies the tissue into which is woven the thread of the poem.

Any one who is familiar with the two poems must know that

---

* *Select Letters of Percy Bysshe Shelley*, edited by Richard Garnett. Kegan Paul Trench & Co., 1882, p. 149.

what Mr. Gladstone has said is true ; and he might have added, not less truly, that when there is any exhibition of domestic life and affection in the " Iliad " the men are dominant, and the women are under their protection, whereas throughout the " Odyssey " it is the women who are directing, counselling, and protecting the men.

Who are the women in the " Odyssey " ?   There is Minerva, omnipresent at the elbows of Ulysses and Telemachus to keep them straight and alternately scold and flatter them.   In the " Iliad " she is a great warrior but she is no woman : in the " Odyssey " she is a great woman but no warrior ; we have, of course, Penelope—masterful nearly to the last and tossed off to the wings almost from the moment that she has ceased to be so ; Euryclea, the old servant, is quite a match for Telemachus, " do not find fault, child," she says to him, " when there is no one to find fault with " (xx. 135).   Who can doubt that Helen is master in the house of Menelaus—of whom all she can say in praise is that he is " not deficient either in person or understanding " (iv. 264) ?   Idothea in Book iv. treats Menelaus *de haut en bas,* all through the Proteus episode.   She is good to him and his men, but they must do exactly what she tells them, and she evidently enjoys " running " them,—for I can think of no apter word.   Calypso is the master mind, not Ulysses ; and, be it noted, that neither she nor Circe seem to have a manservant on their premises.   I was at an inn once and asked the stately landlady if I could see the landlord. She bridled up and answered, " We have no landlord, sir, in this house ; I cannot see what use a man is in a hotel except to clean boots and windows."   There spoke Circe and Calypso, but neither of them seem to have made even this much exception in man's favour.

Let the reader ask any single ladies of his acquaintance, who live in a house of their own, whether they prefer being waited upon by men or by women, and I shall be much surprised if he does not find that they generally avoid having a man about the house at all—gardeners of course excepted. But then the gardener generally has a wife, and a house of his own.

Take Nausicaa again, delightful as she is, it would not be wise to contradict her; she knows what is good for Ulysses, and all will go well with him so long as he obeys her, but she must be master and he man. I see I have passed over Ino in Book v. She is Idothea over again, just as Circe is Calypso, with very little variation. Who again is master—Queen Arête or King Alcinous? Nausicaa knows well enough how to answer this question. When giving her instructions to Ulysses she says :—

"Never mind my father, but go up to my mother and embrace her knees; if she is well disposed towards you there is some chance of your getting home to see your friends again" (vi. 310–315).

Throughout the Phæacian episode Arête (whose name, by the way, I take to be one of the writer's tolerably transparent disguises, and to be intended to suggest Arĕte, or " Goodness ") is a more important person than Alcinous. I do not believe in her myself; I believe Penelope would have been made more amiable if Arête had been as nice a person as the writer says she was; leaving her, however, on one side, so much more important are wives than husbands in the eyes of the author of the " Odyssey " that when Ulysses makes his farewell speech to the Phæacians, she makes him say that he hopes they may continue to give satisfaction to their wives and children (xiii. 44, 45), instead of hoping that their wives and children will continue to give satisfaction to them. A little lower down he wishes Queen Arête all happiness with her children, her people, and lastly with King Alcinous. As for King Alcinous, it does not matter whether he is happy or no, provided he gives satisfaction to Queen Arête; but he was bound to be happy as the husband of such an admirable woman.

So when the Duke of York was being married I heard women over and over again say they hoped the Princess May would be very happy with him, but I never heard one say that she hoped the Duke would be very happy with the Princess May. Men said they hoped the pair would be very happy, without naming one more than the other.

I have touched briefly on all the more prominent female

characters of the " Odyssey." The moral in every case seems to
be that man knows very little, and cannot be trusted not to
make a fool of himself even about the little that he does know,
unless he has a woman at hand to tell him what he ought to
do.   There is not a single case in which a man comes to the
rescue of female beauty in distress ; it is invariably the other
way about.

The only males who give Ulysses any help while he is on his
wanderings are Æolus, who does him no real service and refuses
to help him a second time, and Mercury, who gives him the
herb Moly (x. 305) to protect him against the spells of Circe.
In this last case, however, I do not doubt that the writer was
tempted by the lovely passage of " Il." xxiv., where Mercury
meets Priam to conduct him to the Achæan camp ; one pretty
line, indeed (and rather more), of the Iliadic passage above
referred to is taken bodily by the writer of the " Odyssey " to
describe the youth and beauty of the god.*   With these exceptions, throughout the poem Andromeda rescues Perseus, not
Perseus Andromeda—Christiana is guide and guardian to Mr.
Greatheart, not Mr. Greatheart to Christiana.

The case of Penelope may seem to be an exception.   It may
be urged that Ulysses came to her rescue, and that the whole
poem turns on his doing so.   But this is not true.   Ulysses
kills the suitors, firstly, because they had wasted his substance
—this from the first to last is the main grievance ; secondly,
because they had violated the female servants of his house ;
and only, thirdly, because they had offered marriage to his wife
while he was still alive (xxii. 36–38).   Never yet was woman
better able to hold her own when she chose, and I will show
at full length shortly that when she did not hold it it was
because she preferred not to do so.

I have dealt so far with the writer's attitude towards women
when in the world of the living.   Let us now see what her
instinct prompts her to consider most interesting in the king-
dom of the dead.   When Ulysses has reached the abode of
Hades, the first ghost he meets is that of his comrade

---

* " Od." x. 278, 279 ; cf. " Il." xxiv. 347, 348.

Elpenor, who had got drunk and fallen off the roof of Circe's house just as Ulysses and his men were about to set sail. We are expressely told that he was a person of no importance, being remarkable neither for sense nor courage, so that it does not matter about killing him, and it is transparent that the accident is only allowed to happen in order to enable Ulysses to make his little joke when he greets the ghost in Hades to the effect that Elpenor has got there more quickly by land than Ulysses had done by water. Elpenor, therefore, does not count.

The order, however, in which the crowd of ghosts approach Ulysses, is noticeable. After the blood of the victims sacrificed by Ulysses had flowed into the trench which he had dug to receive it, the writer says :—

" The ghosts came trooping up from Erebus—brides, young bachelors, old men worn out with toil, maids who had been crossed in love, and brave men who had been killed in battle, with their armour still smirched with blood ; they came from every quarter, and flitted round the trench with a strange kind of screaming sound that made me turn pale with fear" (xi. 36–43).

I do not think a male writer would have put the brides first, nor yet the young bachelors second. He would have begun with kings or great warriors or poets, nor do I believe he would make Ulysses turn pale with fear merely because the ghosts screamed a little ; they would have had to menace him more seriously.

What does Bunyan do ? When Christian tells Pliable what kind of company he will meet in Paradise, he says :—

" There we shall see elders with golden crowns ; there we shall see holy virgins with their golden harps ; there we shall see men that by the world were cut in pieces, burnt in flames, eaten of beasts, drowned in the seas, for the love they bore to the Lord of that place ; all well and cloathed with immortality as with a garment."

Men present themselves to him instinctively in the first instance, and though he quits them for a moment, he returns to them immediately without even recognising the existence of women among the martyrs.

Moreover, when Christian and Hopeful have passed through the river of death and reached the eternal city, it is none but men who greet them.

True, after having taken Christian to the Eternal City, Bunyan conducts Christiana also, and her children, in his Second Part ; but surely if he had been an inspired woman and not an inspired man, and if this woman had been writing as it was borne in upon her by her own instinct, neither aping man nor fearing him, she would have taken Christiana first, and Christian, if she took him at all, in her appendix.

Next to Elpenor the first ghost that Ulysses sees is that of his mother Anticlea, and he is sorely grieved that he may not, by Circe's instructions, speak to her till he has heard what the Theban prophet Tiresias had got to tell him. As soon as he has heard this, he enquires how he can make his mother recognise him, and converse with him. This point being answered there follows the incomparably beautiful scene between him and Anticlea, which occupies some seventy or eighty lines, and concludes by his mother's telling him to get home as fast as he can that he may tell of his adventures in Hades—to whom ? To the world at large ? To his kinsmen and countrymen ? No : it is to his wife that he is to recount them and apparently to nobody else (xi. 223, 224). Very right and proper ; but more characteristic of a female than of a male writer.

Who follow immediately on the departure of Anticlea ? Proserpine sends up " all the wives and daughters of great princes "—Tyro, daughter of Salmoneus, Antiope daughter of Asopus, Alcmena, Epicaste (better known as Jocasta), Chloris wife of Neleus, Leda, Iphimedeia, Phædra, Procris, Ariadne, Mæra, Clymene, and Eriphyle. Ulysses says that there were many more wives and daughters of heroes whom he conversed with, but that time would not allow him to detail them further ; in deference, however, to the urgent request of King Alcinous, he goes on to say how he met Agamemnon, Achilles, and Ajax (who would not speak to him) ; he touches lightly also on Minos, Orion, Tityus, Tantalus, Sisyphus, and Hercules.

I have heard women say that nothing can be made out of the

fact that the women in Hades are introduced before the men, inasmuch as they would themselves have been more likely to put the men before the women, and can understand that a male writer would be attracted in the first instance by the female shades.   When women know what I am driving at, they generally tell me this, but when I have got another woman to sound them for me, or when I have stalked them warily I find that they would rather meet the Virgin Mary, Eve, Queen Elizabeth, Cleopatra, Sappho, Jane Austen, St. Elizabeth of Hungary, Helen of Troy, Zenobia, and other great women than even Homer and Shakespeare.   One comfortable homely woman with whom I had taken great pains said she could not think what I meant by asking such questions, but if I wanted to know, she would as lief meet Mrs. Elizabeth Lazenby as Queen Elizabeth or any one of them.   For my own part, had I to choose a number of shades whom I would meet, I should include Sappho, Jane Austen, and the authoress of the " Odyssey " in my list, but I should probably ask first for Homer, Shakespeare, Handel, Schubert, Arcangelo Corelli, Purcell, Giovanni Bellini, Rembrandt, Holbein, De Hooghe, Donatello, Jean de Wespin and many another man—yet the writer of the " Odyssey " interests me so profoundly that I am not sure I should not ask to see her before any of the others.

I know of no other women writers who have sent their heroes down to Hades, but when men have done so they deal with men first and women afterwards.   Let us turn to Dante. When Virgil tells him whom Christ first saved when he descended into Hell, we find that he first rescued Adam. Not a word is there about Eve.   Then are rescued Abel, Noah, Abraham, David, Jacob and his sons—and lastly, just before the *et ceteri*—one woman, Rachel.   When Virgil has finished, Dante begins meeting people on his own account.   First come Homer, Horace, Ovid, and Lucan ; when these have been disposed of we have Electra, Hector, Æneas, Cæsar, Camilla, Penthesilea, Latinus, Lavinia, Brutus, Cato's wife Marcia, Julia, Cornelia, Saladin, Socrates, Plato, Democritus, Diogenes, Heraclitus, Empedocles, Anaxagoras, Thales, Zeno, Dioscorides, Orpheus, Linus, Cicero, Seneca, Euclid, Ptolemy, Hippocrates,

Galen, Avicen, and Averroes.   Seven women to twenty-six
men. This list reminds me of Sir John Lubbock's hundred
books, I shall therefore pursue Dante no further ; I have
given it in full because I do not like him. So far as I can see
the Italians themselves are beginning to have their doubts
about him ; " Dante è un falso idolo," has been said to me
more than once lately by highly competent critics.

Let us now look to the " Æneid."   When Æneas and the
Sibyl approach the river Styx, we read :—

> Huc omnis turba ad ripas effusa ruebat
> Matres atque viri, defunctaque corpora vitâ
> Magnanimûm heroum, pueri, innuptæque puellæ,
> Impositique rogis juvenes ante ora parentum.
>
> " Æn." vi. 305–308.

The women indeed come first, but the *i* in *viri* being short
Virgil could not help himself, and the first persons whom he
recognises as individuals are men—namely two of his captains
who had been drowned, Leucaspis and Orontes—and Palinurus.
After crossing the Styx he first passes through the region
inhabited by those who have died as infants ; then that by
those who have been unjustly condemned to die ; then that by
suicides ; then that of those who have died for love, where he
sees several women, and among them Dido, who treats him as
Ajax treated Ulysses. The rest of those whom Æneas sees or
converses with in Hades are all men.

Lucian is still more ungallant, for in his dialogues of the
dead he does not introduce a single woman.

One other case alone occurs to me among the many that
ought to do so ; I refer to Fielding's *Journey to the next
World*. The three first ghosts whom he speaks to in the
coach are men. When he gets on his journey's end, after a
short but most touching scene with his own little daughter
who had died a mere child only a few months before Fielding
wrote, and who is therefore nothing to the point, he continues :
" The first spirit with whom I entered into discourse, was the
famous Leonidas of Sparta." Of course ; soldier will greet
soldier first.   In the next paragraph one line is given to

Sappho, who we are told was singing to the accompaniment of Orpheus. Then we go on to Homer,* Virgil, Addison, Shakespeare, Betterton, Booth, and Milton.

Defoe, again, being an elderly married man, and wanting to comfort Robinson Crusoe, can think of nothing better for him than the companionship of another man, whereon he sends him Friday. A woman would have sent him an amiable and good-looking white girl whom the cannibals had taken prisoner from some shipwrecked vessel. This she would have held as likely to be far more useful to him.

So much to show that the mind of man, unless when he is young and lovesick, turns more instinctively to man than to woman. And I am convinced, as indeed every one else is, whether he or she knows it or no, that with the above exception, woman is more interested in woman. This is how the Virgin Mary has come to be Queen of Heaven, and practically of more importance than the Trinity itself in the eyes of the common people in Roman Catholic countries. For the women support the theologians more than the men do. The male Jews, again, so I am told, have a prayer in which the men thank God that they were not born women, and the women, that they were not born men. Each sex believes most firmly in itself, nor till we have done away with individualism altogether can we find the smallest reason to complain of this arrangement. A woman if she attempts an Epic is almost compelled to have a man for her central figure, but she will minimise him, and will maximise his wife and daughters, drawing them with subtler hand. That the writer of the " Odyssey " has done this is obvious ; and this fact alone should make us incline strongly towards thinking that we are in the hands not of a man but of a woman.

---

* Talking of Homer Fielding says, " I had the curiosity to ask him whether he had really writ that poem [the " Iliad "] in detached pieces and flung it about all over Greece, according to the report that went of him. He smiled at my question, and asked me whether there appeared any connection in the poem ; for if there did he thought I might answer for myself." This was first published in 1743, and is no doubt intended as a reply to Bentley. See Jebb's *Introduction to Homer*, ed. 1888, note 1 on p. 106.

Chapter IV

NOT only does the writer shew a markedly greater both interest
and knowledge when dealing with women, but she makes it
plain that she is exceedingly jealous for the honour of her sex,
and by consequence inexorable in her severity against those
women who have disgraced it. Goddesses may do what they
like, they are not to be judged by mortal codes ; but a mortal
woman who has fallen must die.

No woman throughout the " Odyssey " is ever laughed at.
Women may be hanged but they must not be laughed at. Men
may be laughed at, indeed Alcinous is hardly mentioned at all
except to be made more or less ridiculous. One cannot say
that Menelaus in Books iv. and xv. is being deliberately made
ridiculous, but made ridiculous he certainly is, and he is treated
as a person of far less interest and importance than his wife is.
Indeed Ulysses, Alcinous, Menelaus, and Nestor are all so
like one another that 1 do not doubt they were drawn from
the same person, just as Ithaca and Scheria are from the same
place. Who that person was we shall never know ; nevertheless
I would point out that unless a girl adores her father he is
generally, to her, a mysterious powerful being whose ways are
not as her ways. He is feared as a dark room is feared by
children ; and if his wife is at all given to laughing at him,
his daughter will not spare him, however much she may cajole
and in a way love him.

But, as I have said, though men may be laughed at, the
women are never taken other than quite seriously. Venus is,
indeed, made a little ridiculous in one passage, but she was a

goddess, so it does not matter ; besides, the brunt of the ridicule was borne by Mars, and Venus was instantly re-adorned and comforted by the Graces. I cannot remember a single instance of a woman's being made to do anything which she could not do without loss of dignity—I except, of course, slaves, and am speaking of the higher social classes.

It has often been observed that the Messenger of the Gods in the " Iliad " is always Iris, while in the " Odyssey " he is no less invariably Mercury. I incline to attribute this to the author's dislike of the idea that so noble a lady as Iris should be made to fetch and carry for anybody. For it is evident Iris was still generally held to have been the messenger of the gods. This appears from the beginning of Book xviii., where we are told that Irus's real name was Arnæus, but that he was called Irus (which is nothing but Iris with a masculine termination) " because he used to carry messages when any one would send him." Writers do not fly in the face of current versions unless for some special reasons of their own.

If, however, a woman has misconducted herself she is to be shewn no mercy. There are only three cases in point, and one of these hardly counts inasmuch as the punishment of the guilty woman, Clytemnestra, was not meted out to her by the authoress herself. The hold, however, which the story of Clytemnestra's guilt has upon her, the manner in which she repeatedly recurs to it, her horror at it, but at the same time her desire to remove as much of the blame as possible from Clytemnestra's shoulders, convinces me that she actually feels the disgrace which Clytemnestra's treachery has inflicted upon all women " even on the good ones." Why should she be at such pains to tell us that Clytemnestra was a person of good natural disposition (iii. 266), and was irreproachable until death had removed the bard under whose protection Agamemnon had placed her ?* When she was left alone—without either husband or guardian, and with an insidious wretch like Ægisthus beguiling her with his incessant flattery, she yielded, and there is no more to be said, except that it was very dread-

---

* The part about the bard is omitted in my abridgement.

ful and she must be abandoned to her fate. I see Mr. Gladstone has wondered what should have induced Homer (whom he holds to have written the " Odyssey " as well as the " Iliad ") to tell us that Clytemnestra was a good woman to start with,* but with all my respect for his great services to Homeric literature, I cannot think that he has hit upon the right explanation. It should not be forgotten, moreover, that this extenuation of Clytemnestra's guilt belongs to a part of the " Odyssey " that was engrafted on to the original design—a part in which, as I shall show later, there was another woman's guilt, which was only not extenuated because it was absolutely denied in the face of overwhelming evidence—I mean Penelope's.

The second case in point is that of the woman who stole Eumæus when he was a child. A few days after she has done this, and has gone on board the ship with the Phœnician traders, she is killed by Diana, and thrown overboard to the seals and fishes (xv. 403–484).

The third case is that of the women of Ulysses' household who had misconducted themselves with the suitors during his absence. We are told that there were fifty women servants in the house, of whom twelve alone were guilty. It is curious that the number of servants should be exactly the same as that of the maidservants in the house of king Alcinous, and it should be also noted that twelve is a very small number for the guilty servants, considering that there were over a hundred suitors, and that the maids seem to have been able to leave the house by night when they chose to do so (xx. 6–8)—true, we are elsewhere told that the women had been violated and only yielded under compulsion, but this makes it more wonderful that they should be so few—and I may add, more terribly severe to hang them. I think the laxity of prehistoric times would have prompted a writer who was not particularly jealous for the honour of women, to have said that there were thirty-eight, or even more, guilty, and only twelve innocent. We must bear in mind on the other hand that when Euryclea brought out the thirty-eight innocent women to see Ulysses

---

* *Studies on Homer and the Homeric age.*—Oxford University Press, 1858, Vol. I., p. 28.

after he had killed the suitors, Ulysses recognised them all (xxii. 501). The youngest of them therefore can hardly have been under forty, and some no doubt were older—for Ulysses had been gone twenty years.

Now how are the guilty ones treated? A man who was speaking of my theory that the " Odyssey " was written by a woman as a mere *mauvaise plaisanterie*, once told me it was absurd, for the first thing a woman would have thought of after the suitors had been killed was the dining room carpet. I said that *mutatis mutandis* this was the very thing she did think of.

As soon as Ulysses has satisfied himself that not a single suitor is left alive, he tells Euryclea to send him the guilty maidservants, and on their arrival he says to Telemachus, Eumæus and Philœtius (xxii. 437–443) :

" Begin to bear away the corpses, and make the women help you. When you have done this, sponge down the seats and tables, till you have set the whole house in order ; then take the maids outside . . . . and thrust them through with your swords."

These orders are faithfully obeyed ; the maids help in the work of removing the bodies and they sponge the chairs and tables till they are clean—Ulysses standing over them and seeing that they lose no time. This done, Telemachus (whose mother, we are told (xxii. 426–427) had never yet permitted him to give orders to the female servants) takes them outside and hangs them (xxii. 462), as a more dishonourable death than the one his father had prescribed for them—perhaps also he may have thought he should have less blood to clean up than if he stabbed them—but see note on p. 98. The writer tells us in a line which she borrows in great part from the " Iliad,"* that their feet move convulsively for a short time though not for very long, but her ideas of the way in which Telemachus hanged them are of the vaguest. No commentator has ever yet been able to understand it ; the only explanation seems to be that the writer did not understand it herself, and did not care to do so. Let it suffice that the women were obviously hanged.

---

* " Od." xxii. 473, cf. " Il." xiii. 573.

No man writing in pre-Christian times would have considered the guilt of the women to require so horrible a punishment. He might have ordered them to be killed, but he would not have carried his indignation to the point of making them first clean up the blood of their paramours. Fierce as the writer is against the suitors, she is far more so against the women. When the suitors are all killed, Euryclea begins to raise a cry of triumph over them, but Ulysses checks her. " Hold your tongue, woman," he says, " it is ill bragging over the bodies of dead men " (xxii. 411). So also it is ill getting the most hideous service out of women up to the very moment when they are to be executed ; but the writer seems to have no sense of this ; where female honour has been violated by those of woman's own sex, no punishment is too bad for them.

The other chief characteristics of the " Odyssey " which incline me to ascribe it to a woman are a kind of art for art's sake love of a small lie, and a determination to have things both ways whenever it suits her purpose. This never seems to trouble her. There the story is, and the reader may take it or leave it. She loves flimsy disguises and mystifications that stultify themselves, and mystify nobody. To go no further than Book i. and iii., Minerva in each of these tells plausible stories full of circumstantial details, about her being on her way to Temesa with a cargo of iron and how she meant to bring back copper (i. 184), and again how she was going to the Cauconians on the following morning to recover a large debt that had been long owing to her (iii. 366), and then, before the lies she had been at such pains to concoct are well out of her mouth she reveals herself by flying into the air in the form of an eagle. This, by the way, she could not well do in either case if she was in a roofed hall, but might be conceived as doing if, as I suppose her to have been in both cases, she was in a roofed cloister that ran round an open court.

There is a flavour of consecutive fifths in these flights,* if

---

* I should explain to the non-musical reader that it is forbidden in music to have consecutive fifths or octaves between the same parts.

indeed they are not downright octaves, and I cannot but think that the writer would have found a smoother progression open to her if she had cared to look for one ; but letting this pass, the way in which white lies occur from the first book to the last, the punctiliousness, omnipresent, with which small religious observances are insisted upon, coupled with not a little unscrupulousness when these have been attended to, the respect for gods and omens, and for the *convenances* generally —all these seem to me to be more characteristic of a woman's writing than a man's.

The seriousness, again, with which Telemachus is taken, the closeness with which he adheres to his programme, the precision with which he invariably does what his father, his mother, Minerva, or any responsible person tells him that he should do, except in one passage which is taken almost *verbatim* from the " Iliad,"* the way in which Minerva beautifies him and preaches to him ; the unobtrusive but exemplary manner in which he discharges all his religious, moral, and social duties —all seem to me to point in the direction of thinking that the writer is a woman and a young one.

How does Minerva preach to him ? When he has washed his hands in the sea he prays that she will help him on his intended voyage in search of news concerning his father. The goddess then comes up to him disguised as Mentor, and speaks as follows :

" Telemachus, if you are made of the same stuff as your father you will be neither fool or coward henceforward, for Ulysses never broke his word nor left his work half done. If, then, you take after him your voyage will not be fruitless, but unless you have the blood of Ulysses and Penelope in your veins I see no likelihood of your succeeding. Sons are seldom as good men as their fathers ; they are generally worse not better ; still, as you are not going to be either fool or coward hence- forward, and are not entirely without some share of your father's wise discernment, I look with hope upon your under- taking " (ii. 270–280).

---

* " Od." i. 356–359, cf. " Il." vi. 490–493. The word " war " in the " Iliad " becomes " speech " in the " Odyssey." There is no other change.

Hence the grandmotherly reputation which poor Mentor is never likely to lose. It was not Mentor but Minerva. The writer does not make Minerva say that daughters were rarely as good women as their mothers were. I had a very dear kind old aunt who when I was a boy used to talk to me just in this way. " Unstable as water," she would say, " thou shalt not excel." I almost heard her saying it (and more to the same effect) when I was translating the passage above given. My uncles did not talk to me at all in the same way.

I may add parenthetically here, but will deal with the subject more fully in a later chapter, that all the time Minerva was lecturing Telemachus she must have known that his going would be worse than useless, inasmuch as Ulysses was, by her own arrangements, on the very eve of his return ; and indeed he was back again in Ithaca before Telemachus got home.

See, again, the manner in which Penelope scolds him in Book xviii. 215, &c., for having let Ulysses and Irus fight. She says :

" Telemachus, I fear you are no longer so discreet and well conducted as you used to be. When you were younger you had a greater sense of propriety ; now, however, that you are grown up, though a stranger to look at you would take you for the son of a well-to-do father as far as size and good looks go, your conduct is by no means what it should have been. What is all this disturbance that has been going on, and how came you to allow a stranger to be so disgracefully ill-treated ? What would have happened if he had suffered serious injury while a suppliant in our house ? Surely this would have been very discreditable to you."

I do not believe any man could make a mother rebuke her son so femininely.

Again, the fidelity with which people go on crying incessantly for a son who has been lost to them for twenty years, though they have still three sons left,* or for a brother whom they have never even seen,† is part and parcel of that jealousy for the sanctity of domestic life, in respect of which women are apt to be more exacting than men.

---

* " Od." ii. 15–23.　　† " Od." iv. 186–188. Neither of these passages is given in my abridgement.

And yet in spite of all this the writer makes Telemachus take no pains to hide the fact that his grievance is not so much the alleged ill-treatment of his mother, nor yet the death of his father, as the hole which the extravagance of the suitors is making in his own pocket. When demanding assistance from his fellow countrymen, he says, of the two great evils that have fallen upon his house :

" The first of these is the loss of my excellent father, who was chief among all you here present and was like a father to every one of you. The second is much more serious, and ere long will be the utter ruin of my estate. The sons of all the chief men among you are pestering my mother to marry them against her will. They are afraid to go to her father Icarius, asking him to choose the one he likes best, and to provide marriage gifts for his daughter, but day after day they keep hanging about my father's house, sacrificing our oxen, sheep, and fat goats for their banquets, and never giving so much as a thought to the quantity of wine they drink. No estate can stand such recklessness " (ii. 46–58).

Moreover it is clear throughout Books iii. and iv., in which Telemachus is trying to get news of his father, that what he really wants is evidence of his death, not of his being alive, though this may only be because he despairs of the second alternative. The indignation of Telemachus on the score of the extravagance of the suitors is noticeably shared by the writer all through the poem ; she is furious about it ; perhaps by reason of the waste she saw going on in her father's house. Under all she says on this head we seem to feel the rankling of a private grievance, and it often crosses my mind that in the suitors she also saw the neighbours who night after night came sponging on the reckless good nature of Alcinous, to the probable eventual ruin of his house.

Women, religion, and money are the three dominant ideas in the mind of the writer of the " Odyssey." In the " Iliad " the *belli causa* is a woman, money is a detail, and man is most in evidence. In the " Odyssey " the *belli causa* is mainly money, and woman is most in evidence—often when she does not appear to be so—just as in the books of the " Iliad " in which the Trojans are supposed to be most triumphant over the Achæans, it is the Trojans all the time whose slaughter is most dwelt upon.

It is strange that the " Odyssey," in which money is so constantly present to the mind of the writer, should show not even the faintest signs of having been written from a business point of view, whereas the " Iliad," in which money appears but little, abounds with evidence of its having been written to take with a certain audience whom the writer both disliked and despised—and hence of having been written with an eye to money.

I will now proceed to the question whether Penelope is being, if I may say so, whitewashed. Is the version of her conduct that is given us in the " Odyssey " the then current one, or is the writer manipulating a very different story, and putting another face on it—as all poets are apt to do with any story that they are re-telling ? Tennyson, not to mention many earlier writers, has done this with the Arthurian Legends, the original form of which takes us into a moral atmosphere as different as can well be conceived from the one we meet with in the *Idylls of the King*.

There is no improbability (for other instances will occur to the reader so readily that I need not quote them) in the supposition that the writer of the " Odyssey " might choose to recast a story which she deemed insulting to her sex, as well as disgusting in itself ; the question is, has she done so or not ? Do traces of an earlier picture show up through the one she has painted over it, so distinctly as to make it obvious what the original picture represented ? If they do not, I will give up my case, but if they do, I shall hold it highly improbable that a man in the Homeric age would undertake the impossible task of making Penelope at the same time plausible and virtuous. I am afraid I think he would be likely to make her out blacker than the last poet who had treated the subject, rather than be at any pains to whiten her.

Least of all would Homer himself have been prompted to make Penelope out better than report says she was. He would not have cared whether she was better or worse. He is fond of women, but he is also fond of teasing them, and he shows not the slightest signs of any jealousy for female honour, or of a desire to exalt women generally. He shows no more sign of this than he does of the ferocity with which punishment is inflicted on the women of Ulysses' household—a ferocity which is in itself sufficient to make it inconceivable that the " Iliad " and the " Odyssey " should be by the same person.

Chapter V

It is known that scandalous versions of Penelope's conduct
were current among the ancients ; indeed they seem to have
prevailed before the completion of the Epic cycle, for in the
Telegony, which is believed to have come next in chrono-
logical order after the " Odyssey," we find that when Ulysses had
killed the suitors he did not go on living with Penelope, but
settled in Thesprotia, and married Callidice, the queen of the
country. He must, therefore, have divorced Penelope, and he
could hardly have done this if he accepted the Odyssean version
of her conduct. According to the author of the *Telegony,*
Penelope and Telemachus go on living in Ithaca, where
eventually Ulysses returns and is killed by Telegonus, a son
who had been born to him by Circe. For further reference
to ancient, though a good deal later, scandalous versions, see
Smith's Dictionary under " Penelope."

Let us see what the " Odyssey " asks us to believe, or rather,
swallow. We are told that more than a hundred young men
fall violently in love, at the same time, with a supposed widow,
who before the close of their suit can hardly have been under
forty, and who had a grown up son—pestering her for several
years with addresses that they know are most distasteful to
her. They are so madly in love with her that they cannot
think of proposing to any one else (ii. 205–207) till she has
made her choice. When she has done this they will go ; till
then, they will pay her out for her cruel treatment of them by
eating her son Telemachus out of house and home. This therefore, they proceed to do, and Penelope, who is a model both
wife and mother, suffers agonies of grief, partly because of the
death of her husband, and partly because she cannot get the
suitors out of the house.

One would have thought all she had to do was to bolt the doors as soon as the suitors had left for the night, and refuse to open them in the morning ; for the suitors never sleep in the same house with Penelope. They sleep at various places in the town, in the middle of which Ulysses' house evidently stands, and if they were meek enough to let themselves be turned out, they would be meek enough to let themselves be kept out, if those inside showed anything of a firm front. Not one of them ever sees Penelope alone ; when she comes into their presence she is attended by two respectable female servants who stand on either side of her, and she holds a screen or veil modestly before her face—true, she was forty, but neither she nor the poetess seem to bear this in mind, so we may take it as certain that it was modesty and nothing else that made her hold up the veil. The suitors were not men of scrupulous delicacy, and in spite of their devotion to Penelope lived on terms of improper intimacy with her women servants—none of whom appear to have been dismissed instantly on detection. It is a little strange that not one of those suitors who came from a long distance should have insisted on being found in bed as well as board, and so much care is taken that not one breath of scandal should attach to Penelope, that we infer a sense on the writer's part that it was necessary to put this care well in evidence. I cannot think, for example, that Penelope would have been represented as nearly so incredulous about the return of Ulysses in Book xxiii., if she had been nearly as virtuous as the writer tries to make her out. The amount of caution with which she is credited is to some extent a gauge of the thickness of the coat of whitewash which the writer considers necessary. In all Penelope's devotion to her husband there is an ever present sense that the lady doth protest too much.

Still stranger, however, is the fact that these ardent passionate lovers never quarrel among themselves for the possession of their middle-aged paragon. The survival of the fittest does not seem to have had any place in their system. They show no signs of jealousy, but jog along cheek by jowl as a very happy family, aiming spears at a mark, playing draughts, flaying goats and singeing pigs in the yard, drinking an untold quantity of wine, and generally holding high feast. They insist that Penelope should marry somebody, but who the happy somebody is to be is a matter of no importance.* No one seems to think it essential that she shall marry himself in particular. Not one of them ever finds out that his case is hopeless and takes his leave ; and thus matters drift on year after year— during all which time Penelope is not getting any younger— the suitors dying of love for Penelope, and Penelope dying only to be rid of them.

Granted that the suitors are not less in love with the good cheer they enjoy at Telemachus's expense, than they are with his mother ; but this mixture of perfect lover and perfect sponger is so impossible that no one could have recourse to it unless aware that he (or she) was in extreme difficulty. If men are in love they will not sponge ; if they sponge they are not in love ; we may have it either way but not both ; when, therefore, the writer of the " Odyssey " not only attributes such impossible conduct to the suitors, but asks us also to believe that a clever woman could not keep at any rate some few of her hundred lovers out of the house, although their presence had been for many years in a high degree distasteful to her, we may know that we are being hoodwinked as far as the writer can hoodwink us, and shall be very inclinable to believe that the suitors were not so black, nor Penelope so white, as we are being given to understand.

As for her being overawed by the suitors, she talks very plainly to them at times, as for example in xviii. 274–280, and again in xix. 322 where she speaks as though she were perfectly able to get rid of any suitor who was obnoxious to her.

Over and above this we may infer that the writer who can tell such a story with a grave face cannot have even the faintest conception of the way in which a man feels towards a woman he is in love with, nor yet much (so far as I may venture to form an opinion) of what women commonly feel

---

* " Od." ii. 127–128 and 203–207.

towards the man of their choice; I conclude, therefore, that she was still very young, and unmarried.   At any rate the story told above cannot have been written by Homer; if it is by a man at all it must be by some prehistoric Fra Angelico, who had known less in his youth, or forgotten more in his old age, than the writer of the "Iliad" is at all likely to have done. If he had still known enough to be able to write the "Odyssey," he would have remembered more than the writer of the "Odyssey" shows any signs of having ever known.

A man, if he had taken it into his head (as the late Lord Tennyson might very conceivably have done) to represent Penelope as virtuous in spite of current scandalous stories to the contrary—a man, would not have made the suitors a band of lovers at all.   He would have seen at once that this was out of the question, and would have made them mere marauders, who overawed Penelope by their threats, and were only held in check by her mother wit and by, say, some three or four covert allies among the suitors themselves.   Do what he might he could not make the permanent daily presence of the suitors plausible, but it would be possible; whereas the combination of perfect sponger and perfect lover which is offered us by the writer of the "Odyssey" is grotesquely impossible, nor do I imagine that she would have asked us to accept it, but for her desire to exalt her sex by showing how a clever woman can bring any number of men to her feet, hoodwink them, spoil them, and in the end destroy them.   This, however, is surely a woman's theme rather than a man's—at least I know of no male writer who has attempted anything like it.

We have now seen the story as told from Penelope's point of view; let us proceed to hear it from that of the suitors. We find this at the beginning of Book ii., and I will give Antinous's speech at fuller length than I have done in my abridgement.   After saying that Penelope had for years been encouraging every single suitor by sending him flattering messages (in which, by the way, Minerva fully corroborates him in Book xiii. 379–381) he continues :

" And then there was that other trick she played us.   She set up a great tambour frame in her room, and began to work on an

enormous piece of fine needlework. ' Sweethearts,' said she,
' Ulysses is indeed dead, still, do not press me to marry again
immediately ; wait—for I would not have my skill in needlework perish unrecorded—till I have completed a pall for the
hero Laertes, to be ready against the time when death shall
take him. He is very rich, and the women of the place will talk
if he is laid out without a pall.'

" This was what she said, and we assented ; whereon we
could see her, working on her great web all day, but at night
she would unpick the stitches again by torchlight. She fooled
us in this way for three years and we never found her out, but
as time wore on and she was now in her fourth year, one of her
maids, who knew what she was doing, told us, and we caught
her in the act of undoing her work ; so she had to finish it,
whether she would or no.

" The suitors, therefore, make you this answer, that both you
and the Achæans may understand : ' Send your mother away,
and bid her marry the man of her own and her father's choice,'
for I do not know what will happen if she goes on plaguing us
much longer with the airs she gives herself on the score of the
accomplishments Minerva has taught her, and because she is so
clever. We never yet heard of such a woman. We know all
about Tyro, Alcmena, Mycene, and the famous women of old,
but they were nothing to your mother any one of them. It
was not fair of her to treat us in that way, and as long as she
continues in the mind with which heaven has now endowed
her, so long shall we go on eating up your estate ; and I do not
see why she should change, for it is she who gets the honour
and glory, and it is you, not she, who lose all this substance.
We however, will not go about our business, nor anywhere
else, till she has made her choice and married some one or
other of us " (ii. 93–128).

Roughly, then, the authoress's version is that Penelope is
an injured innocent, and the suitors', that she is an artful
heartless flirt who prefers having a hundred admirers rather
than one husband. Which comes nearest, not to the truth—
for we may be sure the suitors could have said a great deal
more than the writer chooses to say they said—but to the
original story which she was sophisticating, and retelling in a
way that was more to her liking ? The reader will have noted
that on this occasion the suitors seem to have been in the
house after nightfall.

We cannot forget that when Telemachus first told Minerva about the suitors, he admitted that his mother had not point blank said that she would not marry again. "She does not," he says, "refuse the hateful marriage, nor yet does she bring matters to an end" (i. 249, 250). Apparently not; but if not, why not? Not to refuse at once is to court courtship, and if she had not meant to court it she seems to have been adept enough in the art of hoodwinking men to have found some means of "bringing the matter to an end."

Sending pretty little messages to her admirers was not exactly the way to get rid of them. Did she ever try snubbing? Nothing of the kind is placed on record. Did she ever say, "Well, Antinous, whoever else I may marry, you may make your mind easy that it will not be you." Then there was boring—did she ever try that? Did she ever read them any of her grandfather's letters? Did she sing them her own songs, or play them music of her own composition? I have always found these courses successful when I wanted to get rid of people. There are indeed signs that something had been done in this direction, for the suitors say that they cannot stand her high art nonsense and æsthetic rhodomontade any longer, but it is more likely she had been trying to attract than to repel. Did she set them by the ears by repeating with embellishments what they had said to her about one another? Did she ask Antinous or Eurymachus to sit to her for her web —give them a good stiff pose, make them stick to it, and talk to them all the time? Did she find errands for them to run, and then scold them, and say she did not want them? or make them do commissions for her and forget to pay them, or keep on sending them back to the shop to change things, and they had given ever so much too much money and she wished she had gone and done it herself? Did she insist on their attending family worship? In a word, did she do a single one of the thousand things so astute a matron would have been at no loss to hit upon if she had been in earnest about not wishing to be courted? With one touch of common sense the whole fabric crumbles into dust.

Telemachus in his rejoinder to the suitors does not deny a

single one of their facts. He does not deny that his mother had been in the habit of sending them encouraging messages, nor does he attempt to explain her conduct about the web. This, then, being admitted, and it being also transparent that Penelope had used no due diligence in sending her lovers to the right about, can we avoid suspecting that there is a screw loose somewhere, and that a story of very different character is being manipulated to meet the exigencies of the writer? And shall we go very far wrong if we conclude that according to the original version, Penelope picked out her web, not so much in order to delay a hateful marriage, as to prolong a very agreeable courtship?

It was no doubt because Laertes saw what was going on that he went to live in the country and left off coming into the town (i. 189, 190), and Penelope probably chose the particular form her work assumed in order to ensure that he should not come near her. Why could she not set about making a pall for somebody else? Was Laertes likely to continue calling, when every time he did so he knew that Euryclea would only tell him her mistress was upstairs working at his pall, but she would be down directly? Do let the reader try and think it out a little for himself.

As for Laertes being so badly off as Anticlea says he was in Book xi., there is not one grain of truth in that story. The writer had to make him out poor in order to explain his not having interfered to protect Penelope, but Penelope's excuse for making her web was that he was a man of large property. It is the same with the suitors. When it is desired to explain Telemachus's not having tried in some way to recover from them, they are so poor that it would be a waste of money to sue them; when, on the other hand, the writer wants Penelope to air her woman's wit by getting presents out of them (xviii. 274–280), just before Ulysses kills them, they have any amount of money. One day more, and she would have been too late. The writer knew that very well, but she was not going to let Penelope lose her presents. She evidently looks upon man as fair game, which male writers are much less apt to do. Of course the first present she receives is a new dress.

Returning to Laertes, he must have had money, or how could Ulysses be so rich? Where did Ulysses' money come from? He could hardly have made much before he went to Troy, and he does not appear to have sent anything home thence. Nothing has been heard from him, and in Book x.,* he appears to be bringing back his share of plunder with him—in which case it was lost in the shipwreck off the coast of the Thrinacian island. He seems to have had a dowry of some kind with Penelope, for Telemachus say that if he sends his mother away he shall have to refund it to his grandfather Icarius, and urges this fact as one of the reasons for not sending her (ii. 132, 133); the greater part, however, of Ulysses' enormous wealth must have come to him from Laertes, who we may be sure kept more for himself than he gave to his son. What, then, had become of all this money—for Laertes seems to have been a man of very frugal habits? The answer is that it was still in Laertes' hands, and the reason for his never coming to town now was partly, no doubt, the pall; partly the scandalous life which his daughter was leading; but mainly the writer's inability to explain his non-interference unless she got him out of the way.

The account, again, which Ulysses' mother gives him in Hades (xi. 180, &c.) of what is going on in Ithaca shows a sense that there is something to conceal. She says not one word about the suitors. All she says is that Telemachus has to see a good deal of company, which is only reasonable seeing that he is a magistrate and is asked out everywhere himself (xi. 185-187). Nothing can be more coldly euphemistic, nor show a fuller sense that there was a good deal more going on than the speaker chose to say. If Anticlea had believed her daughter-in-law to be innocent, she would have laid the whole situation before Ulysses.

It may be maintained that the suitors were not yet come to Ithaca in force, for the visit to Hades occurs early in the wanderings of Ulysses, and before his seven years' sojourn with Calypso, so that Anticlea may really have known nothing

---

* " Od." x. 40, this passage is not given in my abridgement.

about the suitors ; but the writer has forgotten this, and has
represented Telemachus as already arrived at man's estate.
In truth, at this point Telemachus was at the utmost only
twelve or thirteen years old, and a children's party was all the
entertainment he need either receive or give. The writer has
made a slip in her chronology, for throughout the poem Telemachus is represented as only just arriving at man's estate in
the twentieth year of Ulysses' absence. It is evident that in
describing the interview with Anticlea the writer has in her
mind the state of things existing just before Ulysses' return,
when the suitors were in full riot. This, indeed, appears still
more plainly lower down, when Agamemnon, also in Hades,
says that Telemachus was a baby in arms when the Trojan
war broke out, and that he must now be grown up (xi. 448, 449).

The silence therefore of Ulysses' mother is wilful so far as
the writer is concerned. She must have conceived of Anticlea
as knowing all about the suitors perfectly well—for she did not
die till Telemachus was, by her own account, old enough to be a
magistrate. The explanation I believe to be, that at the time
Book xi. was written, the writer had as yet no intention of
adding Books i.–iv., and from line 187 of Book xiii. to Book xxiv.
but proposed to ignore the current scandalous stories about
Penelope, and to say as little as possible about her. I will deal
with this more fully when I come to the genesis and development of the poem, but may as well say at once that the difficulty
above pointed out will have to remain unexplained except as
a slip in chronology on the part of a young writer who was
piecing new work on to old. Any one but the writer herself
would have seen it and avoided it ; indeed it is quite possible
that she came to see it, and did not think it worth her while
to be at the trouble of altering it. If this is so I, for one, shall
think none the worse of her.

Chapter VI

FURTHER CONSIDERATIONS REGARDING THE CHARACTER OF
PENELOPE—THE JOURNEY OF TELEMACHUS TO LACEDÆMON.

THE question whether or no the writer of the "Odyssey" is
putting her own construction on grosser versions of Penelope's
conduct current among her countrymen, has such an important bearing on that of the writer's sex, that I shall bring
further evidence to show how impossible she finds it to conceal
the fact that those who knew Penelope best had no confidence
in her.

Minerva with quick womanly instinct took in the situation
at a glance, and went straight to the point. On learning from
Telemachus that Penelope did not at once say she would not
marry again, she wastes no words, but says promptly, "If your
mother's mind is set on marrying again" (and surely this
implies that the speaker had no doubts that it was so set) "let
her go back to her father" (i. 276). From this we may infer
that Minerva had not only formed her own opinion about
Penelope's intentions, but saw also that she meant taking her
time about the courtship, and was not likely to be brought to
the point by any measures less decisive than sending her back
to her father's house.

We know, moreover, what Minerva thought of Penelope
from another source. Minerva appears to Telemachus in a
dream when he is staying with King Menelaus, and gives him
to understand that his mother is on the point of marrying
Eurymachus, one of the suitors (xv. 1–42). This was (so at
least we are intended to suppose) a wanton falsehood on
Minerva's part. Nevertheless if the matter had ended there,
nothing probably would have pleased Telemachus better ; for
in spite of his calling the marriage "hateful," there can be no
question that he would have been only too thankful to get his
mother out of the house, if she would go of her own free will.

Penelope says he was continually urging her to marry and go, on the score of the expense he was being put to by the protracted attentions of the suitors (xix. 530–534). Penelope indeed seems to have been such an adept at lying that it is very difficult to know when to believe her, but Telemachus says enough elsewhere to leave no doubt that, in spite of a certain decent show of reluctance, he would have been glad that his mother should go.

Unfortunately Minerva's story does not end with saying that Penelope means marrying Eurymachus ; she adds that in this case she will probably steal some of Telemachus's property. She says to him :

" You know what women are ; they always want to do the best they can for the man who is married to them at the moment. They forget all about their first husband and the children that they have had by him. Go home, therefore, at once, and put everything in charge of the most respectable housekeeper you can find, until it shall please heaven to send you a wife of your own " (xv. 20–26).

This passage not only betrays a want of confidence in Penelope which is out of keeping with her ostensible antecedents, but it goes far to show that Minerva had read the *Cypria*, in which poem (now lost) we are told that Helen did exactly what is here represented as likely to be done by Penelope ; but leaving this, surely if Penelope's antecedents had been such as the writer wishes us to accept, Telemachus would have made a very different answer to the one he actually made. He would have said, " My dear Minerva, what a word has escaped the boundary of your teeth. My mother steal my property and go off with an unprincipled scoundrel like Eurymachus ? No one can know better than yourself that she is the last woman in the world to be capable of such conduct." And then he would have awoke as from a hideous dream.

What, however, happens in reality ? Telemachus does indeed wake up (xv. 43) in great distress, but it is about his property, not about his mother. " Who steals my mother steals trash, but whoso filches from me my family heirlooms," &c. He kicks poor Pisistratus to wake him, and says they must harness the horses and be off home at once. Pisistratus rejoins that it is pitch dark ; come what may they must really wait till morning. Besides, they ought to say good bye to Menelaus, and get a present out of him ; he will be sure to give them one, if Telemachus will not be in such an unreasonable hurry. Can anything show more clearly what was the inner mind both of Minerva and Telemachus about Penelope—and also what kind of ideas the audience had formed about her ?

How differently, again, do Minerva and Telemachus regard the stealing. Telemachus feels it acutely and at once. Minerva takes it as a matter of course—but then the property was not hers. The authoress of the " Odyssey " is never severe about theft. Minerva evidently thinks it not nice of Penelope to want to marry again before it is known for certain that Ulysses is dead, but she explains that Eurymachus has been exceeding all the other suitors in the magnificence of his presents, and has lately increased them (xv. 17, 18). After all, Penelope had a right to please herself, and as long as she was going to be *bonâ fide* married, she might steal as much as she could, without loss of dignity or character. The writer put this view into Minerva's mouth as a reasonable one for a woman to take. So perhaps it was, but it is not a man's view.

Here I will close my case—as much of it, that is to say, as I have been able to give in the space at my disposal—for the view that the writer of the " Odyssey " was whitewashing Penelope. As, however, we happen to be at Lacedæmon let me say what more occurs to me in connection with the visit of Telemachus to King Menelaus that bears on the question whether the writer is a man or a woman.

When Telemachus and Nestor's son Pisistratus reached Lacedæmon at the beginning of Book iv., Menelaus was celebrating the double marriage of his son Megapenthes and of his daughter Hermione. The writer says :

. . . . . they reached the low lying city of Lacedæmon, where they drove straight to the abode of Menelaus, [and found him in his own house feasting with his many clansmen in honour of the wedding of his son, and also that of his daughter whom he was giving in marriage to the son of that valiant warrior Achilles. He had given his consent and promised her to him while he was still at Troy, and now the gods were bringing the marriage about, so he was sending her with chariots and horses to the city of the Myrmidons over whom Achilles' son was reigning. For his only son he had found a bride from Sparta, the daughter of Alector. This son, Megapenthes, was born to him of a bondwoman, for heaven had vouchsafed Helen no more children after she had borne Hermione who was fair as golden Venus herself.] (iv. 1–14).

I have enclosed part of the above quotation in brackets not because I have any doubt that the whole of it is by the same hand as the rest of the poem, but because I am convinced that the bracketed lines were interpolated by the writer after her work had been completed, or at any rate after Books iv. and xv. had assumed their present shape. The reason for the interpolation I take to be that she could not forgive herself for having said nothing about Hermione, whose non-appearance in Book xv. and in the rest of Book iv. she now attempts to explain by interpolating the passage above quoted, and thus making her quit Lacedæmon for good and all at the very beginning of this last named book. But whatever the cause of the interpolation may have been, an interpolation it certainly is, for nothing can be plainer from the rest of Book iv. than that there were no festivities going on, and that the only guests were uninvited ones—to wit Telemachus and Pisistratus.

True, the writer tried to cobble the matter by introducing lines 621–624, which in our texts are always enclosed in brackets as suspected—I suppose because Aristarchus marked them with *obeli*, though he did not venture to exclude them. The cobble, however, only makes things worse, for it is obviously inadequate, and its abruptness puzzles the reader.

Accepting, then, lines 2–19 and 621–624 of Book iv. as by the writer of the rest of the poem, the reader will note how far more interesting she finds the marriage of Hermione than that of Megapenthes—of whose bride, by the way, there is no trace in Book xv. The marriage of the son is indeed mentioned in the first instance before that of the daughter; but surely this is only because υἱέος ἠδὲ θυγατρός lends itself more readily to a hexameter verse than any transposition of the nouns would do. Having mentioned that both son and daughter are to be married, the writer at once turns to Hermione, and appears only to marry Megapenthes because, as his sister is being married, he may as well be married too. A male writer would have married Megapenthes first and Hermione afterwards ; nor would he have thought it worth while to make a very awkward interpolation in his poem merely in order to bring Hermione into it, for by this time she must have been over thirty, and it would have been easy to suppose that she had been married years ago during Menelaus's absence.

As regards the second and shorter interpolation (iv. 621–624), it refers to the day after the pretended marriages, and runs as follows :

Thus did they converse [and guests kept coming to the king's house. They brought sheep and wine, while their wives had put up bread for them to take with them. So they were busy cooking their dinners in the courts.]

Passing over the fact that on such a great occasion as the marriage of his son and daughter, Menelaus would hardly expect his guests to bring their own provisions with them (though he might expect them, as Alcinous did,* to do their own cooking) I would ask the reader to note that the writer cannot keep the women out even from a mere cobble. A man might have told us that the guests brought meat and wine and bread, but his mind would not instinctively turn to the guests' wives putting up the bread for them.

I say nothing about the discrepancy between the chronology of Telemachus's visit to Sparta, and of Ulysses' journey from the island of Calypso to Ithaca where he arrives one day before Telemachus does. The reader will find it dwelt on in Colonel Mure's *Language and Literature of Ancient Greece*, Vol. I., pp. 439, 440. I regard it as nothing more than a slip on the part of a writer who felt that such slips are matters of very

---

* " Od." viii. 38–40, cf. also 61. It would seem that Alcinous found the provisions which the poorer guests cooked for themselves and ate outside in the court yards. The magnates ate in the covered cloister, and were no doubt cooked for.

small importance; but I will call attention to the manner in which the gorgeousness of Menelaus's establishment as described in Book iv. has collapsed by the time we reach Book xv., though as far as I can determine the length of Telemachus's stay with Menelaus, the interval between the two books should not exceed one entire day.

When Telemachus has informed Menelaus that he must go home at once, Menelaus presses his guests to stay and have something to eat before they start; this, he tells them, will be not only more proper and more comfortable for them, but also cheaper.

We know from " Il." vii. 470–475 that Menelaus used to sell wine when he was before Troy, as also did Agamemnon, but there is a frank *bourgeoisie* about this invitation which a male writer would have avoided. Still franker, however, is the offer of Menelaus to take them on a personally conducted tour round the Peloponesus. It will be very profitable, for no one will send them away empty handed; every one will give them either a bronze tripod or a cauldron, or two mules, or a gold chalice (xv. 75–85). As for the refreshments which they are to have immediately, the king explains that they will have to take potluck, but says he will tell the women to see that there is enough for them, of what there might happen to be in the house.

That is just like Menelaus's usual fussiness. Why could he not have left it all to Helen? After reading the " Odyssey " I am not surprised at her having run away with Paris; the only wonder is that a second great war did ñot become necessary very shortly after the Trojan matter had been ended. Surely the fact that two young bachelors were going to stay and dine was not such a frightful discord but that it might have been taken unprepared, or at any rate without the monarch's personal interference. " Of what there may be in the house " indeed. We can see that the dinner is not going to be profusely sumptuous. If there did not happen to be anything good in the house—and I suspect this to have been the case—Menelaus should have trusted Helen to send out and get something. But there should have been no sending out about it;

Menelaus and Helen ought never to have had a meal without every conceivable delicacy.

What a come down, again, is there not as regards the butler Eteoneus. He was not a real butler at all—he was only a kind of char-butler; he did not sleep in the house (xv. 96), and for aught we know may have combined a shop round the corner with his position in Menelaus' household. Worse than this, he had no footman, not even a boy, under him, for Menelaus tells him to light the fire and set about cooking dinner (xv. 97, 98), which he proceeds to do without one syllable of remonstrance. What has become of Asphalion? Where are the men servants who attended to Telemachus and Pisistratus on their arrival? They have to yoke their own horses now. The upper and under women servants who appear at all Odyssean meals are here as usual, but we hear nothing more of Adraste Alcippe, and Phylo. It seems as though after describing the splendour of Menelaus's house in Book iv. the writer's nerve has failed her, and by Book xv. her instinctive thrift has reasserted itself.

And now let me return, as I said in Chapter iv. that I intended doing, to the very singular—for I do not like to say feminine—nature of the arrangements made by Minerva for her protégé in the matter of his voyage to Pylos and Lacedæmon.

When Minerva first suggested it to him, she knew that Ulysses was on the point of starting from Calypso's island for Scheria, and would be back in Ithaca almost immediately. Yet she must needs choose this particular moment, of all others, for sending Telemachus on a perilous voyage in quest of news concerning him. We have seen how she preached to him; but surely if Telemachus had known that she was all the time doing her very utmost to make his voyage useless, he might have retorted with some justice that whether he was going to be a fool henceforward or no, he should not make such a fool of any young friend of his own as she was now making of himself. Besides, he was to be away, if necessary, for twelve months; yet here before he had been gone more than four or five days, Minerva fills him with an agony of apprehension about his property and sends him post haste back to Ithaca again.

The authoress seems to have felt the force of this, for in xiii. 416–419 she makes Ulysses remonstrate with Minerva in this very sense, and ask :

" Why did you not tell him, for you knew all about it ? Did you want him, too, to go sailing about amid all kinds of hardships when others were eating up his estate ? "
Minerva answered, " Do not trouble yourself about him. I sent him that he might be well spoken about for having gone. He is in no sort of difficulty, but is staying comfortably with Menelaus, and is surrounded with abundance of every kind. The suitors have put out to sea and are on the watch for him, for they mean to kill him before he can get home. I do not much think they will succeed, but rather that some of those who are now eating up your estate will first find a grave themselves."

What she ought to have said was :

" You stupid man, can you not understand that my poetess had set her heart on bringing Helen of Troy into her poem, and could not see her way to this without sending Telemachus to Sparta ? I assure you that as soon as ever he had interviewed Helen and Menelaus, I took—or will take, for my poetess's chronology puzzles my poor head dreadfully—steps to bring him back at once."

At the end of Book iv. Penelope shows a like tendency to complain of the manner in which she is kept in the dark about information that might easily have been vouchsafed to her.

Minerva has sent her a vision in the likeness of her sister Ipthime. This vision comes to Penelope's bedside and tells her that her son shall come safely home again. She immediately says :

" If, then, you are a goddess, or have heard news from Heaven tell me about that other unhappy one. Is he still alive, or is he dead and in the house of Hades ? "
And the vision answered, " I shall not tell you for certain whether he is alive or dead, and there is no use in idle conversation."

On this it vanished through the thong-hole of the door.

I may add that I never quite understood the fastening of the Odyssean bedroom door, till I found my bedroom at the Hotel Centrale, Trapani, fastened in the Odyssean manner.

Chapter VII

FURTHER INDICATIONS THAT THE WRITER IS A WOMAN—
YOUNG, HEADSTRONG, AND UNMARRIED.

I WILL now touch briefly on the principal passages, over and above large general considerations and the details to which I have already called attention, which seem to me to suggest a woman's hand rather than a man's. I shall omit countless more doubtful instances, many of which the reader will have noted, or easily discover.

At the very outset of the poem (i. 13) the writer represents Ulysses as longing to get back to his wife. He had stayed a whole year with Circe, and but for the remonstrances of his men would have stayed no one can say how much longer. He had stayed seven years with Calypso, and seems to have remained on excellent terms with her until the exigencies of the poem made it necessary to send him back to Ithaca. Surely a man of his sagacity might have subtracted Calypso's axe and auger, cut down the trees at the far end of the island, and made his raft years ago without her finding out anything about it ; for she can hardly have wanted either axe or auger very often.

As for the provisions, if Ulysses was not capable of accumulating a private hoard, his cunning has been much overrated. If he had seriously wanted to get back to Penelope his little cunning that is put in evidence would have been exercised in this direction. I am convinced, therefore, that though the authoress chooses to pretend that Ulysses was dying to get back to Penelope, she knew perfectly well that he was in no great hurry to do so ; she was not, however, going to admit anything so derogatory to the sanctity of married life, or at any rate to the power which a wife has over her husband.

An older woman might have been at less pains to conceal the fact that Penelope's hold on Ulysses was in reality very slight, but the writer of the " Odyssey " is nothing if she is not young, self-willed, and unmarried. No matron would set herself down to write the " Odyssey " at all. She would have too much sense, and too little daring. She would have gained too much—and lost too greatly in the gaining. The poem is such a *tour de force* as none but a high-spirited, headstrong girl who had been accustomed to have her own way would have attempted, much less carried to such a brilliantly successful conclusion ; I cannot, therefore, conceive the writer as older than the original of the frontispiece at the beginning of this book—if indeed she was so old.

———

The very beautiful lines in which the old nurse Euryclea lights Telemachus to bed, and folds up his clothes for him (i. 428–442), suggest a woman's hand rather than a man's. So also does the emphasising Laertes' respect for his wife's feelings (i. 430–433). This jealousy for a wife's rights suggests a writer who was bent on purifying her age, and upholding a higher ideal as regards the relations between husband and wife than a man in the Homeric age would be likely to insist on.

———

The price paid for Euryclea (i. 431) is, I do not doubt, a rejoinder to the Iliadic insults of XXIII. 262–264, in which a woman and a tripod are put up in one lot as a prize, and also of XXIII. 702–705, in which a tripod is represented as worth twelve oxen, and a good serviceable maid of all work only four oxen. A matron would have let Homer's passage severely alone, and a man would not have resented it so strongly as to make him write at it by declaring Euryclea to have been bought for twenty oxen.

———

An Iliadic passage of some length is interrupted (iii. 448–455) for the purpose of bringing in Nestor's wife and daughters, and describing their delight at seeing a heifer killed ; the Iliadic passage is then resumed. A man, or older woman, once launched on an Iliadic passage would have stuck to it till it failed them. They would not have cared whether the ladies of Nestor's household liked seeing the heifer killed or no.

_____

When Helen mixes Nepenthe with the wine which was to be handed round to Menelaus, Telemachus, and Pisistratus, we learn its virtues to be so powerful that a man could not weep during all the day on which he had drunk it, not even though he had lost both his father and his mother, or had seen a brother or a son cut to pieces before his eyes (iv. 220–226). From the order in which these relationships present themselves to the writer's mind I opine that her father and mother were the most important persons in her world, and hence that she was still young and unmarried.

_____

A little lower we find Helen more or less penitent for having run away with Paris. Helen was Jove's own daughter, and therefore had a right to do pretty much as she chose ; still it was held better to redeem her as far as possible, by making her more or less contrite. The contrition, however, is of a very curious kind. It was Venus, it seems, who ought to be penitent for having done Helen so great a wrong. It is the wrong that has been done to her that she laments, rather than any misdoing of her own.

_____

Is a man, or matron, likely to have conceived the idea of making Helen walk round the wooden horse, pat it, call out the names of the heroes who were inside, and mimick the voices of their wives (iv. 274–279) ? Ulysses must have told her that the horse was coming, and what it would contain, when he entered Troy in disguise and talked with her. A man might have made Helen walk round the horse, pat it, and even call out the names of the heroes, but he would never have thought of making her mimick their wives.

_____

The writer finds the smell of fish intolerable, and thinks it necessary to relieve Menelaus and his three men from a distressing situation, by getting Idothea to put some scent under each man's nostrils (iv. 441–446). There is, however, an *arrière pensée* here to which I will call attention later (see Chapter XII. near the end). Very daughterly also is the pleasure which Idothea evidently feels in playing a trick upon her father. Fathers are fair game—at all events for young goddesses.

———

The whole of iv. 625–847 is strongly suggestive of a woman's writing, but I cannot expect any one to admit this without reading either the original or some complete translation.

———

Calypso's jealously of Penelope (v. 203, &c.) is too prettily done for a man. A man would be sure to overdo it.

———

Book vi. is perhaps the loveliest in the whole poem, but I can hardly doubt that if it were given to a *Times* critic of to-day as an anonymous work, and he was told to determine the sex of the writer he would ascribe it to a young unmarried woman without a moment's hesitation. Let the reader note how Nausicaa has to keep her father up to having a clean shirt on when he ought to have one (vi. 60), whereas her younger brothers appear to keep her up to having one for them when they want one. These little touches suggest drawing from life by a female member of Alcinous' own family who knew his little ways from behind the scenes.

Take, again, the scene in which Ulysses first meets Nausicaa. A girl, such a girl as Nausicaa herself, young, unmarried, un-attached, and without knowledge of what men commonly feel on such points, having by a cruel freak of fortune got her hero into such an awkward predicament, might conceivably imagine that he would argue as the writer of the " Odyssey " has made Ulysses do, but no man, except such a woman's tailor as could never have written the " Odyssey," would have got his hero into such an undignified position at all, much less have made him talk as Ulysses is made to talk.

How characteristic, again, of the man-hatress is Nausicaa's

attempt to make out that in Ulysses she had found a man to whom she really might become attached—if there were no obstacle to their union.

———

I find it hard to pass over Book vii., especially line 230, &c., where Arēte wants to know how Ulysses came by his clothes, and 294, in which it is said that young people are apt to be thoughtless. Surely this is a girl giving a rap on the knuckles to older people by echoing what she is accustomed to hear them say.

———

In Book viii. the games, which are no doubt suggested by those in " Il." XXIII. are merely labelled " sports," not a single detail being given except that Ulysses' disc made a sound of some sort as it went through the air (viii. 190), which I do not believe it would do. In the " Iliad " details are given of every contest, and the games do not take place as they do in the " Odyssey " immediately after a heavy meal, from which we can hardly suppose that the competitors would be excluded.

I say nothing about the modesty of the female goddesses in not coming to see Mars and Venus caught in the toils of Vulcan (viii. 324), nor yet about the lovely new dress with which the Graces consoled Venus when she had been liberated (viii. 366), for I have omitted the whole of this episode in my abridgement.

———

The love of her own home and parents which is so obvious throughout the poem is never more apparent than in the speech of Ulysses (ix. 34–36). He says that however fine a house a man may have in a foreign land, he can never be really happy away from his father and mother. How different this from the saying which Aristophanes puts into the mouth of Mercury (*Plut.* 1151) to the effect that a man's fatherland is any place in which he is making money ; or again from Euripides, who in a fragment of *Phaethon* says that a man's fatherland is any land that will feed him. It is only a young and affectionate girl who could have made Ulysses (who is not much given to sentiment) speak so warmly. Middle-aged people, whether men or women, are too much spotted with the world to be able to say such things. They think as Aristophanes and Euripides do.

———

In lines 120, 121 of Book ix. the writer tells us that huntsmen as a general rule will face all sorts of hardship in forest and on mountain top. This is quite true, but it is not the way in which men speak of chamois-hunters.

———

As for the Cyclops incident, delightful as it is, it is impossible as a man or matron's writing. It was very kind of Polyphemus, drunk though he was, to stay without moving a muscle, till Ulysses and his men had quite finished boring out his eye with a burning beam that was big enough for a ship's mast, but Baron Munchausen is the only male writer who could offer us anything of the kind, and his is not a case in point. Neither, after all, is Book ix. of the " Odyssey," for the writer is not taking Polyphemus seriously.

———

The distress which Polyphemus caused to Ulysses and his men by flinging down a bundle of firewood is too graphic a touch not to have been drawn from life. I have often fancied that the whole Cyclops incident may have been suggested by one of those *merende,* or pic-nics which Italians and Sicilians are still so fond of, and that the writer of the " Odyssey " went with her friends to Pizzolungo and the cave where the scene is laid, which was then really much what an *alpe* is now—an abode of shepherds who made cheese in the cave itself. I like to fancy (for I know that it is nothing more than fancy) that the writer of the " Odyssey " was delighted with all she saw, but that as she was looking at the milk dishes some huge unkempt shepherd came in with a load of firewood on his back, and gave a sudden shock to her nervous system by flinging it down too violently. Him she transformed into the local giant that exists on Mt. Eryx now under the name of Conturràno.*

———

* See Chapter x.

It is very hard to say what the authoress thought that Polyphemus did in the matter of his ewes and lambs. The lambs were in the yards all day, for Ulysses' men saw them there and wanted to steal them (ix. 226, 227). Besides, Polyphemus could not have got any milk from the ewes if their lambs had been with them in the day-time. Having driven the ewes into his cave (I omit the she-goats for brevity) he milked them, and then put their lambs with them (ix. 245). The question is, did he take them away again after they had got what they could from a milked ewe, or did he leave them with their mothers all night?

On the one hand we have no hint of their removal, which would be a long and troublesome task; on the other we are told in line 309 that he milked the ewes in the morning, and again gave each one of them her lamb; on the evening of the same day he repeats this process (line 342), and he could hardly give the ewes their lambs unless he had first removed them.

The difficulty is that if he removed them they would certainly die in a very few days of such diet as Polyphemus allows them, for whatever he did was κατὰ μοῖραν, according to his usual practice; while if he did not remove them, he could not have got any milk. Whatever he did, we may be sure that the writer of the " Odyssey " had got it wrong, and there is not much to be gained by trying to find out what she thought, for it is obvious that she did not think.

I asked my friend, Sig. Giuseppe Pagoto of Mt. Eryx, what was the practice of Sicilian shepherds now, and received the following answer :

In Sicily they do not milk ewes that have lately lambed; they keep the lambs shut up and take the ewes to feed. In the evening they let the lambs suck, and then shut them up again. During the night the ewes make a great deal of milk, and this is again sucked by the lambs in the morning, and not milked. Our shepherds do not take any of the milk until the lamb has been killed. Perhaps in those days the pastures were so abundant that the ewes gave milk enough to nourish the lambs, and still have some for milking. This is the only way in which what Polyphemus did can be explained.

I believe the true explanation to be that the shepherd from whose *alpe* the scene was in part drawn, drove in a number of ewes some of which had lambs, while the lambs of others had been already killed and eaten. The authoress saw the shepherd milk a number of ewes, and then bring in a number of lambs, but she did not understand that the ewes which had been milked had got no lambs, while those that had lambs still living had not been milked. I think she knew she was hazy about it, otherwise she would not have cut her version short with a πάντα κατὰ μοῖραν—" all in due course."

———

It being evident that Circe is quite as capable a prophet as Tiresias, why should poor Ulysses be sent down to Hades? Obviously because the writer had set her heart on introducing colloquies with the dead. Granted; but a writer who was less desirous of making out that women know as much as men would not have made Circe know quite so much. Why, as soon as Ulysses has returned from Hades, repeat to him the warning about the cattle of the Sun which Tiresias had given him in the same words, and add a great deal more of her own? Why, again, did she not tell Ulysses to be particularly careful to ask Tiresias about the Wandering Cliffs, in respect of which she had confessed that her information was deficient? Ulysses does not appear to' have said anything, but he must have thought a good deal. Young people are impatient of such small considerations. Who, indeed, can let fancy, *naiveté*, and the charm of spontaneity have free and graceful play, if he or she is to be troubled at every touch and turn by the suggestions of common sense? The young disdain precision too contemptuously; while older people are apt to think of nothing else.

———

The same desire to exalt the capabilities of woman appears in making the Sun leave his sheep and cattle in the sole charge of the two nymphs Lampetie and Phaëthusa (xii. 132) who, by the way, proved quite unable to protect them. But then the Sun was a man, and capable of any folly.

———

The comparison of Ulysses to a hungry magistrate (xii. 439,

440), which is obviously humorous, is neither a man's nor a matron's simile for such a thrilling situation. To me it suggests the hand of a magistrate's daughter who had often seen her father come home tired and cross at having been detained in court.

The present from Helen to Telemachus of a wedding dress (xv. 125–129) was more likely to occur to a young woman than to a man. I think also that a male writer would have given something to poor Pisistratus, who has been very good and amiable all through. It does not appear that Telemachus tipped Eteoneus or any other of Menelaus' servants, though from xx. 296, 297 it is plain that it was quite usual for visitors to give something to the servants of a house at which they were staying. He is very rude about not saying good-bye to Nestor (xv. 199–201), and he never says good-bye to Pisistratus as he ought.

Ulysses, again, seems to have no sense of obligation whatever to Circe or Calypso. He has no other idea than that of taking as much and giving as little as he can. So in Hades he does not begin by asking how Penelope is, but how she is behaving, and whether she is protecting his estate (xi. 177, &c.).

In Book xvii. 495 the old nurse and housekeeper, who has hitherto always been Euryclea, suddenly becomes Eurynome, a name which we have not yet had. Eurynome from this point is frequently mentioned, though the context always suggests, and sometimes compels, the belief that Euryclea is intended. In Book xx. 4, for example, we are told that Eurynome threw a cloak over Ulysses after he had lain down to rest, but in line 143 of the same Book, Euryclea says she threw the cloak over him herself—for surely this is intended, though the plural according to very common custom is used instead of the singular. The alternation of the two names becomes very baffling, till finally in Book xxiii. 289–293 both Eurynome and Euryclea appear on the scene together, which cobbles the difficulty, but does not make a good job of it—for one woman would have been quite enough to do all that there was to do.

What happened, I take it, was this. In the first line where we meet with Eurynome, the name Euryclea could not be made to scan very easily, and the writer, thinking she would alter it later, wrote Eurynome. Having done so once, she used the names Eurynome and Euryclea according as metrical convenience inspired her. This went on for some time, till in the end she found it would be a great deal of trouble to re-write all the passages in which Eurynome had appeared; she therefore determined to brazen it out, and pretend that she had all along meant Euryclea and Eurynome to be two people. To put their separate existence beyond question, she brings them both on together. I do not say that this is feminine, but I can find nothing like it in the " Iliad." I have sometimes thought the last six or seven Books, though they contain some of the most exquisite passages in the whole poem, were written in greater haste than the earlier ones, while the last hundred lines or so of Book xxiv. suggest that the writer was determined to end her work without much caring how. I have also wondered whether the husband who in Book vi. was yet to find may not have been found before Book xxiv. was written ; but I have nothing to urge in support of this speculation.

———

Argus (xvii. 292) is not a very good name for a dog. It is the stock epithet for hounds in both " Iliad " and " Odyssey," and means " fleet." The whole scene between Ulysses and Argus is perhaps the most disappointing in the " Odyssey." If the dog was too old or feeble to come to Ulysses, Ulysses should have gone up to him and hugged him—fleas or no fleas ; and Argus should not have been allowed to die till this had been put in evidence. True, Ulysses does wipe away one tear, but he should have broken utterly down—and then to ask Eumæus whether Argus was any use, or whether he was only a show dog—this will not do even as acting. The scene is well conceived but badly executed ; it betrays the harder side of the writer's nature, and has little of the pathos which Homer would have infused into it.

———

When Eumæus says what kind of man he would be likely

to ask to the house if he was free to choose, he puts a divine first, a physician next, then a carpenter, and then a bard (xvii. 384). The only wonder is that the writer did not put the bard before the carpenter, and doubtless she would have done so had she not wanted to give the bard a whole line to himself. A woman, writing at the present day would be apt to consider the clergyman, and the doctor, as the first people who should be invited, but a man in the Homeric age would hardly have chosen as Eumæus is made to do.

I do not believe that any man living could wash Ulysses' feet and upset the bath so delightfully as Euryclea does (xix. 386, &c.), and at the same time make Penelope sit by and observe nothing of what was going on. He could not rise to the audacity of saying that Minerva had directed Penelope's attention elsewhere, notwithstanding the noise which Ulysses' leg made, and the upsetting of a bath full of water, which must have run over all that part of the cloister. A man would have made Penelope desire suddenly to leave the cloister, just before the accident happened, and lie down upon that couch which she had never ceased to water with her tears, &c. ; she could then have come back, remembering that she had forgotten something, after the foot-bath had been refilled and the mess cleaned up. But he could not have done it at all.

It will be observed that the stronger the indications become that Ulysses is on the point of returning, the more imperative Penelope finds it to marry one of the suitors without a day's delay. She has heard about the hawk tearing the dove ; she has heard Telemachus sneeze ; she has been assured that Ulysses was among the Thesprotians, quite near, and would be in Ithaca immediately ; she has had a dream which would have made any one wait, say, for at least a week longer, unless determined to take the gloomiest possible view of the situation ; but no ; on the following day she must marry and leave the house. Her words seem to me like those of a woman gloating over the luxury of woe, as drawn by another woman who has never known real trouble. Nothing can better show the hollowness of Penelope's distress from first to last. A woman who felt herself really drowning would have clutched at any one of the straws above mentioned, and made it buoy her up for weeks or months ; and any writer who had known real sorrow would also know how certain she would be to do this. A man could only so draw his heroine if he was laughing at her in his sleeve ; whereas the writer of the " Odyssey " is doing her very utmost to take herself seriously.

———

Penelope seems firmly convinced that she is keeping excellent guard over her son's estate all the time, and that if she were to leave the house everything would go to rack and ruin. She implies this to Ulysses when he is disguised as a beggar (xix. 524). One wonders how Ulysses could restrain himself from saying, " Well, Madam, if you cannot prove more successful as a guardian than you have been doing this many years past, the sooner you leave the house the better for Telemachus."

———

No great poet would compare his hero to a paunch full of blood and fat, cooking before the fire (xx. 24–28). The humour, for of course it is humorously intended, is not man's humour, unless he is writing burlesque. This the writer of the " Odyssey " is not doing here, though she has intentionally approached it very nearly in a great part of the Phæacian episode.

The only other two points which suggest a female hand in Book xx.—I mean with especial force—are the sympathy which the writer betrays with the poor weakly woman who could not finish her task (105, &c.), and the speech of Telemachus about his mother being too apt to make much of second rate people (129–133).

———

The twelve axes set up in Book xxi. remain in the court during the whole time that the suitors are being killed. How, I wonder, is it that not one of the suitors picked up a single axe ? A dozen men with a dozen axes should have made short work of Ulysses and his men. True, by my own hypothesis the heads had been taken off the handles, but they must have been wedged, or bound, either on to the handles or to some other like pieces of wood, so as to raise them high enough for anyone to shoot through the handle-holes. It should have been an easy matter either to fix the heads on to the handles again, or to extemporise new ones. If the writer had not forgotten all about the axes in her desire to begin with the shooting, she would have trumped up a difficulty of some kind. Perhaps she thought that the audience, hearing nothing more about them, would forget all about the axes too—and she was not far wrong.

The instinctive house-wifely thrift of the writer is nowhere more marked than near the beginning of Book xxii., where amid the death-throes of Antinous and Eurymachus she cannot forget the good meat and wine that were spoiled by the up-setting of the tables at which the suitors had been sitting.

The killing of the suitors is aggressive in its want of plausi-bility. If Melanthius could go to the store-room, no matter how, the other suitors could have followed him and attacked Ulysses from behind ; for there is evidently a passage from the store-room to the place where Ulysses is standing.

Again, the outer yard was open to the suitors all the time. Surely with the axes still at command they could have cut the Byblus-fibre rope that was the only fastening of the main gate ; some of them at any rate might have got out. The first ninety lines of the book are as fine as the " Iliad," but from line (say) 100 to line 330 the writer is out of her depth, and knows it. The most palpably feminine part is where Minerva comes to help Ulysses disguised as Mentor (xxii. 205–240). The suitors menace her, and in a rage she scolds not them but Ulysses, whom she rates roundly. Having done this, she flies away and sits on a rafter like a swallow.

All readers will help poets, playwrights, and novelists, by making believe a good deal, but we like to know whether we are in the hands of one who will flog us uphill, or who will make as little demand upon us as possible. In this portion of

Book xxii. the writer is flogging us uphill. She does not care
how much she may afflict the reader in his efforts to believe
her—the only thing she really cares for is her revenge. She
must have every one of the suitors killed stone dead, and all
the guilty women hanged, and Melanthius first horribly tortured and then cut in pieces. Provided these objects are
attained, it is not necessary that the reader should be able to
believe, or even follow, all the ins and outs of the processes
that lead up to them.

I will therefore not pursue the absurdities with which
the killing of the suitors abounds. I would, however, point
out that in Book xvi. 281, &c., where the taking away of
the armour from the cloister walls was first mooted, it was
proposed that enough to arm Ulysses and Telemachus should
be left accessible, so that they might snatch it up in a moment
without having to go all the way down into the store-room
after it, at the risk of Telemachus's forgetting to shut the
door—as young people so often do. I suppose Ulysses forgot
all about this sensible precaution, when he and Telemachus
were hiding the armour at the beginning of Book xix. Or
shall we suppose that the idea of catching Melanthius in the
store-room had not occurred to the poetess when she was
writing Book xvi., but had struck her before she reached
Book xix., and that she either forgot or did not think it worth
while, or found it inconvenient, to cancel lines 295, 296 of
Book xvi. ? From what I have seen of the authoress I incline
to this last opinion, and hold that she made Ulysses omit to
leave a little of the armour accessible to himself and Telemachus, because she had by this time determined to string
Melanthius up in the store-room, and did not see how to get
him inside it unless she made Telemachus go there first and
leave the door open ; and, again, did not see how to get Telemachus down to the store-room if she left armour near at
hand, for him to snatch up.

As for Telemachus bringing up four helmets, four shields,
eight spears, he was already fully armed when the fight began
(xxi. 434), so three helmets, three shields and six spears should
have done. Four helmets, four shields, and eight spears

is a heavy load ; but Melanthius carried twelve shields, twelve helmets, and twelve spears apparently all at one time.

We are in an atmosphere of transpontine melodrama, but the only wonder is that the absurdities are not even grosser than they are, seeing that the writer was a young woman with a strong will of her own. Woman she must have been ; no male writer could have resisted the temptation to kill Eumæus. It is the faithful servant's rôle to be mortally wounded on occasions of this sort. There are very few more suitors to be killed, and Minerva is going to raise her ægis immediately, so that he could be perfectly well spared ; possibly the writer felt that she should be shorthanded with the cleaning up of the blood and the removal of the dead bodies, but more probably she hated the suitors so bitterly that she would not let them score a single point.

How evidently relieved she feels when she has got the killing over, and can return to ground on which she is strong, such as the saving of Phemius and Medon, and the cleaning down of the house.

What are we to say of making Penelope, whose room looked out upon the cloister, sleep soundly all through the killing of the suitors ? What of her remarks to Euryclea when she has been waked ? What, again, of her interview with Ulysses, and the dance which Ulysses presently advises ? what, indeed, of the whole Book ? Surely it is all perfectly right as coming from some such person as the one portrayed in my frontispiece, but who can conceive the kind of man or matron who could write it ? The same applies to Book xxiv. What man or middle-aged woman could have written the ineffably lovely scene between Ulysses and Laertes in the garden ? or have made Ulysses eat along with Dolius, whose son and daughter he had killed on the preceding day ? A man would have been certain to make Ulysses tell Dolius that he was very sorry, but there had been nothing for it but to hang his daughter and to cut his son's nose and ears off, draw out his vitals, and then cut off his hands and feet.   Probably, however, he would have kept Dolius and his sons out of the Book altogether.

———

When Ulysses and Penelope are in bed (xxiii. 300–343) and are telling their stories to one another, Penelope tells hers first. I believe a male writer would have made Ulysses' story come first and Penelope's second.

———

Chapter VIII

THAT ITHACA AND SCHERIA ARE BOTH OF THEM DRAWN FROM TRAPANI AND ITS IMMEDIATE NEIGHBOURHOOD.

I HAVE now given, though far more briefly than the subject requires, some of my reasons for believing that from the first Book of the " Odyssey " to the last we are in the hands of a young woman. Who, then, was she ? Where did she live and write ? She was of flesh and blood, lived in time and place, looked on sea and sky, came and went somewhither and somewhen—but where ? and when ? and above all, who ? It will be my object to throw what light I can upon these subjects in the following chapters.

I will follow the same course that I have taken earlier, and retrace the steps whereby I was led to my conclusions.

By the time I had finished Book x. I was satisfied that the " Odyssey " was not a man's work, but I had seen nothing to make me think that it was written rather at one place than at another. When, however, I reached xiii. 159–164, in which passage Neptune turns the Phæacian ship into a rock at the entrance of the Scherian harbour, I felt sure that an actual feature was being drawn from, and made a note that no place, however much it might lie between two harbours, would do for Scheria, unless at the end of one of them there was a small half sunken rock. Presently I set myself to consider what combination of natural features I ought to look for on the supposition that Scheria was a real place, and made a list of them as follows :—

1. The town must be placed on a point of land jutting out as a land's end into the sea between two harbours, or bays in which ships could ride (vi. 263) ; it must be connected with the mainland by a narrow neck of land, and as I have just said, must have a half sunken formidable rock at the entrance of one of the harbours.

2. There must be no river running into either harbour, or Nausicaa would not have had to go so far to wash her clothes. The river when reached might be nothing but a lagoon with a spring or two of fresh water running into it, for the clothes were not, so it would seem, washed in a river ; they were washed in public washing cisterns (" Od." vi. 40, 86, 92) which a small spring would keep full enough of water " to wash clothes even though they were very dirty." The scene is laid close on the sea shore, for the clothes are put out to dry on a high bank of shingle which the sea had raised, and Nausicaa's maidens fly from Ulysses along the beach and spits that run into the sea.

3. There must be a notable mountain at no great distance from the town so as to give point to Neptune's threat that he would bury it under a high mountain. Furthermore, the whole combination above described must lie greatly further west of Eubœa than Ithaca was, and hence greatly west of Ithaca (vii. 321). Surely, if a real place is being drawn from, these indications are ample to ensure its being easily found.

Men of science, so far as I have observed them, are apt in their fear of jumping to a conclusion to forget that there is such a thing as jumping away from one, and Homeric scholars seem to have taken a leaf out of their book in this respect. How many striking points of correspondence, I wonder, between an actual place and one described in a novel, would be enough to create a reasonable assurance that the place in which they were combined was the one that was drawn from ? I should say four well marked ones would be sufficient to make it extremely improbable that a like combination could be found elsewhere ; make it five and unless we find something to outweigh the considerations which so close a correspondence between the actual place and the one described in the novel would suggest, or unless by some strange coincidence the same combination in all its details can be shown to occur in some other and more probable locality, we may be sure that the novel was drawn from the place ; for every fresh detail in the combination required decreases the probability of error in geometrical ratio if it be duly complied with.

Let us suppose that a policeman is told to look out for an elderly gentleman of about sixty ; he is a foreigner, speaks a little English but not much, is lame in his left foot, has blue eyes, a bottle nose, and is about 5 ft. 10 in. high. How many of these features will the policeman require before he feels pretty sure that he has found his man ? If he sees any foreigner he will look at him. If he sees one who is about 5 ft. 10 in. high he will note his age, if this proves to be about sixty years, and further, if the man limps on his left foot, he will probably feel safe in stopping him. If, as he is sure to do, he finds he has a bottle nose, he will leave the blue eyes and broken English alone, and will bring the man before the magistrate.

If it is then found that the man's eyes are hazel, and that he either speaks English fluently or does not speak it at all— is the magistrate likely to discharge the prisoner on account of these small discrepancies between him and the description given of him, when so many other of the required characteristics are found present ? Will he not rather require the prisoner to bring forward very convincing proof that it is a case of mis- taken identity ?

Or to take another illustration, which is perhaps more strictly to the point as involving comparison between an actual place and one described in a novel. Here is an extract from a novel :—

Grammerton, like other fair cities, was built on a hill. The highest point was the fine old Elizabethan School, then, and now, of European reputation. Opposite it was the old shat- tered and ruined castle, overlooking the bubbling and boiling shallows of the broad and rapid river Saber. . . . From the hill the town sloped rapidly down on every side towards the river, which made it a peninsula studded with habitations. (*The Beauclercs, Father and Son*, by Charles Clarke, Chapman and Hall. Vol. 1. p. 28.)

Is there any man of ordinary intelligence and acquainted with Shrewsbury who will doubt that Shrewsbury was the place that Mr. Clarke was drawing from ?

When I have urged the much more numerous and weightier points of agreement between Scheria as described in the " Odyssey," and Trapani as it still exists, eminent Homeric scholars have told me, not once nor twice—and not meekly, but with an air as though they were crushing me—that my case rests in the main on geographical features that are not unknown to other parts of the coast, and upon legends which also belong to other places.

Grammerton, they argue—to return to my illustration— must not be held as Shrewsbury, for at Harrow as well as Shrewsbury the School is on the highest part of the town. There is a river, again, at Eton, so that Eton may very well have been the place intended. It is highly fanciful to suppose that the name Saber may have been a mere literary travesty of Sabrina. At Nottingham there is a castle which was in ruins but a few years since, and from which one can see the Trent. Nottingham, therefore, is quite as likely to be the original of Grammerton as Shrewsbury is.

And so on *ad infinitum*. This line of argument consists in ignoring that the force of the one opposed to it lies in the demonstrable existence of a highly complex combination, the component items of which are potent when they are all found in the same place, but impotent unless combined. It is a line which eminent Homeric scholars almost invariably take when discussing my Odyssean theory, but it is not one which will satisfy those before whom even the most eminent of Homeric scholars must in the end bow—I mean, men of ordinary common sense. These last will know that Grammerton can only be dislodged from Shrewsbury on proof either that the features of Shrewsbury do not in reality correspond with those of Grammerton, or else that there is another town in England which offers the same combination, and is otherwise more acceptable.

So with Trapani and Scheria. Eminent Homeric scholars must show that I have exaggerated the points of correspond- ence between the two places—which in the face of Admiralty charts and of the " Odyssey " they will hardly venture ; or they must bring forward some other place in which the same points of correspondence are found combined—which they will not attempt ; or they must show reason for thinking that the very numerous and precise correspondences between Trapani and all

Scherian and Ithacan scenes are referable to mere accident—and this will satisfy those only who will believe that a man has held thirteen trumps in his hand three deals running, without having tampered with the cards. I need not discuss this last supposition, and as for the other two, I can only assure the reader that no attempt has been made to establish either of them during the close on six years since my theory was first put before the public.

Neither will it ever be made. For Scheria should be looked for on some West coast to the West of Greece, and there are no such West coasts except those of Italy and Sicily, both of which I know well enough to be sure that if the Scherian combination could be found elsewhere than at Trapani I should long since have found it. Even could such a place be found with its rock Malconsiglio, legend and all, before it could compete with Trapani in claiming the " Odyssey " it would have to offer the Ithacan combination as well as the Scherian ; for surely a place which provides us with both Ithacan and Scherian topography would have a greater right to be considered as that from which the " Odyssey " was drawn, than one which could only offer the details of Scheria.

Furthermore, could they find another place with all both Scherian and Ithacan features, my opponents would be only half way through their troubles ; for Trapani could still hold its own against it, unless it also had four islands (neither more nor fewer) lying off it, one of them long and narrow, and all of them corresponding with the inaccurate Odyssean description of the Ionian islands. Nor would it even then begin to be on equal terms with Trapani, till it was shown that the effective part of the voyages of Ulysses begins and ends with it. When all this has been done, but not before, it will be time to weigh the comparative claims to the two sites.

For I rest my case on the harmonious concurrence of four lines of argument, each requiring the fulfilment of many and very rigorous conditions, and each by itself sufficient to raise a strong presumption that Trapani was the place which was most prominent in the mind of the writer of the " Odyssey." They are :

1. That Scheria is drawn from Trapani. This I will substantiate by bringing forward a much stronger combination
of correspondences than exists between Grammerton and
Shrewsbury.

2. That Ithaca also is drawn from Trapani and its immediate
neighbourhood. My case for this will be found even stronger
if possible than that by which I established that Scheria was
Trapani.

3. That the Ionian islands as described in the " Odyssey "
cannot have been drawn from the actual Ionian islands, nor
from any others but those off Trapani ; and that the writer
sinned against her own knowledge in order to force these
islands into her narrative.

4. That the voyages of Ulysses practically resolve themselves into a voyage from Troy to the neighbourhood of Sicily,
and thenceforward into a sail round Sicily, beginning with
Trapani and ending with the same place.

It will be necessary that no argument adduced in support of
any of these propositions should clash with those in support of
any other, but all the four lines of argument must corroborate
each other, so that they fit into one another as the pieces of a
child's puzzle. It is inconceivable that anything but a true
theory should comply with conditions so exacting. I will now
proceed to show that Scheria is Trapani, and will return to the
steps by which I arrived at this conclusion.

Armed with the list of points I had to find in combination,
as given at the beginning of this chapter, I went down to the
map room of the British Museum intending to search the
Mediterranean from the Troad to Gibraltar if necessary ; but
remembering that I ought to look (for reasons already given)
some distance West of Greece, and also that the writer of the
" Odyssey " appeared to have lived on a coast that looked West
not East, I resolved to search the West coasts first. I knew that
Colonel Mure and a respectable weight of ancient testimony
had placed the Cyclopes on Mt. Eryx, and it seemed to me
that the island where Ulysses hunted the goats, and the whole
Cyclopes incident suggested drawing from life more vividly
than any other part of the voyages. I knew, moreover, that

the writer was a young woman who was little likely to have travelled, and hence felt sure that if one place could be found, none of the others would be long in finding ; I asked, therefore, for the map of the Lilybæan promontory, as the West coast West of Greece that offered the greatest prospect of success, and hardly had I got it in my hand before I found the combina-

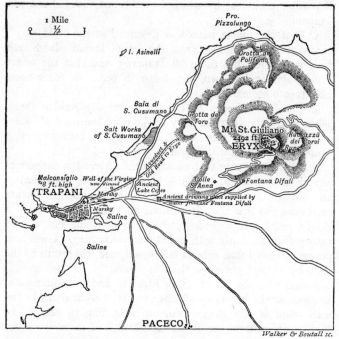

TRAPANI AND MT. ERYX

tion I wanted for Scheria lying right under Mt. Eryx. The land's end jutting into the sea—the two harbours one on either side of it—the narrow entrance between two marshes—the high mountain hard by—the rock at the entrance of one of the harbours—the absence of any river—will be found in the map here given, which Messrs. Walker & Boutall have made for me from the Italian Government survey, and from our own Admiralty chart.

But this was not all. Not only was the rock of the right height, and so turned as to give the idea of a ship coming into port, but it bore the strange name of Malconsiglio, or " Evil counsel." I was so much struck with this that I wrote to Trapani enquiring whether there existed any local tradition in connection with the rock, and was told that there were two— the one absurd, and the other to the effect that the rock had been a ship of Turkish Pirates who were coming to attack Trapani, but were turned into stone at the entrance of the harbour by the Madonna di Trapani. I did not doubt that the name and the legend between them preserved the Odyssean version, in a Christianised form—the legend recording the fact of a ship's having been turned into stone as it was entering harbour, and the name telling us the other fact that this had been brought about in consequence of an evil counsel.

I believe the above sufficient for reasonable assurance that Scheria was drawn from Trapani, and will, therefore, proceed to establish that the Ithaca scenes are drawn also from the same place and its immediate neighbourhood.

To this end it will be incumbent upon me to find that near Trapani, though not actually at the town, there exists, or can be shown to have in all reasonable probability existed, a harbour which has, or had, a current in it, and which lies hard by the foot of a mountain. This harbour should have a shelving bottom, for the Phæacian crew which brought Ulysses to Ithaca ran half the ship's length on shore before the way was off it. At no great distance there must be two caves near together (xiii. 103-112 and 347-349). One of them must have two entrances—one turned towards the North, by which people can go down into the cave, and the other towards the South, by which the gods alone can enter. It must have water in it, and also prehistoric implements should be found there. From near it one must be able to see harbours (in the plural), and it should be on the side of a mountain. Here Ulysses hid the treasures that the Phæacians had given him. The other cave need present no special features.

A man ascending the mountain from these caves, and keeping along the top of it should come to a place on ground commanding an extensive prospect, where there is a spring and a rock that is called Raven. This site must be bitterly cold in winter, and must be about two hours' walk from Trapani; the path to the town must be so rugged that a man in ordinary vigour would not like to take it without having a stick; and lastly, it must pass a notable mound or hill much nearer Trapani than the high ground above alluded to, and commanding a full view of the city and harbour. The reader who turns to the abridgement of Books xiii., xiv., xv., xvi. and xvii. given in this work, will find that all these points are necessary.

They all of them exist at this day, even to the calling of the rock " Raven," except one—I mean the mouth of the harbour where the Phæacians entered; this is now silted up, like the harbour of Selinunte,* which I might almost call on the same coast. The inner part of the harbour is still full of sea water, but has been converted into Salt Works† which are slightly below the level of the sea. The bed of the old exit is clearly seen, and there are still rushes in it though it is quite dry: it is very narrow, is often full in winter, and is marked with dotted lines in the Italian Ordnance Map, but not so in our Admiralty Chart.

The existence of this bed was pointed out to me by Signor Sugameli, of Trapani. He assured me that till 1848 when the Salt Works were made, the whole space covered by them was an open mere where his father used to go to shoot wild ducks. One great difficulty in making the Salt Works was the abundance of fresh water springs, which made it necessary to cement the salt pans in order to keep the fresh water from mixing with the salt. It was perhaps from some of these springs that the πλυνοί, or washing cisterns, of vi. 40 were supplied—unless indeed Nausicaa washed the clothes in sea water as I have seen women in the island of Pantellaria still do.

Given a mass of water, nearly a mile long and a quarter of a mile broad, with a narrow exit, and the tide, which here has a rise and fall of from two to three feet, would cause a current

---

* A few years ago the stone work at the entrance to the harbour of Selinunte was excavated, but it was silted over again in a single winter. † Shown in the plan as the Salt Works of S. Cusumano.

THE HARBOUR RHEITHRON, NOW SALT WORKS OF S. CUSUMANO

MOUTH OF THE HARBOUR RHEITHRON, NOW SILTED UP

that at times would be strong, and justify its being described as a river and also as a harbour with a current in it ; returning for a moment to Scheria, I suppose this to be the river at the mouth of which Ulysses landed, and the river's staying his flow (v. 451), I take to mean that he arrived there just at the turn of the tide. I may also say that this harbour is used five times in the " Odyssey " :

1. As the " flowing harbour, in the country beyond the town, under Mt. Neritum "—reading, as explained earlier, Νηρίτῳ for Νηίῳ—where Minerva said she left her ship, when she was talking with Telemachus i. 185, 186. 2. As the place where Ulysses landed in Scheria and where Nausicaa washed her clothes. 3. As the place where Ulysses landed in Ithaca. 4. As the place where Telemachus landed in Ithaca on his return from Pylos (xv. 495, &c.). 5. As the spot pointed to by Ulysses as the one where his ship was lying " in the country beyond the town " (xxiv. 308).

I will now return to the two caves which ought to be found at no great distance from the head of this harbour. It is clear from the text that there were two not one, but some one has enclosed in brackets the two lines in which the second cave is mentioned, I presume because he found himself puzzled by having a second cave sprung upon him when up to this point he has been only told of one.

I venture to think that if he had known the ground he would not have been puzzled, for there are two caves, distant about 80 or 100 yards from one another, at the place marked in the map as the *grotta del toro*. The one is conspicuous, but without special feature ; the other, which is not very easily seen, and which is called by the peasants the *grotta del toro*, looks due North, and is universally believed to contain a treasure, which a bull who lives in its recesses is continually grinding, but which can only be found by a virgin, who will eat a whole pomegranate without spilling a single pip. I suspect the *toro* to be a children's corruption of *tesoro*. The bull having thus got into the cave has never got out again, and as the treasure is also confidently known to exist—well—what can the bull be there for but to turn a mill and grind the treasure ?

The cave runs due South into the rock by a passage so rough and narrow that no one is likely to go more than a very few feet with it. No one, therefore, can enter the cavern from the South —it is only the gods who can do so.

In August, 1894, I visited the ground with some Sicilian friends, and we discoursed with the *contadino* who had charge of the farm on which the caves are found. While we were talking there came up a nice intelligent lad on a donkey, and he seemed much interested in our conversation.

" Is there," we asked, pointing to the *grotta del toro,* " a treasure in the cave ? "

" Certainly," was the immediate answer. Here the boy broke in. He was quite sure there was one. Everybody knew it. It could not be doubted.

" Is there a treasure in the other cave ? "

" Oh, no."

" Which of the two caves is called the *grotta del toro ?* "

" That one "—from both peasant and boy, who pointed at once to the cave that corresponded with the " Odyssey."

" You are quite sure that the other cave is not called ' la grotta del toro ' ? "

" Quite."

" Where does the *grotta del toro* go to ? "

" It gets narrow and goes far into the rock."

" Has any one ever been to the end of it ? "

" No, no ; no one knows where it ends. There was a cattle driver who went in once to explore it, but he never came back, and they say that after this there was a wall built to stop any one from going further."

" Have you ever been inside the cave yourself ? "

" Yes."

" Have you been as far as the wall ? "

" No."

" How far did you go ? "

" Not very far ; I was afraid."

" Then you have no idea how far the cave goes ? "

" No."

" Is there water in the cave at all times ? "

" Yes."

" Have you seen it ? "

" I was there in May last, and there was water then."

" Is there water there now ? "

" I should think so, but cannot be certain."

" Can you take us to it ? "

" No ; the key of the ground is at Trapani."

" They say there is a bull in the further recesses of the cavern ? "

" They say so, but we have never seen him ; all we know for certain is that there is a treasure."

Here the boy again brightened up, and said that this was certain.

When we had finished our questions the *contadino* took one of our party aside, and said, confidentially, " Be sure of me, for I have a strong stomach " (*i.e.*, I can keep a secret). " When you come to remove the treasure, which I can see that you intend to do, you must take me with you and give me my share. If you come by night the dogs will bark, and I shall know that you are there. I will then come down and help you, but you must give me my share."

I wrote the above conversation down, in Italian, immediately on my return to Trapani, and my Sicilian friends signed it, at my request, as a correct report. It occurs to me to add that there is no other cave near Trapani to which any story of a hidden treasure attaches.

Last year (May, 1896) I visited the cave again, this time with my friend Mr. H. Festing Jones, who has gone over the whole of the ground described in this book, to make sure that I have not overstated my case. We were accompanied by Signor Sugameli of Trapani, to whom I owe the correction of my error in believing the more conspicuous of the two caves to be called the *grotta del toro*—for so, on my first visit to Trapani in 1892, my friends in the town had assured me, not knowing the existence of the one which really bears the name. Jones and Signor Sugameli scrambled into the interior of the cavern, but I, being elderly and somewhat lame, did not venture. They found the cave end, after about thirty feet, in a mass of solid rock; but few who have gone above ten or twelve feet will be likely to go any further, and I can well believe that the writer of the " Odyssey," like the peasants of to-day, believed that no one could get to the end of it. My friends found water.

The cave is full of bees' nests in summer, as are all the caves hereabouts. They are small, solitary, of red clay, and about the size of the cup of an acorn. All the caves in the neighbourhood of Mt. Eryx abound in remains of stone-age man, some fine examples of which may be seen in the museum at Palermo. These remains would doubtless be more common and more striking three thousand years or so ago than they are at present, and I find no difficulty in thinking that the poetic imagination of the writer of the " Odyssey " ascribed them to the nymphs and naiads.

From hard by both the caves one can see, of course, the precipices of Mt. Eryx, which I suppose to be Neritum in the mind of the writer (xiii. 351), the straight paths on the cultivated land some couple of hundred feet below, the harbour of the old merman Phorcys, and also the harbours of Trapani, all which are requisite by lines xiii. 195, 196, and 345–351.

The reader will note that while more than one Scherian detail is given casually and perhaps unintentionally, as for example the harbour where Ulysses landed in Scheria, and the harbours, which I do not doubt are the two harbours of Trapani, there is no Ithacan detail given so far which conflicts with any feature in the description of Scheria.

The number and value of the points of correspondence between the cave in which Ulysses hid his treasure, and the *grotta del toro* greatly exceed those between Grammerton and Shrewsbury. Nevertheless it will be well to see whether his movements on leaving the cave confirm my view or make against it.

I suppose him to have ascended the steep, and then, doubtless, wooded slopes of Mt. Eryx and to have passed along its high and nearly level summit (δι' ἄκριας, xiv. 2) to the other end of the mountain, where the Norman Castle stands now 2500 feet above the sea level. Here he descended some two or three hundred feet to the spot now called *i runzi,* where there is a spring near a precipice which is still called *il ruccazzū dei corvi, i.e.* " the rock of the ravens," it being on this part of the mountain that these birds breed most freely. This walk would take him about two hours, more or less.

The site is seen from far and wide, it is bitterly cold in winter, and is connected with Trapani by a rough mountain path which Ulysses may well have been afraid to travel without a stick (xvii. 195).* The path passes close to the round-topped *Colle di Sta Anna* which answers perfectly to the Ἕρμαιος λόφος of xvi. 471. The time it takes to walk from the *runzi* to Trapani corresponds with all the indications furnished us in the " Odyssey " concerning the distance between Eumæus's hut and the town of Ithaca—which seems roughly to have been a winter's day walk there and back.

The reader will see, therefore, that we have the whole road taken by Ulysses from his landing in the harbour of Phorcys to the cave (with all its complex requirements) in which he hid his presents, up Mt. Neritum, along its long top to the spring and the Raven Rock, and finally the path passing the hill of Mercury down to Ithaca, as accurately presented to us by the road from the *saline di S. Cusumano* to the *grotta del toro,* Mt. Eryx, the fountain, the Raven Rock, and the road to Trapani, as though the " Odyssey " had been written yesterday. When the reader can find me in all literature, ancient or modern, any like chain of correspondences between an actual place and one described in a work of fiction as an effect of mere chance, I will accept the coincidences to which I have called attention as possibly accidental only ; but I am convinced that no such case nor anything approaching it can be adduced.

I, therefore, claim that Ithaca, like Scheria, must be taken as drawn from Trapani. There is, however, this important point to be remembered, that though the writer, when she has to consider Ithaca *ab extra,* as an island and nothing more, pictures it to herself as the high and striking island of

---

* Of recent years an excellent carriage road has been made from Trapani to the town on the top of Mt. Eryx, but pedestrians still use the old path, which in places is very rough.

Marettimo some 22 miles off Trapani, when she wants details she takes them from her own immediate neighbourhood on the mainland.

Young people when transferring familiar stories to their own neighbourhood, as almost all young people do, never stick at inconsistencies. They are like eminent Homeric scholars, and when they mean to have things in any given way they will not let the native hue of resolution be balked by thought, and will find it equally easy to have an Ithaca in one place and also in another, and to see the voyages of Columbus to the tropics in their own sliding over a frozen pool. So Lord Selborne writes :

As we grew, the faculty of imagination increased in power. It coloured all our childish pleasures ; it accompanied us on the ice and into the woods ; it mixed the dreams of the supernatural with the most ordinary things. Our resting-places when sliding over a frozen pool were the islands discovered by Columbus or Cook, in whose voyages we delighted.

(*Memorials, &c.*, by Roundell Palmer, Earl of Selborne, Macmillan, 1896, pt. 1. p. 66.)

Before I leave the Ithaca scenes I ought to show that there may well have existed at Trapani a sheet of water which cattle would be likely to cross in a boat, as described in " Od." xx. 186–188. The land on the East side of Trapani was artificially raised in 1860, till which time the two seas on either side the town were often joined in winter after a continuance of Northerly Winds. Several people have assured me that they remember having to be carted over the water between Trapani and the mainland. I was at first tempted to believe that Philœtius had come to the town when the narrow entrance to it was flooded ; but a few lines above we find that Eumæus had also come to the town with three pigs, and Melanthius with some goats. These men had both unquestionably come from Mt. Eryx, and the text seems to forbid the idea that they too had had to cross the water. There is nothing, however, to imply that Philœtius had come from Mt. Eryx ; indeed, it is more likely that his cattle would feed on the flat land south of the harbour, which he had crossed by boat to save the long

détour which would have been otherwise necessary. If the
water had been that of any such river as is to be found in
Asia Minor, Greece, or Sicily, one man would probably have
been enough, whereas there seem to have been several plying
for hire, as in a port or harbour.

The fact that Scheria and Ithaca would be perfectly well-
known by the audience as drawn from their own neighbourhood
explains another difficulty. " How," some hypercritical listener
might ask, " could so sagacious and experienced a mariner as
Ulysses have failed to note that he was only travelling two
miles, or even less, from Scheria to Ithaca ? And how again
could he fail to recognise the place at which he landed as the
one where he had met Nausicaa a few days previously ? "

The writer of the " Odyssey " admits with some *naiveté* that
the Phæacian mariners were already acquainted with the
harbour in which they left Ulysses. They probably would be.
But how prevent Ulysses from remonstrating both during the
voyage and on being landed ? It is not easy to see what better
course the writer could take than the one she actually did take,
i.e., put Ulysses to sleep as soon as ever he was on board, and
not wake him till after the sailors were gone. A sleep, therefore, is prepared for him (vii. 318, and viii. 445) and he falls
into it apparently before even leaving the harbour ; it is so
profound that it is more like death than sleep (xiii. 80).
Nothing, not even the men lifting him off the ship next
morning, laying all his treasures hard by him and going away,
can disturb him till the Phæacian sailors are beyond all reach
of question. Then, of course, the sooner he wakes up the
better.

As for the other difficulty of his not seeing that he was only
at the spot where he had met Nausicaa two days earlier, this
was got over by making it a misty morning, and muddling
Ulysses generally so that he does not even recognise the place
as Ithaca, much less as Scheria, till Minerva meets him and
has a long talk with him, in the course of which the audience
slides into the situation, and accepts the neighbourhood of
Trapani for that of Ithaca without more demur.

Chapter IX

IN a later chapter I propose to show that the writer of the
" Odyssey " had the " Iliad " before her in the state in which we
have it now, unimportant copyists' errors alone excepted. I
shall show that those Books on which most doubt has been
cast by eminent Homeric scholars both on the Continent and
in England, are just as fully and freely quoted from as those
that are admitted to have been by Homer. I have seen no
sufficient reason alleged for doubting that the Catalogues of
" Il." II. 484–877 formed part of the poem as Homer left it,
though it is quite likely that he may have got some one with
greater knowledge of Greece to help him. I intend returning
to this question, but for the present will ask the reader to
accept my assumption that the writer of the " Odyssey " knew
the Catalogues above referred to. The group of the Echinades
and the Ionian islands are described as follows in the Catalogue
of the Achæan forces :

And they of Dulichium, with the sacred Echinean islands,
who dwelt beyond the sea off Elis—these were led by Meges,
peer of Mars, the son of Phyleus, who had erewhile migrated
to Dulichium in consequence of a quarrel with his father. And
with him there came forty ships.

Ulysses led the brave Cephallenians, who held Ithaca,
wooded Neritum, Crocylea, rugged Ægilips, Zacynthus, and
Samos,* with the mainland also that is over against the
islands. These were led by Ulysses, peer of gods in counsel,
and with him came twelve ships (" Il." ii. 625–637).

---

* In the " Odyssey " more generally called Same.

The reader will note that Dulichium, which means " Long Island," does not belong to the Ionian islands, but to the

Neritum or Leucas
now
Sta. Maura

3700

19580 Kalomo

Crocylea now Arkudi

Ægilips
now
Atakos

Ithaca
2060 Vathi
2435

Makri
supposed to be
Dulichium

3601

3212

2174 Samos   Same or Samos
2800   now
5218   Cephalonia

MAP OF THE
IONIAN ISLANDS
12 Miles
0 2 4 6 8 10 12

Zacynthus
(Zante)   Peloponese

Walker & Boutall sc.

neighbouring group of the Echinades. Let us now see how the islands in the neighbourhood of Ithaca are described in the " Odyssey." Ulysses says (ix. 21–26) :

" I dwell in Ithaca, an island which contains a high mountain called Neritum. In its neighbourhood there are other islands near to one another, Dulichium, Same and Zacynthus. It lies on the horizon all highest up in the sea towards the west, while the other islands lie away from it to the east."

In the " Odyssey " there are never more than three islands besides Ithaca. When mentioned all together they are always named in the order given above—probably for reasons of scansion —but Dulichium is the most important in the eyes of the writer, being more frequently mentioned separately, and sending fifty-two suitors as against twenty-four from Same, twenty from Zacynthus, and twelve from Ithaca itself (xvi. 247–251).

A glance at the map given above will show that there is no

island in the neighbourhood of Ithaca which can with poetical propriety be held to have sent nearly as many suitors as the other three put together. Least of all could Dulichium be so held. It seems, then, that it was the name, and not the island, that the writer wanted ; and further that she wanted this so badly as to lay violent hands upon it and raid it from another group.

Why should she strain so considerable a point in order to get hold of it ? The Iliadic catalogue omits three or four but leaves us six Ionian islands. After suppressing the small islands of Crocylea and Ægilips, there remained four, which it seems was the exact number that the writer of the " Odyssey " meant to introduce ; why, then, should not Neritum have been good enough for her ? It evidently did not answer her purpose, or she would not, in the face of the catalogue, have stowed it away inside Ithaca and gone further afield for her dominant island. These things are never done without a reason, and in this case a reason is particularly necessary, for it would have been more easy and also suitable, considering the insignificance of the real Dulichium, to make the fifty-two suitors come from the very considerable island of Neritum.

All difficulty is removed by supposing that the writer lived at Trapani and was drawing the Ionian islands from the, to her, familiar Ægadean group. A glance at the foregoing map will shew that she cannot have been drawing from the real Ionian islands. Ithaca cannot be tortured into lying " all highest up in the sea towards the West." It is completely covered by Samos. Nor do the other islands lie away from it to the East. It is clear, then, that the Ionian islands were not those present to the mind of the writer, but we may infer in passing, firstly, that her audience lived at a sufficient distance from Greece to make the infraction of topographical accuracy a matter of no importance, and secondly, that the islands from which she was in reality drawing lay, like the true Ionian group, off a West coast.

I will now give a map of the islands off Trapani. I see that Professor Freeman, in his map of the West coast of Sicily, as he supposes it to have been in ancient times, has joined the

Isola Grande to the neighbouring main land, but he gives no authority for doing so. I can find none in ancient writers, and having examined the ground see nothing to indicate any change in the distribution of land and water, as having taken place within measurable distance of our own times.

The lofty and rugged island of Marettimo did duty in the writer's mind for Ithaca, though, as I have said, when details are wanted they are taken from Trapani and Mt. Eryx. The long island, now the Isola Grande—low lying and wheat growing—was her Dulichium; this must have been far the most important of the four as regards Trapani, being accessible in all weathers, and probably already pregnant with the subsequently famous city of Motya, of which hardly anything remains, but which stood on the Southernmost of the two islands that lie between Isola Grande and the mainland. The other two islands stood for Same and Zacynthus, but which was which I have not been able to determine. Marettimo can hardly be seen from Trapani, being almost entirely hidden by Levanzo. From the heights, however, of Mt. Eryx, with which, for other reasons, I suppose the writer to have been familiar, it is seen " on the horizon, all highest up in the sea towards the West." I do not doubt the poetess was describing it as she knew it from the top of Mt. Eryx, and as the reader may still see it. The rough sketch on the following page will explain πανυπερτάτη εἰν ἁλὶ better than words can do ; the two small islands shown just over Trapani are the Formiche, which I take to be the second rock thrown by Polyphemus.

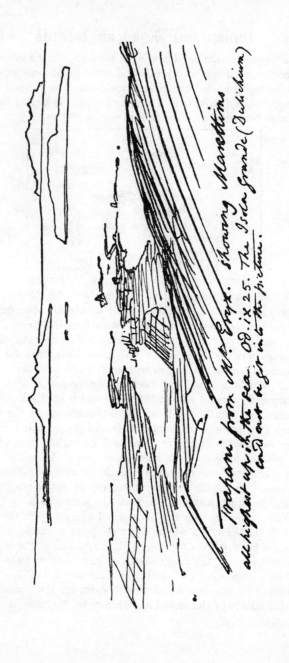

Trapani from Mt. Eryx. showing Marettimo
all highest up in the sea. 09.ix.25. The Isola Grande (Bülchium)
and out to S^r in to the picture.

If what I have said above is not enough to satisfy the reader that the writer of the " Odyssey " was drawing the Ionian islands from the Ægadean, nothing that I can add is likely to convince him. I will therefore now go on to my fourth point, namely, that the voyages of Ulysses are, as nearly as the writer could make them, a voyage round Sicily, from Trapani by the North coast, through the straits of Messina, to the island of Pantellaria, and so back to Trapani, beyond which we need not go, for Ithaca and Scheria are, both of them, Trapani, as I have already shown.

The main episodes of the voyage occur in the following order. 1. The Cicons. 2. The Lotus-eaters, arrived at after passing the island of Cythera. 3. The island where Ulysses and his men hunted the goats, and the adventure with Polyphemus. 4. The island of Æolus, and a ten days' sail towards the East with a fair wind all the time, till Ithaca is well in sight, followed by an immediate return to the island from which Ulysses had started. This sail to Ithaca over the toe of Italy and the island of Samos has no topographical significance except as showing that the writer conceived of the island of Æolus as lying a long way West of Ithaca. The episode is introduced merely for the purpose of bringing the cup close to Ulysses' lips and then dashing it from them. 5. The Læstrygonians. 6. The island of Circe and the journey to Hades, which last is again without topographical significance, being nothing but a peg on which to hang colloquies with the dead, and bringing us back to the island of Circe. 7. The Sirens. 8. Scylla and Charybdis. 9. The cattle of the Sun. 10. The island of Calypso. 11. Scheria and Ithaca.

There is no difference of opinion among scholars as to the sites of the Cicons, the island of Cythera, and the Lotus-eaters ; the reader will, therefore, see that we are taken without waste of time to a point at no great distance from Sicily—the contrary winds off Cape Malea (ix. 81) being apparently raised on purpose to take us away from Greece. It is not quite easy to see why the Cicons were introduced unless it was that Ulysses might become possessed of the wondrous wine of

Ismarus with which he intoxicated Polyphemus. The wine of this neighbourhood was famous many centuries after the " Odyssey " was written, and presumably was so in the time of the " Odyssey " itself. A gasconading story of this wine may well have existed among the people of Trapani which might prompt the writer to introduce it, poke fun at it and make Polyphemus drunk with it.

Or again, knowing as we do from Thucydides (vi. 2) that the original Sican inhabitants of this part of Sicily received an influx of fugitives from the neighbourhood of Troy after the fall of that city, it is possible that traditions may have existed among the writer's audience to the effect that some of them were of Cicon origin, and she may have wished to flatter them by telling them that they had repulsed Ulysses. Nothing can be said with any confidence upon this head ; all we may note is that the country is quite featureless, and hence does not suggest drawing from personal knowledge, any more than does the land of the Lotus-eaters.

On leaving the land of the Lotus-eaters the full consent which has accompanied us so far fails us ; nevertheless a considerable weight of authority, ancient, medieval, and modern, carries us to the island of Favognana, anciently called Ægusa or Goat Island, as the one on which Ulysses and his men hunted the goats. Indeed this incident seems introduced as though purposely to suggest the Ægadean or " goat " islands to the audience, as also does the line iv. 606 in which Ithaca— that is to say, in reality, the island of Marettimo—is said to be an island fit for goats.*

A very considerable consent accompanies us also to Mt. Eryx as the site of the adventure with Polyphemus. Here, and with the island on which the goats were hunted, the local colour is stronger than anywhere else in Ulysses' voyages, as indeed might be reasonably expected from a writer whom I have shown to have been so intimately acquainted with the neighbourhood of Trapani.

---

* The name Favognana is derived from Favonius, this wind blowing on to Trapani from off the island. It is, however, also and perhaps most frequently called Favignana.

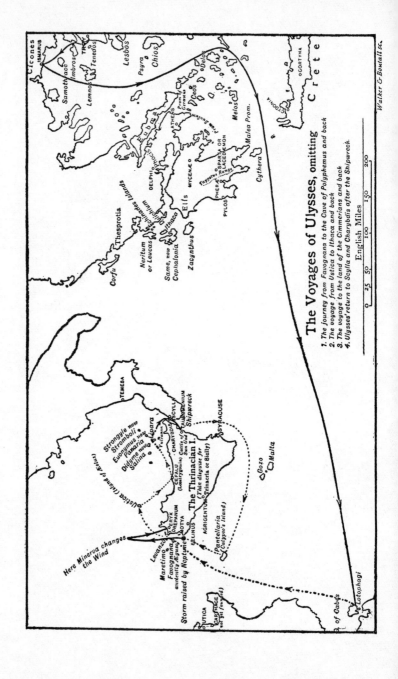

The Voyages of Ulysses, omitting

1. The journey from Favoygnana to the Cave of Polyphemus and back
2. The voyage from Ustica to Ithaca and back
3. The voyage to the land of the Cimmerians and back
4. Ulysses' return to Scylla and Charybdis after the Shipwreck.

English Miles

0   25   50   100   150   200

Walker & Boutall sc.

Even partial consent, however, now fails us. The island of Æolus and the country of the Læstrygonians have been placed in almost as many sites as there have been writers upon the "Odyssey." I shall return to these on a later page, as also to the island of Favognana and the Cyclopes. My present object is to show how much of the voyage we may consider as known, how much as supported by considerable authority, and how much we have yet to find.

The partial consent which we lost at the cave of Polyphemus returns to us with the island of Circe, the Sirens and the Wandering Cliffs, which are generally considered to have been the Lipari islands, and universal consent rejoins us for Scylla and Charybdis. I can hardly say that consent is universal for placing the cattle of the Sun on the East coast of Sicily, some-where about Tauromenium now Taormina ; but it is very general, and is so obviously well founded that I shall claim this point as certain ; for the name of the island sufficiently indicates Sicily, the winds that detain Ulysses show him to have been on an East coast, and the South wind that blew him back to Charybdis in a night shows that he was supposed to be at no great distance South of the Straits of Messina.

The island of Calypso has been generally held to be Malta, but on no foundation either internal or external to the "Odyssey," I shall, therefore, consider Calypso's island as yet to find.

I have no consent for Scheria being Trapani, but after what I have written above shall claim this point too as certain. The map, therefore, which I here give will show the reader how we stand as regards assent and otherwise ascertained points. I have used strong lines for the parts of the voyage that may be claimed as certain, interrupted lines for the parts that are backed by considerable authority, and dotted lines for those which I would supply. I have made Ulysses approach Trapani from the South, on the strength of Calypso's directions to him that he was to sail towards the Great Bear, keeping it on his left hand (v. 276, 277).* This indicates certainly a

---

* Gr. Τὴν γὰρ δή μιν ἄνωγε Καλυψὼ δῖα θεάων
ποντοπορευέμεναι ἐπ' ἀριστερὰ χειρὸς ἔχοντα.

Northerly, and one would say a N.N. Easterly, course ; at any rate such a course would in no way conflict with Calypso's instructions. Perhaps I had better give the words of the poem which run :

He sat keeping his eyes upon the Pleiades,* late setting Boötes, and on the Bear, also called the Wain, which turns round and round facing Orion, and alone never sinks beneath the sea—for Calypso had bidden him steer by this, keeping it on his left hand (v. 272–277).

All the places in Ulysses' voyage have been generally referred to some actual locality, which was present to the writer's mind either under its own or a fictitious name ; and when we have once got into Sicilian waters, all those about which there is any considerable amount of consent, or which we may now, with or without consent, claim as ascertained— I mean Circe's island, the Sirens, Scylla and Charybdis, the Thrinacian island, Scheria and Ithaca are on, or hard by, the coast of Sicily. Is not the temptation irresistible to think that the three unknown sites—the island of Æolus, the Land of the Læstrygonians and the island of Calypso—are also real places however fictitious the names may be, and to hold that they should be looked for on, or near, the coast of Sicily in the same order as that in which we find them described ?

If, on the hypothesis that Favognana and Mt. Eryx are the true sites of the island on which Ulysses and his men hunted the goats, and of the cave of Polyphemus, we are immediately led to others, in due order of sequence, which commend themselves as being those of the island of Æolus, the Land of the Læstrygonians, Circe's island, the other established sites, and

---

* We may neglect the Pleiades, as introduced simply because they are in the Iliadic passage (xviii. 486–489) which the writer of the " Odyssey " is adopting with no other change than taking out the Hyades and Orion, and substituting Boötes. This she was bound to do, for she could not make Ulysses steer towards both the Bear and Orion, when she is just going to tell us, as the " Iliad " does, that Orion is on the other side of the sky. The Pleiades she has allowed to stand—which of us knows in what quarter of the heavens (let alone the Precession of the Equinoxes) they are to be looked for ?— and it is made quite clear that the Bear is the constellation by which Ulysses is steering.

lastly Calypso's island, should we not conclude, at any rate provisionally, that the hypothesis is a true one ?

I will so conclude, and proceed to look for the island of Æolus in some island, apparently solitary, a good way to the West of the Lipari islands, and at no great distance from Mt. Eryx.

I should first correct a very general misapprehension. The word πλωτῇ (x. 3) has been unduly pressed into meaning that the island floated about, and thus changed its place. But if so singular a phenomenon were intended more would have been made of it. It would not have been dealt with in a single word, admitting easy explanation as mere metaphor. No one presses the " swiftly moving " islands of xv. 299 into meaning that the islands actually moved. All that is meant is that they " seemed to move " as the ship flew past them, and so with the island of Æolus—" it seemed to float on the horizon." It shows no signs of having moved during the month that Ulysses stayed on it, and when he returns to it after an absence of three weeks, we have no hint given of its having changed its place.* I conclude, therefore, that it was as fixed as any other island, and proceed to look for it.

This is no hard matter, for the island of Ustica offers itself at once. In clear weather it can be faintly seen from Mt. Eryx, and would naturally have impressed itself on the mind of a writer to whom Eryx and its neighbourhood was all in all. It is in the quarter from which the winds blow most fiercely on Trapani during the winter months, and may fitly have been selected by a Trapanese writer as the home of the winds. The distance, a long way West of the Lipari islands, and a greatly longer distance West of Ithaca, is all as it should be. I accept it, therefore, and go on to look for the land of the Læstrygonians, and their city Telepylus, at some point on the North coast of Sicily between Ustica and the Lipari islands.

---

* At Messina a few months since I saw a printed handbill about the hours when the boat would start for Reggio, in which Italy was called " Terra firma," as though a sense of instability attached itself to any island.

The name of the Læstrygonians or Workers in Stone,* like all names of places or people inside Sicily, is fictitious. If there had ever been any people really so called in Sicily Thucydides would have been able to find out some little, at any rate, about them; whereas he declares (vi. 2) that he cannot do so, and subrisively refers his readers to the poets, or whatever other source of information they can command. Clearly he does not believe in them except as poetical fictions concerning the most ancient inhabitants of Sicily—of whom none are known to him as more ancient than the Sicans.

But why should not the writer of the "Odyssey" be referring under names of her own coinage to these same Sicans, for both the Cyclopes and the Læstrygonians? The name of the Læstrygonian city, Telepylus, is certainly fictitious. It means "with gates far asunder," which can only be an *ex post facto* name: a city receives its name long before it is known what it will prove to be in the matter of growth. All that we can gather from the name is that the writer of the "Odyssey" intended her audience to understand that the city was large.

Its inhabitants, like the Cyclopes, are giants and ogres. They being giants, we should look for remains of megalithic buildings, and being ogres we should suspect identity of race between them and the Cyclopes whom they so closely resemble. The writer hates them both, and looks down upon the Cyclopes much as the Normans looked down upon the Saxons for some generations after the Conquest.

The Cyclopes appear to have been subdued and outlawed; not so the Læstrygonians. These last are a flourishing and very industrious people, who work by night as well as by day (x. 84–86). There is a poor little prehistoric joke about them, to the effect that in their country a man could earn double wages if he could only do without sleep. Moreover they were so wealthy and luxurious that they used to have relays of fresh

---

* The name seems derived from λᾶας, τρυγάω, and αἶα, as Œnotria is from οἶνος, τρυγάω, and αἶα. I have read, but forget where, that Œnotria is only a Greek rendering of Italia, which is derived from *vites, alo,* and some Latin equivalent for αἶα. The modern Italian word *lastricare,* "to pave roads with stone," is probably derived from the same roots as *Læstrygonian.*

WALL AT CEFALÙ, RISING FROM THE SEA

MEGALITHIC REMAINS ON THE MOUNTAIN BEHIND CEFALÙ

milk (x. 82, 83), instead of being contented with a morning supply, as Sicilian towns generally are even at the present day. More than this I cannot collect about them from the " Odyssey."

Can we, then, find a place answering to the description of Telepylus, on the North coast of Sicily between Ustica and the island of Lipari ? I have no hesitation in saying that Cefalù will give us all we want. It has two fine examples of megalithic work. They must both of them be centuries earlier than the " Odyssey." They are about three quarters of a mile apart, one, a wall rising from the sea, the other a building on the hill, behind the town, in part polygonal, and very rude, and in part of much later and singularly exquisite work—the later work being generally held to be of the Mycenæan age.

The city, therefore, must have been for those days extensive. The whole modern town is called among the common people Portazza, *i.e.*, *portaccia*, or " wide gate," which is too like a corrupt mistranslation of Telepylus to allow of my passing it over.

There can, I think, be no doubt that Eryx and Cefalù were built in a very remote age by people of the same race. I have seen no other megalithic remains in Sicily than at the two places just named ; I have seen remains of ancient buildings at Collesano about fifteen miles S.W. of Cefalù, which are commonly called Cyclopean, but they are very doubtful, and Dr. Orsi suspects them, I have little doubt correctly, to be Byzantine. I have also seen a few, neither striking nor yet certain ones, at Capo Schisò near Taormina. What little is left of the walls of Segesta is of a greatly later age, and I find it very difficult to think that Segesta was in existence when the " Odyssey " was being written.* I have heard of the remains of a Cyclopean acropolis behind Termini, a monograph about which by Sigr. Luigi Mauceri will be found in the British Museum. At Isnello two hours inland from Collesano a very early necropolis has been discovered not long since, and the

---

* Segesta would have been seen from the top of Mt. Eryx gleaming in the summer sunset, and I think there would have been some kind of allusion to it.

efforts of local archæologists will, I doubt not, lead to the finding of others at or near many of the little known mountain sites in the North of Sicily ; Dr. Orsi, indeed, has recently discovered the remains of a megalithic house at Pantalica some forty miles inland from Syracuse. No megalithic work, however, that has yet been found will compare in importance with the remains at Eryx and Cefalù, nor does it seem likely that any other such remains will be discovered.

Bearing in mind, then, the situation of Cefalù both as regards Ustica and Lipari, the affinity between its founders and those of Eryx as evidenced by existing remains, its great extent, and the name it still bears among the common people, I do not hesitate to accept it as the city of the Læstrygonians, nor does it affect me that the details of the harbour as given in the " Odyssey " have no correspondence with the place itself. I may mention that when my friend, Mr. H. F. Jones, and myself were at Cefalù in the spring of 1896, we met a flock of goats coming into the town to be milked about five in the afternoon, and on our return from a walk we met another flock coming out after having been just milked. These two flocks must have met, and the shepherds must have saluted one another as in x. 82, 83, but unfortunately we did not happen to be at their point of meeting.

On enquiry we found that relays of fresh milk come into the town from six till eight in the morning, and from five till seven in the afternoon, and were told that there was no other town known to our informant which had more than a morning supply. At Trapani, a town with 30,000 inhabitants, there is no evening supply, and though I have no doubt that fresh milk can be had in the evening at Palermo, Catania, and Syracuse, it is not easily procurable even in these large towns, while in smaller ones, so far as I know them, it is not to be had at all. At Rome I asked the landlord of my hotel whether the goats came to be milked in the evening as in the morning, and he said it would be only in exceptional cases that they would do so.

I have now only to find the island of Calypso, which in the " Odyssey " is called the "navel " of the sea (i. 50), a metaphor absolutely impossible of application to any but a solitary island, and prohibitive of either Gozo or Malta, or of the other two small islands of the same group. Calypso lives by herself and is cut off from every one else—Ulysses cannot be supposed to have other islands in sight as he sits on the sea shore weeping and looking out upon the waves. Moreover, Scheria being fixed at Trapani, Ulysses could never get there from either Gozo or Malta if he followed the directions of Calypso and steered towards the Great Bear, keeping it on his left hand. We are, therefore, compelled to look for some other island, which shall be more solitary and more S.S.W. of Trapani.

The island of Pantellaria fulfils both these conditions ; true, in clear weather the coast of Africa can sometimes be just made out—I have seen it from Pantellaria, but it is not sufficiently near or sufficiently often seen to have obtruded itself on Ulysses' notice ; still less so is Mt. Eryx, which can also be seen sometimes, but very rarely. No doubt the island is represented as being a good deal further off Scheria than it really was, but the liberty taken in this respect is not greater than is generally conceded in poetry.

As, therefore, the writer begins the voyage, when Ulysses is once clear of Trapani, with an island interesting to herself and her audience as being well within their ken, so she ends it with another island which has like claims on her and their attention.

Chapter X

WHAT I have said in the preceding chapter should be enough to establish that the course taken by Ulysses was the one indicated in my map, but I have remarks to make on the Cyclopes, the wall round the island of Æolus, the Sirens, the Wandering Cliffs, and other matters connected with the voyages which I have reserved in order to keep the general view more broad and simple.

The habitat of the Cyclopes on Mt. Eryx is the point which it is most incumbent on me to establish, for if this be conceded, and both Scylla and Charybdis, and Scheria be taken as found, all the other places fall so spontaneously on to the sites I have marked for them, that I fear no dispute concerning them. Let us turn, then, to Favognana and accept it for the moment as the island on which Ulysses hunted the goats.

Why, I wonder, was the author so careful to invoke a thick darkness, so pompous and circumstantial, and to pilot Ulysses into the harbour of this island by divine assistance, rather than permit him to look about him and see the land, which was " not very far " off.

The answer is " not very far " to seek. If Ulysses had seen the main land of Sicily as he approached it from that of the Lotus-eaters, he would have been sure to have followed it up, and in this case he would have been taken straight into Trapani harbour. Now, though the writer, as all the audience would know, had already dealt with Trapani, as the last point in all Ulysses' vogages, Ulysses himself ought not to know anything about it till he comes to it in due course.

The cave of Polyphemus—still called among the peasants *la grotta di Polifemo*—was some six or seven miles North of

Trapani; Ulysses had got to be taken there, and if possible, without unsettling either his own mind or that of the audience by showing him a city which eight years later he was to know as Scheria. He could, with the help of a little mist, be just supposed to go from the island of Favognana to the promontory of Pizzolungo and the cave of Polyphemus, without seeing the city of the Phæacians if he did not look particularly hard in that direction, but even Ulysses would have been compelled to take note of Scheria if he had been allowed to go on till he reached its harbour. It was better, therefore, that some god should take him to the island without letting him see any other land at all, and hence the intense darkness which the writer has been so careful to describe. We shall see that later on (as regards the supposed time, though earlier in the structure of her poem) she invokes a darkness which makes it impossible for Ulysses to form any idea of his whereabouts, in exactly the same place, and for the same reasons (v. 291–294)— for here too it is necessary to get Ulysses from a point South of Trapani, to another on the North side of it without seeing the town.

My map of the Ægadean islands (p. 177) combined with that of Trapani and Mt. Eryx (p. 164) will show the course Ulysses would make from Favognana to the *Grotta di Polifemo*—which is far the largest cave near Trapani, and is still used as a place in which to keep a large flock of sheep by night. The two rocks which Polyphemus threw should be seen, the first as the Asinelli,* and the second as the two small islands called Formiche, which, being close together, are taken as one.

I find, therefore, in the care taken to prevent Ulysses from seeing Trapani, a considerable argument for the belief that Favognana was the island where Ulysses hunted the goats, and that the cave of Polyphemus was on Mt. Eryx.

Another indication, though one of no great strength, seems to suggest that the Cyclopes were still near neighbours of the Phæacians.

---

* The Asinelli is a single islet much in the shape of a ship heading straight for Favognana. There is nothing plural about it, and one does not see why it should have a plural name. Who were the " asses " or " fools " ?

At the beginning of Book vi. we learn that the Phæacians used to live at a place called Hypereia, " near the lawless Cyclopes," but had of late years been moved to Scheria, which, as I have said, means Jutland. In a passage which I have not given in my abridgement Alcinous says casually (vii. 205, 206) that the Phæacians are as closely related to the gods as the Cyclopes and the giants are. Passing over the fact that Alcinous, being grandson to Neptune, was half nephew to Polyphemus, the spontaneousness with which the Cyclopes rise to his mind suggests that though less near than they had been, they were still about the nearest neighbours that he had.

The giants are only the Cyclopes over again, and are doubtless the descendants of the people who built the noble megalithic walls of Eryx. Hypereia, or Upper-town, was probably at the Eastern end of the top of Mt. Eryx on a site where a very ancient wall, of totally different character to those of the Sican city at the West end of the mountain, may yet be traced. The remains of this wall are just above the *Ruccazzù dei Corvi*, in Count Pepoli's grounds, and were first shown me by the Count. A stranger is little likely to find them unless conducted by one who has seen them.

As regards Hypereia I would repeat that all the names of places in Sicily with one partial exception are fictitious, even Trinacria, which Thucydides tells us was the most ancient name of Sicily, becoming " the Thrinacian," or " three-pointed," island ; whereas as soon as we are outside Sicily the names are real. This affords ground for thinking that the writer was drawing real people as well as real places, and travestying them under flimsy disguises that she knew her audience would see through. Once only is the mask dropped for a moment, when Ulysses says that he had just come from Sicania (xxiv. 307), but this does not count, for Ulysses is supposed to be lying.

The name Cyclopes, for example, or " round faces "—for there is nothing in the word to show that it means anything else than this, and I see from Liddell & Scott that Parmenides calls the moon Cyclops—is merely an author's nick name. If $\mu\hat{\eta}\lambda\omega\psi$ means " apple-faced," $\kappa\acute{\upsilon}\kappa\lambda\omega\psi$ should mean " circle-faced." As there is nothing in the word, so neither is there in the " Odyssey," to suggest that the Cyclopes were a people with only one round eye in the middle of their foreheads. Such a marked feature does not go without saying,* and that it did not go with the earliest Greek artists appears from the fact that they always gave Polyphemus two eyes. It is not till later times that he becomes monophthalmic, and the " Odyssey " gives him eyebrows in the plural (ix. 389), which involve eyes in the plural also. True, the writer only blinds one eye, but she could trust to the sympathetic inflammation which so serious an injury would excite in the other eye, and would consider that she had sufficiently blinded both by roasting one of them. One eye alone was blinded, not because Polyphemus had not got two, but because his pole had not got two prongs, and the writer saw neither how to get a bifurcated instrument into the cave, nor how to wield it now that so many of the men had been eaten.

" Cyclopes," therefore, we may be sure, mean nothing more than " moon-faced." The name Polyphemus is found as that of a hero in the " Iliad," and is perhaps a pseudonym for the local giant (if there was one) taken from that poem. Whatever his name may have been, and whether he was a pre-Odyssean giant, or whether the writer of the " Odyssey " called him into being, he exists now under the name of Conturràno. I have sometimes wondered whether this name may have any connection with the Greek words κόντος and οὐρανός, and may indicate that the giant was so tall as to be able to knock a hole in the sky with his staff. Should this be so, his name as likely as not was Conturràno, or something near it, in the days of the " Odyssey," and it was with the κόντος commemorated in his own name that Ulysses blinded him. The giant has grown greatly since the " Odyssey " was written, and large as the *grotta di Polifemo* is, he could never get inside it ; for he rests

---

* Virgil does not let it pass unnoticed. He writes :
" Cernimus adstantes nequidquam lumine torvo
    Ætnæos fratres,........"
                                    " Æn." iii. 677, 678.
He calls the Cyclopes " Ætnæan " because he places them on Mt. Etna.

his feet on the plain while he props his stomach on the top of Mt. Eryx, and bending forward plunges his huge hands into the sea between Bonagia and Cofàno, to catch tunnies. When disturbed he tears great rocks from the top of Mt. Eryx, and dashes them at all who interrupt him.

To repeat and to sum up, for I will argue this point no further; I take the Cyclopes to be the conquered remnant of the old Sican inhabitants of Mt. Eryx. They owe their gigantic stature to the huge size of the stones with which the walls of their city on Mt. Eryx were built. These stones show few or no signs of having been worked with a tool of hardened bronze or iron, save in so far as the Phœnicians may have trimmed them here and there when they rebuilt the walls, in part, *de novo*, with stones some of which bear quarry-men's marks in Phœnician characters.* The old Sican work, a good deal of which has been allowed to stand, belongs to the true megalithic age, when it was cheaper to carry than to cut; later generations, failing to consider the revolution which the introduction of improved methods of cutting had effected, argued that the men who built with such large stones must have been large men, whereas in reality they were only economical men.

As soon as it became cheaper to cut than to carry, the huge unwieldy blocks that we see at Eryx, at Cefalù, and at Segni, Arpino, Allatri, and many another city in Southern Italy, became obsolete, but it was still long before all irregularity in the courses was abandoned for that perfect regularity which we find at Syracuse, Selinunte, the temple of Segesta, and nearly all the Greek and Roman architecture of historic times. Indeed I know many buildings as late as the tenth century after Christ, in which the courses are far from regular; nevertheless the tendency, almost immediately after cutting had become cheaper, was towards greater regularity of courses and the use of smaller stones, until there arose another megalithicism, of a kind diametrically opposed to that of the earlier builders—I mean the megalithicism of display.

---

* There is no Phœnician work in the bastion shown in my illustration, the restorations here are medieval.

H. FESTING JONES ESQ. (height 6ft. 2in.) IN FLUTE OF COLUMN AT SELINUNTE

REMAINS OF MEGALITHIC WALLS ON MT. ERYX

There are stones at Selinunte, used in buildings of the fifth century before Christ, that are larger than the largest at Eryx or Cefalù ; there are columns thirteen feet in diameter at the base, and in a flute of which my friend Mr. H. F. Jones could stand ; but they are written all over in clear though invisible characters with the word " Glory," whereas the stones at Eryx bear not less clearly the word " Economy." I do not think that any true megalithic polygonal walls not worked with metal can be dated much earlier than 2000 B.C. By the time we reach such buildings as the Treasury of Atreus at Mycene, or the Iliadic wall of Hissarlik (which, however, is built in far less regular courses), cutting, whether with chisels of hardened bronze, or more probably by that time with iron, has ceased to be troublesome ; nevertheless as late as Hesiod, who is not generally dated earlier than 1000 B.C., the memory of an age when " as yet swart iron was not," had not been lost. (*Works and Days*, 148–151.)

Furthermore, I would ask the reader to remark how closely the description of the Cyclopes in the " Odyssey " tallies with that of the modern Sicilian brigands published in the *Times* of September 24th, 1892.

The writer—Mr. Stigand—says :

S. Mauro, the headquarters of the brigands, is a town on the top of a mountain 3000 feet high, and in sight of Geraci Siculo, another town of about the same height, and of Pollina, also on the summit of another mountain. The roads among the mountains, connecting these towns, are mere mule paths. The mountains abound in caves known only to the brigands and shepherds.

The " Odyssey " says of the Cyclopes :

They have neither places of assembly nor laws, but live in caves on the tops of high mountains ; each one of them rules over his own wife and children, and they take no account of any one else (ix. 112–115).

I saw several families of cave-dwellers at a place called *le grotte degli Scurati* on Cofàno about fifteen miles North of Trapani. There was, however, nothing of the Cyclops about them. Their caves were most beautifully clean and as comfortable as the best class of English cottages. The people, who were most kind and hospitable, were more fair than dark, and might very well have passed for English. They provided us with snow white table cloths and napkins for the lunch which we had brought from Trapani, and they gave us any quantity of almonds fried in a little salt and butter ; most unexpected of all, the salt they brought us was mixed with chervil seed. There was an atrocious case of brigandage on Cofàno about a fortnight later than our pic-nic. A Palermo merchant was kept a whole month on the mountain till he was ransomed, but I am sure that our cave-dwellers had nothing to do with it. The caves bore traces of prehistoric man by way of ancient meals now petrified.

It is noticeable that forms of the word σπέος or ἄντρον (cave) appear forty-five times in the " Odyssey " as against only six in the " Iliad," which, allowing for the greater length of the last named poem, is about in the proportion of 10 : 1. We may surmise, therefore, that the " Odyssey " hails from a district in which caves abounded.

As regards " the wall of bronze " which the writer of the " Odyssey " tells us ran round the island of Æolus, it is hard to say whether it was purely fiction or no. We may be sure that it was no more made of bronze than Æolus was king of the winds, but all round the island of Marettimo, wherever the cliffs do not protect it naturally, there existed a wall of long pre-Odyssean construction, traces of which were shown me by Sigr. Tedesco and Professor Spadaro, without whose assistance I should not have observed them. I have sometimes wondered whether the writer may not have transferred this wall to Ustica, as we shall see later that she transferred the hump on Thersites' back to that of Eurybates ; but no traces of any such wall exist so far as I know on Ustica, nor yet on the islands of Favognana or Levanzo. The ancient name of Marettimo was Hiera, and about 1900 feet above the sea I was shown ruins (not striking) of exceedingly ancient walls on a small plateau which the inhabitants dare not cross by night, and which is believed to have been the site of the cult that gave its name to the island.

What I have to say about Circe's island is so speculative that I write it in fear and trembling. I see that Circe's house is, like Eumæus's pig farm, " in a place that can be seen from far " (x. 211), and I see also that Ulysses approaches it " over the top of the mountain " (x. 281), as he does Eumæus's hut (xiv. 2). I remember the pigs, and I cannot refrain from thinking that though the writer tells us in the first instance that the island was a low one (x. 196), her inability to get away from her own surroundings is too much for her, and she is drifting on to the top of Mt. Eryx and Eumæus's pig farm. She does not mean to have pigs at first—the men whom Circe bewitched on previous occasions were turned into wolves and lions—but the force of association is too strong for her, and Ulysses' men are turned into pigs after all.

The fall of Elpenor from the top of Circe's house is a very singular way of killing him. If he had been at Eumæus's hut she could not have killed him more naturally than by letting him tumble off the precipice that overhangs it, and on the top of which the temple of Venus stood in later ages. I suspect not without shame, that the wall of Circe's house is made to do duty for this precipice.

On the island of Panaria, anciently Euonymus, among the Lipari group, there is a small bay called La Caletta dei Zummari, which suggests a corruption of Cimmerii, but I have already explained that no attempt should be made to localise the journey to Hades.

The two Sirens can be placed with, I should say, confidence, on the island of Salina, anciently called Didyme from the two high mountains, each about 3000 feet high, of which it consists. Sudden cat's paws of very violent wind descend at times from all high points near the sea in this part of the Mediterranean, as from Cofàno near Trapani, where there is a saying among the fishermen " ware Cofàno." My friend, Signor E. Biaggini, whose loss I have to deplore within the last twelve months, and who has furnished me over and over again with local details, told me that he once was all but capsized by a gust from Cofàno, that came down on his boat in perfectly calm weather, and lasted hardly more than a few seconds. I take it that the two Sirens—who are always winged in the earlier Greek representations of them—were, as indeed their name suggests, the whistling gusts or avalanches of air that descended without the slightest warning from the two mountains of Didyme. The story turned from poetry into prose means, "Woe to him who draws near the two treacherous mountains of Didyme; the coast is strewn with wreckage, and if he hears the wind from off them shriek in his rigging his bones will whiten the shore." The reader will remember that the Sirens' island is very near Circe's.

Speaking of the Æolian islands Admiral Smyth says:

Whether from the heat of the water by volcanic springs, the steam of Vulcanella, the incessant hot injections from Stromboli, or all of them added to the general temperature, it is certain that there are more frequent atmospherical changes among this group than in the neighbourhood (*The Mediterranean*, Parker, 1854, p. 250).

Speaking, again, of the Straits of Messina, he says:

Precautions should also be taken against the heavy gusts, which at times, from the mountainous nature of the coasts, rush down the Fuimare, and are dangerous to small vessels. I have twice, with grief, seen the neglect of them prove fatal (*Sicily and its Islands*, Murray, 1824, p. 111).

The reason why the poetess found herself in such difficulties about the Wandering Cliffs, is because the story, as Buttmann has said, does not refer to any two islands in particular, but is derived from traveller's tales about the difficulties of navigating the Lipari islands as a whole. "They close in upon you," it was said, "so quickly one after another that a bird can hardly get through them." The "hurricanes of fire," moreover (xii. 68), suggest an allusion to the volcanic nature of the Æolian islands generally. Still more so does the dark cloud that never leaves the top of Scylla's rock (xii. 74) neither in summer nor winter.

The terrors of Scylla and Charybdis are exaggerated in the same poetic vein as the Sirens and the Wandering Cliffs. Instead of its being possible to shoot an arrow from the one to the other, they are about eight miles apart. We ought not to

look for the accuracy of one of Mr. Murray's handbooks in a
narrative that tells us of a monster with six heads and three
rows of teeth in each. It is enough if there are a few grains of
truth, and these there are : for Scylla is a high rock looking
West, and Charybdis is (for those days) a formidable whirlpool,
on the other side the Straits, off lower ground, and hard by the
approach to a three pointed island. According to Admiral
Smyth it is just outside Messina harbour, and is now called
Galofaro. Admiral Smyth says of it :

To the undecked boats of the Rhegians, Locrians, Zancleans,
and Greeks, it must have been formidable ; for even in the
present day small craft are sometimes endangered by it, and
I have seen several men-of-war, and even a seventy-four-gun
ship, whirled round on its surface ; but by using due caution
there is generally very little danger or inconvenience to be
apprehended (*Sicily and its Islands*, Murray, 1824, p. 123).

I do not doubt that the Galofaro is the nucleus round which
the story of Charybdis gathered, but I have seen considerable
disturbance in the sea all through the Straits of Messina.
Very much depends upon the state of the winds, which sometimes bank the water up in the angle between the toe of Italy
and the North coast of Sicily, on which a current and strong
eddies occur in the Straits of Messina. At other times there is
hardly anything noticeable.

Passing over the nine days drifting in the sea, which take
Ulysses from Charybdis to the island of Calypso, *i.e.* Pantellaria—and we may be sure he would have been made to take
longer time if the writer had dared to keep him longer without
food and water—it only remains for me to deal at somewhat
fuller length than yet I have done with the voyage from
Pantellaria to Trapani. On the eighteenth day after Ulysses
had left Pantellaria, steering towards the Great Bear, but
keeping it on the left, he saw the long low line of the Lilybæan
coast rising on the horizon. He does not appear to have seen
the island of Favognana, which must have been quite near,
and it was perhaps as well that he did not, for he could hardly
have failed to recognise it as the one on which he had hunted

the goats some eight or nine years previously, and this might have puzzled him.

But though he is allowed to see the land he must not be permitted to follow it up, or, as I have explained already, he would have gone straight into the harbour of Scheria, whereas he is particularly wanted to meet Nausicaa on the North side of the town, and to know nothing about Scheria till she brings him to it. Neptune, therefore, is made to catch sight of him at this moment and to raise a frightful hurricane ; sea and sky become obscured in clouds, with a darkness as dense as night (v. 291–294), and thus Ulysses is carried a long distance apparently to the North, for when he has been taken far enough, Minerva blows him two days and two nights before a North wind, and hence Southwards, till he reaches the harbour near which Nausicaa can meet him.

There are no other such noticeable darknesses in the "Odyssey," as this and the one of Book ix. 144, alluded to on p. 188. They both occur in the same place, and for the same reason—to keep the town of Scheria in reserve.

I have now shown that all the Ithacan scenes of the "Odyssey" are drawn with singular fidelity from Trapani and its neighbourhood, as also all the Scherian ; moreover, I have shown that the Ionian islands are in reality drawn from the Ægadean group off Trapani ; lastly I have shown that the voyage of Ulysses in effect begins with Trapani and ends with Trapani again. I need not deal with Pylos and Lacedæmon beyond showing that they were far removed from the knowledge of either writer or audience.

There is not a single natural feature mentioned in either case. The impossible journey of Telemachus and Pisistratus from Pheræ to Lacedæmon in a chariot and pair over the lofty, and even now roadless, ranges of Mt. Taygetus, causes no uneasiness to the writer. She gives no hint of any mountain to be crossed—from which we may infer, either that she knew nothing of the country between Pylos and Lacedæmon, or that at any rate her audience would not do so. It may, however, be remarked that the West wind which Minerva provided in order to take Telemachus from Ithaca to Pylos, was more suitable for taking him from Sicily. A North wind would have been better for him if he had been coming from the real Ithaca, but Minerva manages things so strangely that I would not press this point.

Chapter XI

WHO WAS THE WRITER?

I BELIEVE the reader will by this time feel no doubt, from my earlier Chapters that the " Odyssey " was written by one woman, and from my later ones that this woman knew no other neighbourhood than that of Trapani, and therefore must be held to have lived and written there.

Who, then, was she?

I cannot answer this question with the confidence that I have felt hitherto. So far I have been able to demonstrate the main points of my argument; on this, the most interesting question of all, I can offer nothing stronger than presumption.

We have to find a woman of Trapani, young, fearless, self-willed, and exceedingly jealous of the honour of her sex. She seems to have moved in the best society of her age and country, for we can imagine none more polished on the West coast of Sicily in Odyssean times than the one with which the writer shews herself familiar. She must have had leisure, or she could not have carried through so great a work. She puts up with men when they are necessary or illustrious, but she is never enthusiastic about them, and likes them best when she is laughing at them; but she is cordially interested in fair and famous women.

I think she should be looked for in the household of the person whom she is travestying under the name of King Alcinous. The care with which his pedigree and that of his wife Arête is explained (vii. 54–77), and the warmth of affectionate admiration with which Arête is always treated, have the same genuine flavour that has led scholars to see true history and personal interest in the pedigree of Æneas given in " Il." xx. 200–241. Moreover, she must be a sufficiently intimate member of the household to be able to laugh at its

head as much as she chose. No pedigree of any of the other
dramatis personæ of the " Odyssey " is given save that of Theoclymenus, whose presence in the poem at all requires more
explanation than I can give. I can only note that he was of
august descent, more than sub-clerical, and of a different stamp
from any other character to whom we are introduced.

The fact that the writer should be looked for in a member
of King Alcinous' household seems further supported by the
zest with which this household and garden are described (vii.
81–132), despite the obviously subrisive exaggeration which
pervades the telling. There is no such zest in the description
of any other household, and the evident pleasure which the
writer takes in it is more like that of a person drawing her
own home, than either describing some one else's or creating
an imaginary scene. See how having begun in the past tense
she slides involuntarily into the present as soon as she comes
to the women of the house and to the garden. She never does
this in any other of her descriptions.

Lastly, she must be looked for in one to whom the girl
described as Nausicaa was all in all. No one else is drawn
with like livingness and enthusiasm, and no other episode is
written with the same, or nearly the same, buoyancy of spirits
and resiliency of pulse and movement, or brings the scene
before us with anything approaching the same freshness, as
that in which Nausicaa takes the family linen to the washing
cisterns. The whole of Book vi. can only have been written by
one who was throwing herself into it heart and soul.

All the three last paragraphs are based on the supposition
that the writer was drawing real people. That she was drawing a real place, lived at that place, and knew no other, does
not admit of further question ; we can pin the writer down
here by reason of the closeness with which she has kept to
natural features that remain much as they were when she
portrayed them ; but no traces of Alcinous's house and
garden, nor of the inmates of his household will be even looked
for by any sane person ; it is open, therefore, to an objector to
contend that though the writer does indeed appear to have
drawn permanent features from life, we have no evidence that

she drew houses and gardens and men and women from anything but her own imagination.

Granted ; but surely, in the first place, if we find her keeping to her own neighbourhood as closely as she can whenever the permanency of the feature described enables us to be certain of what she did, there is a presumption that she was doing the same thing in cases where the evidence has been too fleeting to allow of our bringing her to book. And secondly, we have abundant evidence that the writer did not like inventing.

Richly endowed with that highest kind of imagination which consists in wise selection and judicious application of materials derived from life, she fails, as she was sure to do, when cut off from a base of operation in her own surroundings. This appears most plainly in the three books which tell of the adventures of Ulysses after he has left Mt. Eryx and the Cyclopes. There is no local detail in the places described ; nothing, in fact, but a general itinerary such as she could easily get from the mariners of her native town. With this she manages to rub along, helping herself out with fragments taken from nearer home, but there is no approach to such plausible invention as we find in *Gulliver's Travels, Robinson Crusoe*, or *Pilgrim's Progress ;* and when she puts a description of the land of Hades into the mouth of Circe (x. 508–515)—which she is aware must be something unlike anything she had ever witnessed—she breaks down and gives as a scene which carries no conviction. Fortunately not much detail is necessary here ; in Ithaca, however, a great deal is wanted, and feeling invention beyond her strength she does not even attempt it, but has recourse with the utmost frankness to places with which she is familiar.

Not only does she shirk invention as much as possible in respect of natural features, but she does so also as regards incident. She can vilipend her neighbours on Mt. Eryx as the people at Trapani continue doing to this day, for there is no love lost between the men of Trapani and those of Mte. S. Giuliano, as Eryx is now called. She knows Ustica : the wind comes thence, and she can make something out of that ; then there is the other great Sican city of Cefalù—a point can be

made here; but with the Lipari islands her material is
running short. She has ten years to kill, for which, however, eight or eight-and-a-half may be made to pass. She
cannot have killed more than three months before she lands
her hero on Circe's island; here, then, in pity's name let
him stay for at any rate twelve months—which he accordingly
does.

She soon runs through her resources for the Sirens' island,
and Scylla and Charybdis; she knows that there is nothing
to interest her on the East coast of Sicily below Taormina—
for Syracuse (to which I will return) was still a small pre-
Corinthian settlement, while on the South coast we have no
reason to believe that there was any pre-Hellenic city. What,
she asked herself, could she do but shut Ulysses up in the most
lonely island she could think of—the one from which he would
have the least chance of escaping—for the remainder of his
term? She chose, therefore, the island which the modern
Italian Government has chosen, for exactly the same reasons,
as the one in which to confine those who cannot be left at
large—the island of Pantellaria; but she was not going to
burden Calypso for seven long years with all Ulysses' men, so
his ship had better be wrecked.

This way out of the difficulty does not indicate a writer of
fecund or mature invention. She knew the existence of Sardinia, for Ulysses smiles a grim Sardinian smile (xx. 302). Why
not send him there, and describe it with details taken not from
the North side of Trapani but from the South? Or she need
not have given details at all—she might have sent him very
long journeys extending over ever so many years in half a page.
If she had been of an inventive turn there were abundant
means of keeping him occupied without having recourse to the
cheap and undignified expedient of shutting him up first for a
year in one island, and then for seven in another. Having
made herself so noble a peg on which to hang more travel and
adventure, she would have hung more upon it, had either
strength or inclination pointed in that direction. It is one of
the commonplaces of Homeric scholars to speak of the voyages
of Ulysses as "a story of adventurous travel." So in a way

they are, but one can see all through that the writer is trying to reduce the adventurous travel to a minimum.

See how hard put to it she is when she is away from her own actual surroundings. She does not repeat her incidents so long as she is at home, for she has plenty of material to draw from ; when she is away from home, do what she may, she cannot realise things so easily, and has a tendency to fall back on something she has already done. Thus, at Pylos, she repeats the miraculous flight of Minerva (iii. 372) which she had used i. 320. On reaching the land of the Læstrygonians Ulysses climbs a high rock to reconnoitre, and sees no sign of inhabitants save only smoke rising from the ground—at the very next place he comes to he again climbs a high rock to reconnoitre, and apparently sees no sign of inhabitants but only the smoke of Circe's house rising from the middle of a wood. He is conducted to the house of Alcinous by a girl who had come out of the town to fetch a pitcher of water (vii. 20) ; this is repeated (x. 105) when Ulysses' men are conducted to the house of the Læstrygonian Antiphates, by a girl who had come out of the town to fetch a pitcher of water. The writer has invented a sleep to ruin Ulysses just as he was well in sight of Ithaca (x. 31, &c.). This is not good invention, for such a moment is the very last in which Ulysses would be likely to feel sleepy—but the effort of inventing something else to ruin him when his men are hankering after the cattle of the Sun is quite too much for her, and she repeats (xii. 338) the sleep which had proved so effectual already. So, as I have said above, she repeats the darkness on each occasion when Ulysses seems likely to stumble upon Trapani. Calypso, having been invented once, must do duty again as Circe—or *vice versâ,* for Book x. was probably written before Book v.

Such frequent examples of what I can only call consecutive octaves indicate a writer to whom invention does not come easily, and who is not likely to have recourse to it more than she can help. Having shown this as regards both places and incidents, it only remains to point out that the writer's dislike of invention extends to the invention of people as well as places. The principal characters in the " Odyssey " are all of them

Scherian. Nestor, Ulysses, Menelaus and Alcinous are every one of them the same person playing other parts, and the greater zest with which Alcinous is drawn suggests, as I have said in an earlier Chapter, that the original from whom they are all taken was better known to the writer in the part of Alcinous than in that of any of the other three. Penelope, Helen, and Arēte are only one person, and I always suspect Penelope to be truer to the original than either of the other two. Idothea and Ino are both of them Nausicaa ; so also are Circe and Calypso, only made up a little older, and doing as the writer thinks Nausicaa would do if she were a goddess and had an establishment of her own. I am more doubtful about these last two, for they both seem somewhat more free from that man-hatred which Nausicaa hardly attempts to conceal. Still, Nausicaa contemplates marrying as soon as she can find the right person, and, as we have seen, neither Circe nor Calypso had a single man-servant of their own, while Circe was in the habit of turning all men who came near her into pigs or wild beasts. Calypso, moreover, is only made a little angry by being compelled to send Ulysses away. She does not seem to have been broken-hearted about it. Neither of them, therefore, must be held to be more fond of men than the convenience of the poem dictated. Even the common people of Ithaca are Scherians, and make exactly the same fault-finding ill-natured remarks about Penelope (xxiii. 149–151) as the Phæacians did about Nausicaa in Book vi. 273–288.

If, then, we observe that where the writer's invention is more laboured she is describing places foreign to her own neighbourhood, while when she carries conviction she is at or near her own home, the presumption becomes very strong that the more spontaneous scenes are not so much invention as a rendering of the writer's environment, to which it is plain that she is passionately attached, however much she may sometimes gird at it. I, therefore, dismiss the supposition of my supposed objector that the writer was not drawing Alcinous' household and garden from life, and am confirmed in this opinion by remembering that the house of Ulysses corresponds perfectly with that of Alcinous—even to the number of the women servants kept in each establishment.

Being limited to a young woman who was an intimate member of Alcinous' household, we have only to choose between some dependant who idolised Nausicaa and wished to celebrate her with all her surroundings, or Nausicaa (whatever her real name may have been) herself. Or again, it may be urged that the poem was written by some bosom friend of Nausicaa's who was very intimate with the family, as for example Captain Dymas's daughter.

The intimate friend theory may be dismissed at once. High spirited girls, brilliant enough to write the " Odyssey " are not so self effacing as to keep themselves entirely out of sight. If a friend had written the washing day episode, the friend would have come a washing too—especially after having said she would in Nausicaa's dream.

If, again, a dependant had written it, Nausicaa would neither have had the heart nor the power to suppress her altogether ; for if she tried to do so the dependant—so daring and self-willed as the writer proves herself to be—would have been more than a match for her mistress. We may be sure that there were not two such spirits in Trapani, as we must suppose if we make Nausicaa able to bow the will of the authoress of the " Odyssey." The fact that in the washing day episode, so far as possible, we find Nausicaa, all Nausicaa, and nothing but Nausicaa, among the female *dramatis personæ*, indicates that she was herself the young woman of Trapani, a member of the household of King Alcinous, whom we have got to find, and that she was giving herself the little niche in her work which a girl who was writing such a work was sure to give herself.

A dependant would not have dared to laugh at Alcinous with such playful malice as the writer has done. Again she would have made more of Nausicaa herself in the scenes that follow. At present she is left rather as a ragged edge, and says good bye to Ulysses in Book viii. 460, &c., with much less detail, both as regards her own speech and that of Ulysses in reply, than a courtier-like dependant would have permitted.

She does not hear Ulysses' account of his adventures—which she might perfectly well have done under her mother's wing. She does not appear to take her meals with the rest of the family at all. When she returns from washing, Eurymedusa brings her supper into her own room. She is not present at any of Alcinous' banquets, nor yet at the games, and her absence from the farewell scene in Book xiii. is too marked to be anything but intentional. It seems as though she wished the reader to understand that she lived apart, and however much she might enjoy an outing with her maids, would have nothing to do with the men who came night after night drinking her father's best wine, and making havoc of his estate. She almost calls these people scoundrels to their faces by saying that they always made the final drink offering of the evening not to Jove but to Mercury, the god of thieves (vii. 137). In passing, I may say that the strangeness of the manner in which Nausicaa says good bye to Ulysses is one of the many things which convince me that the " Odyssey " has never been recast by a later hand. A person recasting the work would have been tolerably sure to have transferred the leave-taking to Book xiii.

Nausicaa, again, would have been more than human if she had permitted any one but herself to put into her mouth the ill-natured talk about her which she alleges to pass current among the Phæacians. She would not mind saying it herself when her audience, private or public, would know that she was doing so, but a dependant would have been requested to be less pungent.

I admit as I have already done that these arguments are not absolutely demonstrative, but it being, I may say, demonstrated that we must choose between Nausicaa and some other young woman of Trapani who lived in, or was very closely intimate with, the household of King Alicnous, I have no hesitation in saying that I think Nausicaa herself more likely than this other unknown young woman to have been the writer we are seeking.

Let the reader look at my frontispiece and say whether he would find the smallest difficulty in crediting the original of the portrait with being able to write the " Odyssey." Would he refuse so to credit her merely because all he happened to know about her for certain was that she once went out washing clothes with her attendants ? Nausicaa enjoyed a jaunt on a fine spring morning and helped her maids at the washing cisterns ; therefore it is absurd to suppose that she could have written the " Odyssey." I venture to think that this argument will carry little weight outside the rank and file of our Homerists—greatly as I dislike connecting this word however remotely with the " Odyssey."

No artist can reach an ideal higher than his own best actual environment. Trying to materially improve upon that with which he or she is fairly familiar invariably ends in failure. It is only adjuncts that may be arranged and varied—the essence may be taken or left, but it must not be bettered. The attempt to take nature and be content with her save in respect of details which after all are unimportant, leads to Donatello, Giovanni Bellini, Holbein, Rembrandt, and De Hooghe—the attempt to improve upon her leads straight to Michael Angelo and the *barocco*, to Turner and the modern drop scene. There is not a trace of the *barocco* in my frontispiece ; we may be confident, therefore, that such women, though doubtless comparatively rare, yet existed, as they exist in Italy now, in considerable numbers. Is it a very great stretch of imagination to suppose that one among them may have shown to equal advantage whether as driver, washerwoman, or poetess ? At the same time I think it highly probable that the writer of the " Odyssey " was both short and plain, and was laughing at herself, and intending to make her audience laugh also, by describing herself as tall and beautiful. She may have been either plain or beautiful without its affecting the argument.

I wish I could find some one who would give me any serious reason why Nausicaa should not have written the " Odyssey." For the last five years I have pestered every scholar with whom I have been able to scrape acquaintance, by asking him to explain why the " Odyssey " should not have been written by a young woman. One or two have said that they could see none whatever, but should not like to commit themselves to a definite opinion without looking at the work again. One well-known

and very able writer said that when he had first heard of the
question as being mooted, he had supposed it to be some
paradox of my own, but on taking up the " Odyssey " he had
hardly read a hundred lines before he found himself saying
" Why of course it is." The greater number, however, gave
me to understand that they should not find it a difficult matter
to expose the absurdity of my contention if they were not
otherwise employed, but that for the present they must wish
me a very good morning. They gave me nothing, but to do
them justice before I had talked with them for five minutes I
saw that they had nothing to give with which I was not already
familiar. The " Odyssey " is far too easy, simple, and straight-
forward for the understanding of scholars—as I said in the
Life of Dr. Butler of Shrewsbury, if it had been harder to
understand, it would have been sooner understood—and yet I
do not know ; the " Iliad " is indeed much harder to understand, but scholars seem to have been very sufficiently able to
misunderstand it.

Every scholar has read a Book or two of the " Odyssey " here
and there ; some have read the whole ; a few have read it
through more than once ; but none that I have asked have so
much as been able to tell me whether Ulysses had a sister or
no—much less what her name was. Not one of those whom
I have as yet had the good fortune to meet in England—for I
have met with such in Sicily—have saturated themselves with
the poem, and that, too, unhampered by a single preconceived
idea in connection with it. Nothing short of this is of the
smallest use.

Chapter XII

THE DATE OF THE POEM, AND A COMPARISON OF THE STATE OF
THE NORTH WESTERN PART OF SICILY AS REVEALED TO US IN
THE ODYSSEY, WITH THE ACCOUNT GIVEN BY THUCYDIDES OF
THE SAME TERRITORY IN THE EARLIEST KNOWN TIMES.

THE view that the " Odyssey " was written at Trapani will
throw unexpected light upon the date of the poem. We can
never date it within a hundred years or so, but I shall attempt
to show that we must place it very little, if at all, later than
1050, and not earlier than 1150 B.C.

I see that I may claim Professor Jebb's authority as to some
extent, at any rate, supporting the later of these two dates.
He writes :

With regard to the age of the " Odyssey," we may suppose
that the original " Return " was composed in Greece Proper
as early as the Eleventh Century B.C., and that the first enlarge-
ment had been made before 850 B.C.*

I have shown why I cannot admit that any part of the
" Odyssey " was written in Greece Proper, and while admitting
that the poem has been obviously enlarged by the addition of
Books i.–iv. and line 187 of Book xiii.–xxiv., with which I will
deal fully in a later Chapter—I cannot think that the enlarge-
ment was by another hand than that of the authoress of the
poem in its original form. Nevertheless I am glad to claim
Professor Jebb's support as far as it goes, for dating the inception of the " Odyssey " as in the eleventh century B.C.

I will begin by giving my reasons for thinking that the
" Odyssey " must at any rate be earlier than 734 B.C.

When Eumæus is telling the story of his childhood to
Ulysses (xv. 403, &c.), he says that he was born in the Syrian

---

* *Introduction to Homer*, ed. 1888, pp. 172, 173.

island over against Ortygia, and I have rendered " the Syrian island " " the island of Syra," guided by the analogy of the " Psyrian island " (iii. 171), which unquestionably means the island of Psyra.

The connection of an island Syra with a land Ortygia, suggests Syracuse; in spite of the fact that in reality Ortygia was an island, and Syracuse both on the island and on the adjacent mainland—for as I have already too often said all Sicilian places in the " Odyssey " are travestied, however thinly.

The impression that Syracuse* is being alluded to is deepened by our going on to read that " the turnings of the sun " are " there "—which I presume may be extended so as to mean " thereabouts." Now what are " the turnings of the sun " ? I looked in Liddell and Scott, for whose work no one can feel a more cordial admiration, nor deeper sense of gratitude, and found that the turnings of the sun are " the solstices, or tropics, i.e., the turning points of midsummer and midwinter." This may do very well as regards time, but not as regards place. In reference to the Odyssean passage, I read that " the turning of the sun denotes a point in the heavens probably to the Westward."

But we want the sun to turn not at a point in the heavens, but in the neighbourhood of Syra and Ortygia, and to do so here in a way that he does not do elsewhere. The simplest way of attaining this end will be to suppose that the writer of the " Odyssey " was adopting a form of speech which we often use on a railway journey, when we say that the sun has turned and is coming in at the other window—meaning that the line has taken a sharp turn, and that we are going in a new direction. Surely I am not wrong in thinking that the author meant nothing more recondite than that near the two places named the land turns sharply round, so that sailors who follow it will find the sun on the other side of their ship from what it has hitherto been.

A glance at the map will show that the site which the combination of Syra and Ortygia has suggested is confirmed

---

* On its earlier coins Syracuse not unfrequently appears as Syra.

by the fact that shortly South of it the coast of Sicily turns abruptly round, and continues thenceforward in a new direction. Indeed it begins to turn sharply with the promontory of Plemmyrium itself. Eumæus, therefore, should be taken as indicating that he was born at the place which we know as Syracuse, and which was then, so he says, an aggregate of two small towns, without many inhabitants. It seems to have been a quite easy-going little place, where every one had enough to eat and drink, and nobody died except of sheer old age, diseases of all kinds being unknown. Business must have been carried on in a very leisurely fashion, for it took the Phœnicians a twelvemonth to freight their vessel, and the largest ship of those times cannot have been very large.

This is not the description of a busy newly founded settlement, as Syracuse would be in 734 B.C. Still less will it apply to any later Syracusan age. The writer modernises when dealing with an earlier age as frankly as Shakspeare : I have never detected a trace in her of any archæological instinct. I believe, therefore, that she was telling what little she knew of the Syracuse of her own day, and that that day was one prior to the arrival of the Corinthian Colony. I think it likely also that she made Eumæus come from Syracuse because she felt that she rather ought to have done something at Syracuse during the voyage of Ulysses, but could not well, under the circumstances, break his journey between Charybdis and Calypso's Island. She, therefore, took some other way of bringing Syracuse into her story.

It may be urged that we have no other evidence of any considerable civilisation as having existed at Syracuse before the one founded by the Corinthians, and as regards written evidence this is true, so far at least as I know ; but we have unwritten evidence of an even more conclusive kind. The remains of pottery and implements found at, or in the near neighbourhood of, Syracuse go back in an unbroken line from post-Roman times to the age of stone, while commerce with the Peloponnese, at any rate from the Mycenæan age, is shown by the forms and materials of the objects discovered in countless tombs. I had the advantage of being shown over the

Museum at Syracuse by Dr. Orsi, than whom there can be no more cautious and capable guide on all matters connected with the earliest history of Sicily, and he repeatedly insisted on the remoteness of the age at which commerce must have existed between the South East, and indeed all the East, coast of Sicily, and the Peloponnese. The notion, therefore, too generally held in the very face of Thucydides himself, that there were no people living at or near Syracuse till the arrival of the Corinthians must be abandoned, and I believe we may feel confident that in the story of Eumæus we have a peep into its condition in pre-Corinthian times.

The two communities of which Eumæus tells us were probably, one, on the promontory of Plemmyrium, and the other, at a place between three and four miles distant, now called Cozzo Pantano, on each of which sites Dr. Orsi has discovered the burying ground of an extensive village or town (*borgo*) to which he had assigned the date xii.–xi. centuries B.C. before his attention had been called to the existence of a reference to prehistoric Syracuse in the " Odyssey." Many examples of implements found on these two sites may be seen in the museum at Syracuse. I did not gather that any other prehistoric burying grounds had been found at or in close proximity to Syracuse.

Whether the people whose burying grounds have been found at the above named places were Greeks, who were displaced later by Sicels, as the Sicels in their turn were displaced by the Corinthians, or whether they were Sicels of an earlier unrecorded immigration, I must leave Dr. Orsi and others to determine, but the name of the sea which washes the East coast of Sicily points to the existence at one time of extensive Ionian settlements on East Sicilian shores. The name, again, Aci, which is found in *Aci reale, Aci Castello,* and *Aci trezza,* and which among the common people is now always sounded Iaci, suggests a remote Ionian origin—for we may assume that there was no Ionian migration later than 734 B.C. of sufficient importance to give the name Ionian to Sicilian waters, towns, and islands. The reader will be reminded in the following Chapter that 'Ιακός means Ionian.

Eumæus was so young when he was carried off that even though Greek was not his native language, he would have become Grecised in a few years; I incline to think, however, that the writer of the " Odyssey " would have said something about his being a Sicel if she had so conceived of him in her own mind. She seems to think of him as a Greek by birth.

The Sicels, however, also probably spoke Greek. The inhabitants of Temesa, on the toe of Italy, do not indeed seem to have done so (" Od." i. 183); but we do not know that they were Sicels. No writing has been found at Plemmirio nor yet at Cozzo Pantano; we have therefore very little to go upon.

But postulating that we may accept Thucydides—whose accuracy as regards Syracusan details proves that even though he had not been at Syracuse himself, he had at any rate means of informing himself on Sicilian history—who is evidently taking pains, and whose reputation is surpassed by that of no other historian—postulating that we may accept his statement (vi. 2) that the great irruption of Sicels which changed the name of the country from Sicania to Sicelia took place about 300 years before B.C. 734, I think we may safely put back the date of the " Odyssey " to a time before B.C. 1000.

For the " Odyssey " conveys no impression as though Sicily at large had been lately subdued and overrun by Sicels. Locally, indeed, the city at the top of Mt. Eryx had, as we have seen (" Od." vii. 60), been conquered and overthrown; but I shall bring Thucydides, as well as other evidence, to show that in this case the victors are more likely to have been Asiatic Greeks than Sicels. The poem indicates a time of profound present peace and freedom from apprehension, and on the one occasion in which the writer speaks of Sicily under its own name, she calls it by its pre-Sicelian name of Sicania.* The old Sicel woman who waited on Laertes (xxiv. 211 and elsewhere) is not spoken of as though there were any ill-will on the part of the writer

---

* The fact that Σικανίης (xxiv. 307) should not have got corrupted into Σικελίης—which would scan just as well—during the many centuries that the island was called Σικελία, suggests a written original, though I need hardly say that I should not rely on so small a matter if it rested by itself.

towards the Sicels, or as though they were a dominant race.
Lastly, one of the suitors (xx. 382) advises Telemachus to ship
Theoclymenus and Ulysses off to the Sicels. Now if the writer
had the real Ithaca in her mind, the Sicels could only have
been reached by sea, whether they were in Italy or Sicily ; but
I have already shown that she never pictured to herself any
other Ithaca than the one she had created at Trapani ; the
fact, therefore, that Theoclymenus and Ulysses were to be put
on board ship before they could reach the Sicels, shows that
she imagined these last as (except for an occasional emigrant)
outside the limits of her own island.

If the foregoing reasoning is admitted, 1050 B.C. will be about
as late as it is safe to place the date of the " Odyssey " ; but a
few years later is possible, though hardly, I think, probable. Unfortunately this date will compel us to remove the fall of Troy
to a time very considerably earlier than the received date. For
a hundred years is, one would think, the shortest interval that
can be allowed between the " Odyssey " and the " Iliad."
The development of myth and of the Epic cycle, of which we find
abundant traces in the " Odyssey," is too considerable to render
any shorter period probable. I therefore conclude that 1150 B.C.
is the latest date to which we should assign the " Iliad."

The usually received date for the fall of Troy is 1184 B.C.
This is arrived at from a passage in Thucydides (i. 12) which
says that sixty years after the fall of Troy, the Bœotians were
driven from Arne and settled in what was originally called
Cadmeis, but subsequently Bœotia. Twenty years later, he tells
us, the Dorians and the Heraclidæ became masters of the
Peloponnese ; but as he does not fix this last date, probably
because he could not, so neither does he fix that of the fall of
Troy.

The date commonly accepted for the return of the Heraclidæ
and their conquest of the Peloponnese is 1104,* but those who
turn to Müller's *History of the Doric Race*,† Vol. I., p. 53,
will see that there is no authority for this date which is worth
a moment's consideration ; and with the failure of authority

---

* See Prof. Jebb's *Introduction to Homer*, ed. 1888, Note 1 on p. 43.
† Murray, 1830.

here, we are left absolutely without authority for 1184 B.C. as the date of the fall of Troy.

Admitting for the moment 1150 B.C. as the latest date to which we should assign the " Iliad," the question arises : How much later than the fall of Troy did Homer write ? Mr. Gladstone has argued very ably in support of the view that he wrote only some forty or fifty years after the events he is recording, in which case it would seem that he must date the " Iliad " hardly at all later than the latest date to which I would assign it, for he does not appear to dispute the received date for the fall of Troy, though he does not say that he accepts it. I should only be too glad to find that I can claim Mr. Gladstone's support so far, but farther I cannot expect to do so ; for the impression left upon me by the " Iliad " is that Homer was writing of a time that was to him much what the middle ages are to ourselves.

If he had lived as near the Trojan War as Mr. Gladstone supposes, he would surely have given us some hint of the manner in which Troy fell, whereas he shows no signs of knowing more than the bare fact that the city had fallen. He repeatedly tells us this much, but always more curtly and drily than we should expect him to do, and his absolute silence as to the way in which the capture of the city was effected, goes far to prove either that all record of the *modus in quo* had perished—which would point to a very considerable lapse of time—or else to suggest a fact which, though I have often thought it possible, I hardly dare to write—I mean that Troy never fell at all, or at any rate that it did not fall with the close of the Trojan War, and that Homer knew this perfectly well.

The infinite subtlety of the " Iliad " is almost as unfathomable as the simplicity of the " Odyssey " has so far proved itself to be, and its author, writing for a Greek audience whom he obviously despised, and whom he was fooling to the top of their bent though always sailing far enough off the wind to avoid disaster, would take very good care to tell them that—if I may be allowed the anachronism—Napoleon won the battle of Waterloo, though he very well knew that it was won by Wellington. It is certain that no even tolerably plausible account of the fall

WALL AT HISSARLIK,
SHOWING CONTRAST BETWEEN WEATHERED AND PROTECTED COURSES

THE ILIADIC WALL

A COIN BEARING ON THE OBVERSE THE LEGEND IAKIN, AND ON
THE REVERSE A REPRESENTATION OF THE BROOCH DESCRIBED BY ULYSSES
Enlarged to about double the actual diameter

of Troy existed among the Greeks themselves ; all plausibility ends with their burning their tents and sailing away baffled (" Od." viii. 500, 501)—see also the epitome of the " Little Iliad," given in the fragment of Proclus. The wild story of the wooden horse only emphasises the fact that nothing more reasonable was known.

But let us suppose that Troy fell, and that Homer's silence was dictated by the loss of all record as to the manner of its falling. In this case one would think that two, or even three, hundred years must have passed between the fall of Troy and the writing of the " Iliad." Let us make it the same distance of time as that between the Parliamentary Wars and the present day. This would throw back the Trojan War to about 1400 B.C., and if we accept Homer's statement that the wall of Troy (*i.e.* that which Dr. Dörpfeld excavated in 1893—for that this is the Iliadic wall may be taken as certain) was built in the time of Priam's father Laomedon, we should date the wall roughly as 1450 B.C. I may add, that it seems to me to be of somewhat earlier date than the co-called Treasury of Atreus at Mycene, and hence still earlier than that which bears the name of Clytemnestra.

I see by the latest work on the subject* that Dr. Dörpfeld dates it as between 1500 and 1000 B.C. I know how perilous it is to date a wall by the analogy of other walls in distant countries, which walls are themselves undateable with anything like precision, but having seen the Iliadic wall as also those of Tiryns and Mycene, as well as most of the so-called Pelasgic walls that remain in the Latin and Volscian cities, I should say that the wall of Troy was much later than those of the megalithic ages, but still not by any means free from the traditions of megalithic builders. I should date it roughly at not later than 1300 B.C. and hardly earlier than 1500 B.C.†

---

* *The Mycenæan Age*, by Dr. Chrestos Tsountas and Dr. J. Irving Manatt, Macmillan, 1897, p. 369.

† The dark line across my illustration is only due to an accident that happened to my negative. I believe (but am not quite sure, for my note about it was not written on the spot) that the bit of wall given in my other illustration has nothing to do with the Iliadic wall, and is of greatly later date. I give it to show how much imagination is necessary in judging of any wall that has been much weathered.

I will, however, date the Iliadic wall as 1400 B.C. The Trojan war will then be supposed to have taken place from 1360–1350 B.C. ; the writing of the " Iliad " will be about 1150 ; and that of the " Odyssey " about 1050 B.C. This is a tight fit, and I should be glad to throw the Iliadic wall back to the earlier of the two dates between which Dr. Dörpfeld has placed it, but precision is out of the question; 1400 B.C. will be as near the truth as anything that we are likely to get, and will bring the archæological evidence as derivable from the wall of Troy, the internal evidence of the " Iliad " and " Odyssey," the statement of Thucydides that the last and greatest inroad of the Sicels occurred about 1030 B.C., and our conclusion that the " Odyssey " was written before that date, into line with one another.

The date 1050 B.C. will explain the absence of all allusion in the " Odyssey " to Utica, the land near which, on certain rare days, can be seen from Mt. Eryx. The Phœnicians are known in the " Odyssey," disliked and distrusted, but they do not seem to be feared as they would surely be if so powerful a maritime nation were already established so near the writer's own abode. She does not seem to know much about the Phœnicians after all, for in iv. 83 she makes Menelaus say that he had gone to Cyprus, Phœnicia, and the Egyptians, and in the next line she adds that he had also been to the Ethiopians and the Sidonians, as though she was not aware that Sidon was a Phœnician city.

The absence of all allusion to Olympia when Telemachus was on his return from Pylos is most naturally explained by supposing that Olympia was not yet famous. The principal hero at Athens appears to be the earliest known object of the national cult, I mean Erechtheus (vii. 81) ; the later, though still very early, cult of Theseus is not alluded to. There is no allusion, however vague, to any event known as having happened in Greek history later than 1100 B.C., and though the absence of reference to any particular event may be explained by indifference or forgetfulness, the absence of all reference to any event whatever suggests, I should say strongly, that none of the events to one or other of which reference might be expected had as yet happened.

While, however, placing 1050 B.C. as the latest limit for the
" Odyssey " I do not see how we can place it earlier than 1150
without throwing the date of the Iliadic wall farther back
than we can venture to do, for we can hardly date it earlier
than 1500 B.C., and 350 years is as short an interval as we can
well allow between the building of that wall and the writing
of the " Odyssey."

Let us now compare the history of the N.W. corner of Sicily
as revealed to us in the " Odyssey "—always assuming that
the pedigree of Alcinous and Arēte in Book vii. is in its main
facts historic—with the account given by Thucydides concerning
the earliest history of the same district.

In the " Odyssey " we have seen the Sicans (whom I think
that I have sufficiently identified) as originally in possession of
Mt. Eryx under a king whose Odyssean name is Eurymedon.
He, it seems, was overthrown, and the power of his people was
broken, by enemies whose name is not given, about a hundred
years before the writing of the " Odyssey," as nearly as we can
gather from the fact of his having been Nausicaa's great great
grandfather.

The writer of the " Odyssey " wrote in a language mainly
Ionian, but containing a considerable Æolian element. It must
be inferred, therefore, that her family and audience—that is to
say the Phæacians—spoke a dialect in which these characteristics are to be found. The place of all others where such a
dialect might be looked for is Phocæa, a little South of the Troad ;
for Phocæa was an Ionian city entirely surrounded on its land
sides by Æolian territory. I see from Professor Jebb's *Introduction to Homer** that Aristarchus when editing the " Iliad "
and " Odyssey," and settling the text to all intents and purposes
as we now have it, by comparison of the best copies known,
made most frequent use of the civic edition of Marseilles which
contained both " Iliad " and " Odyssey." It will be remembered that Marseilles was a Phocæan colony.

---

* Ed. 1888, note on p. 91.

The name Phæacians is not unsuggestive of a thin disguise for Phocæans ; lines iv. 441–443, moreover, will gain greatly in point, if we imagine that the seals, or Phocæ, with their disgusting smell, are meant for the writer's countrymen whom she evidently dislikes, and that the words, " who, indeed, would go to bed with a sea monster if he could help it ? " are her rejoinder to the alleged complaint of the young Phæacians that she would marry none of them (vi. 276 &c.). Apart, therefore, from any external evidence, I should suspect the Phæacians to have been Phocæans, who had settled on this part of the island.* From the fact that the Phæacians in the time of the " Odyssey " were evidently dominant on Mt. Eryx as well as at Trapani, I conclude that they must have had, to say the least of it, a considerable share in the overthrow of Eurymedon and of the Sican power in that part of the island. If they had allies with them, these allies seem to have gone on to other sites on which Elymite cities are known to have existed, for we find no reference in the " Odyssey " to any other people as sharing Hypereia and Scheria with the Phæacians.

Though the power of the Sicans at Eryx was broken, and the Phæacians were established at Hypereia, also on the top of Mt. Eryx and less than a mile from the Sican city, the Sicans were still troublesome neighbours ; there seems, however, to have been a marriage between some chief man among the Phæacians and Periboea, youngest daughter of the old king Eurymedon, and this no doubt would lead to some approach to fusion between the two peoples. The offspring of this marriage, Nausithous, is said in the poem to have been by Neptune, from which I infer that the marriage may have been of a more or less irregular kind, but there can be no doubt that Nausithous came of a Phæacian father and would speak the Phæacian dialect, which the Sicans, though in all probability a Greek-

---

* Herodotus tells us (I. 163) that the Phocæans were the first people to undertake long voyages, exploring the Tuscan sea, and going as far as Cadiz. He says that their ships were not the round ones commonly used for commerce, but long vessels with fifty oarsmen. The reader will recollect that this feature of Phocæan navigation is found also among the Phæacians, who sent Ulysses to the place that we are to take as Ithaca, in a vessel that had fifty oarsmen.

speaking race, cannot be supposed to have done. Nausithous seems to have been a capable man ; finding the continued raids of semi-outlawed Sicans still harassing, perhaps, also, induced by the fact that the promontory on which Trapani stands was better suited to a race of mariners than the lofty and inhospitable top of Mt. Eryx, he moved his people down to the seaside and founded the city that now bears the name of Trapani—retaining, however, the site of Hypereia as his own property on which his pigs and goats would feed, and to which also his family would resort, as the people of Trapani still do, during the excessive heat of summer.

The reader will have noted that Eumæus, who we must never forget is drawn not from Ithaca but from Mt. Eryx, when watching over his pigs by night thought it necessary to be fully armed (xiv. 526). He seems also from xvi. 9, to have had neighbours, from which we may infer that the old Sican city of Eryx was not yet entirely abandoned ; nevertheless, Eumæus would not be there at all unless the fusion between the Sicans and the Phocæans had been fairly complete. The Sicans appear in the " Odyssey " under the names of Cyclopes and Læstrygonians, and the Sicels are not yet come. This is all that we can collect from the " Odyssey."

We will now see what support the sketch given above will derive from Thucydides (vi. 2). According to him the Læstrygonians and the Cyclopes, mentioned as the earliest inhabitants of Sicily, are mere poetical fictions. This, however, does not preclude their having had their prototype in some real Sicilian people who bore another name ; and at any rate, however fictitious they may be, he locates them in Sicily.

He continues that the oldest historic inhabitants of the island were the Sicans, who by their own account had been there from time immemorial. This he denies, for he says they were Iberians, and he says it as though he had satisfied himself after due inquiry, but since he gives no hint as to the date of their arrival, he does not impugn their statement that their settlement in the island dated from a remote time. It is most likely that he is right about the Sicans having come from Spain ; and indeed at Tarragona, some fifty or sixty miles

North of the mouth of the river Iberus, there are megalithic walls that bear, so far as I can judge from photographs, a very considerable analogy with those of Eryx. In Thucydides' own times there were still Sicans in the Western part of Sicily.

He then goes on to say that after the fall of Troy, but he does not say how much after, some of the Trojans who had escaped the Greeks migrated to Sicily. They settled in the neighbourhood of the Sicans and were all together called Elymi, their cities being Eryx and Segesta. There were also settled with them—but whether at the same date, or earlier or later, and if so, how much, Thucydides does not say—certain Phocians of the Trojan branch, *i.e.*, Phocæans—Phocæa having been founded by Phocians from the gulf of Corinth under the leadership of the Athenian chiefs Philogenes and Damon (*Strab.* xiv. 633; *Pausan.* vii. 3, 10; cf. *Herod.* I. 146). These Phocæans had been carried first by a tempest to Libya,* and thence to Sicily.

We need not follow him to the arrival of the Sicels, for I have already, I hope, satisfied the reader that the " Odyssey " belongs to a pre-Sicelian age, and I am only dealing with the period which the " Odyssey " and Thucydides cover in common.

I should perhaps put it beyond doubt that Thucydides means Phocæans and not Phocians. In the first place it is difficult to understand how Phocians, who were on the Achæan side (" Il." II. 518), should amalgamate with Trojans; and in the next Thucydides' words cannot be made to bear the meaning that is generally put upon them, as though the Phocians in question were on their way back from Troy to Phocis. His words are Φωκέων τινὲς τῶν ἀπὸ Τροίας, and this cannot be construed as though he had said Φωκέων τινὲς τῶν ἀνερχομένων ἐν νόστῳ ἀπὸ Τροίας. If ἀπό is to imply motion from, it should have a verb or participle involving motion before it; without this it is a common way of expressing residence in a place. For example, Ὀρέστης ἤλυθεν...ἀπ' Ἀθηνάων (iii. 307) means Orestes

---

* One cannot help wondering whether the episode of the Lotus-eaters may not be due to the existence of tradition among the Phæacians that their ancestors had made some stay in Libya before reaching Sicily.

came from Athens, whereas 'Ορέστης ὁ ἀπ' 'Αθηνάων would mean
" Orestes the Athenian, or quasi-Athenian," as Λακεδαιμόνιοι
οἱ ἀπὸ Σπάρτης means " the Lacedæmonians who live at Sparta,"
Neither of these last two passages can be made to bear the
meaning " Orestes, who was on his way from Athens," or " the
Lacedæmonians, who were on their way from Sparta." The
reader who looks out ἀπὸ in Liddell & Scott will find plenty of
examples. To Thucydides, Phocæans in Asia Minor and
Phocians on the gulf of Corinth would be alike Phocians in
virtue of common descent, but to avoid misapprehension he
calls the Phocæans " Phocians of the Trojan stock," by " Trojan"
meaning not very far from Troy. It should be noted that the
Phocians of the gulf of Corinth are called Φωκῆες, not Φωκέες
in " Il." II. 517, XV. 516, XVII. 307. I see that Dobree (*Adver-
saria in Thucyd.*) is suspicious of the reading Φωκέων in the
passage of Thucydides which we are now considering. He
evidently considers that Φωκέων must mean Phocians from the
gulf of Corinth, and so it would, if it were not qualified by
the words τῶν ἀπὸ Τροίας which negative the possibility of
European Phocians being intended.

Thucydides says nothing about any invasion of Sicily by a
people called Elymi. He does not see the Elymi as anything
more than the combined Asiatic and Sican peoples, who came
to be called Elymi. If he had believed in the Elymi as a
distinct batch of immigrants he would have given us a line or
two more about them.

It is just possible that the known connection between
Phocians and Phocæans may explain why Ulysses' maternal
grandfather should have been made to live on Mt. Parnassus,*
which is in Phocis. Ulysses, to the writer of the " Odyssey,"
was a naturalised Phæacian, for her native town had become
in her eyes both Scheria and Ithaca. It would not be un-
natural, therefore, that she should wish to connect his ancestry
with Phocis, the ancestral seat of the Phocæans.

Returning to Thucydides, the only point in which he varies
the Odyssean version is that he makes other Trojans migrate

---

* " Od." xix. 410, 432.

to Eryx as well as the Phocæans, whereas the writer of the "Odyssey" mentions only the Phæacians without saying anything about their having been of Phocæan descent. She has, however, betrayed herself very sufficiently. Thucydides again does not tell us that the Phocæans re-settled themselves at Drepanum, but a man who is giving a mere outline of events which happened some seven hundred years before he was writing, can hardly be expected to give so small a detail as this. The wonder is that the "Odyssey" should bear him out and confirm his accuracy in so striking a way as it does. We now, therefore, see that instead of there being any cause for surprise at finding an Ionic-Æolian poem written near Mt. Eryx, this is the very neighbourhood in which we might expect to find one.

Finally, let us turn to Virgil. His authority as a historian is worthless, but we cannot suppose that he would make Æneas apparently found Drepanum, if he held the presence of a Greek-speaking people at Drepanùm even before the age of Homer to be so absurd as it appears to our eminent Homeric scholars. I say "apparently found Drepanum," for it is not quite easy to fix the site of the city founded by Æneas (*Æn.* v. 755–761), for at the close of *Æn.* III. Anchises dies at Drepanum, as though this city was already in existence. But whether the city founded by Æneas was actually Drepanum, or another city hard by it, it is clear that Virgil places Greek-speaking people at Drepanum, or close to it, immediately after the fall of Troy. He would hardly do this unless Drepanum was believed in his time to be a city of very great antiquity, and founded by Greek-speaking people. That the Trojan language was Greek will not be disputed.

Chapter XIII

FURTHER EVIDENCE IN SUPPORT OF AN EARLY IONIAN SETTLE-
MENT AT OR CLOSE TO TRAPANI.

I AM often asked how I explain the fact that we find no trace
in ancient authors of any tradition to the effect that the
" Odyssey " was written at Drepanum or that the writer was a
woman. This difficulty is laid before me as one that is almost
fatal. I confess, however, that I find it small in comparison
with that of explaining how both these facts should have failed
of being long since rediscovered. Neptune indeed did not
overwhelm Scheria under Mt. Eryx, but he, or some not less
spiteful god, seems to have buried both it and its great poetess
under another mountain which I fear may be found even more
irremovable—I mean a huge quasi-geological formation of
academic erudition.

The objection is without sufficient foundation in its implied
facts ; for that the Phæacians were a real people who lived at
a place bearing the name of Drepane (which is near enough to
Drepanum for all practical purposes),* has never been lost
sight of at all—except by those who find it convenient to lose
sight of it. Thucydides (i. 25) tells us that the inhabitants of
Corfu were the descendants of the Phæacians, and the rock
into which their ship was turned as it was entering the harbour
after having escorted Ulysses to Ithaca is still shown at Corfu
—as an island 58 feet high with a monastery on the top of it.
But the older name of Corfu was Drepane,† and when the
Carthaginians had established themselves at the Sicilian
Drepanum, it would be an easy matter for the inhabitants of
the Corfu Drepane to claim Phæacian descent, and—as they

---

* Drepanum means a curved sword or scimitar. Drepane is a
sickle.

† See Smith's *Dictionary of Classical Geography*, under
Corcyra, where full references will be found.

proceeded to do—to call their island Scheria, in spite of its offering no single point of correspondence with the description given in the " Odyssey."

I grant that no explicit tradition exists to the effect that the " Odyssey " as a whole was written at or in Corfu, but the Phæacian episode is the eye of the poem. I submit, then, that tradition both long has, and still does, by implication connect it with a place of which the earliest known name was to all intents and purposes the same as that of the town where I contend that it was written.

The Athenian writers, Thucydides included, would be biassed in favour of any site which brought Homer, as they ignorantly called the writer of the " Odyssey," nearer their own doors. The people, moreover, of Eryx and Segesta, and hence also of Drepanum, were held to be barbarians, and are so called by Thucydides himself (vi. 2) ; in his eyes it would be little less than sacrilege to hesitate between the Corfu Drepane and the Sicilian Drepanum, did any tradition, however vague, support Corfu. But it is not likely that Thucydides was unaware of the Sicilian claim not only to the Phæacian episode, but to the entire poem, for as late as 430 B.C., only a little before the date of his own work, there were still people on or near Mt. Eryx who present every appearance of having claimed it, as I will almost immediately show.

As for losing sight of its having been written by a woman, the people who could lose sight of the impossibility of its having been written by Homer could lose sight of anything. A people who could not only do this, but who could effectually snuff out those who pointed out their error, were nót likely to know more about the difference underlying the two poems than the average English layman does about those between the synoptic gospels and that of St. John.

I will now return to my assertion that in the time of Thucydides there seem to have been not a few who knew of, and shared in, the claim of Drepanum to the authorship of the " Odyssey."

The British Museum possesses a unique example of a small bronze coin which is classed with full confidence among those of Eryx and Segesta. It is of the very finest period of the numismatic art, and is dated by the museum authorities as about 430 B.C.

The reader will see that the obverse bears the legend IAKIN, and the reverse a representation of the brooch described by Ulysses (" Od." xix. 225–231). A translation of this passage is given on page 80.

The cross line of the A is not visible in the original, but no doubt is felt at the Museum about its having existed.

There seems, however, to be more doubt whether the legend should be IAKIN, or ΓIAKIN—Γ being the older form of Π. Possibly from a desire to be right in either case, the Museum catalogue gives it as IAKIN in the illustration, and ΓIAKIN in the descriptive letterpress. The one reading will do nearly as well as the other for my argument, which only requires that the coin should belong to the Eryx and Segesta group and be dated about 430 B.C.—neither of which points are doubted. I will, however, give the reasons that convince me that IAKIN is the true reading.

Firstly, neither I nor some artist friends of mine whose opinion is infinitely better worth having than my own, can find any trace of a Γ between the lowermost boss and the neck. I am aware that some experts of the highest competence profess to be able to detect such traces, but the artist who figured the coin in the Museum Catalogue evidently could not do so, and the experts do not seem to have had such confidence in their own opinion as to make him alter his drawing.

Secondly, the composition is obviously and intentionally symmetrical. It would be abhorrent to the instincts of the man who could design so exquisite a coin to destroy its balance by crowding a Γ into the place which must be assigned to it if it exists at all.

Thirdly, Piacus, to which town the coin had been ascribed by the dealer from whom the Museum bought it, is mentioned very briefly by Stephanus Byzantinus, but by no other writer, as a Sicilian city, and he expressly states that its citizens were called ΠΙΑΚΗΝΟΙ ; so that the coin, if it was one of theirs, should bear the legend ΓIAKHN instead of the alleged ΓIAKIN.

Stephanus Byzantinus did not write till about 500 A.D., and in the absence of any statement from him to the effect that Piacus was an old city, it argues some recklessness to conclude that it had existed for at least a thousand years when he mentioned it ; there is no evidence from any quarter to support such a conclusion, and a safer one will be that the dealer above referred to, not knowing where the coin came from, and looking for a city in Stephanus Byzantinus, found he could get nothing nearer than Piacus—whereon he saw a Γ as the smallest thing he could do in Π's, into his coin, and sold it to the British Museum probably for a song as compared with the value which it now proves to have. Thus the Museum authorities having got it into part of their notes (for they seem to have got IAKIN into another part) that the legend was ΓIAKIN, have very naturally been led to see more on the coin than those who have no notes will quite bear them out in seeing. But I will add no more. The legend is obviously IAKIN.

This is an abbreviation for IAKINΩN, as ΕΡΥΚΙΝ and ΚΕΝΤΟΡΙΠΙΝ are for ΕΡΥΚΙΝΩN and ΚΕΝΤΟΡΙΠΙΝΩN, not to quote further examples. It means that the people who struck it were called IAKINEΣ, and though we cannot determine the precise name of their city we may infer with confidence that it was some derivative of IAKOΣ, which is given in Liddell & Scott as meaning Ionian. The name may very likely have been IAΞ though I cannot find any authority for the existence of such a town.

I hold, therefore, that as late as B.C. 430 there was near Trapani a town still more or less autonomous, which claimed Ionian descent and which also claimed to be in some special way connected with the " Odyssey " ; for I am assured that nothing would be allowed on a coin except what had an important bearing on the anterior history of those who struck it. Admitting that the reverse of the coin in question must be taken as a reproduction of Ulysses' brooch—and I found no difference of opinion among the numismatists at the Museum on this head—it is hard to see what more apposite means of saying " Odyssey " upon a coin can be suggested than to stamp it with the subject which invites numismatic treatment more than any other in the whole poem. It seems to me, then, that though the theory that there was an Ionian city in the neighbourhood of Eryx which could claim connection with the " Odyssey " will stand perfectly well without the coin, the coin cannot stand without involving the existence of an Ionian city near Eryx which claimed connection with the " Odyssey." Happily, though the coin is unique, there is no question as to its genuineness.

To those, therefore, who ask me for monuments, ruins of buildings, historical documents to support a Sicano-Ionian civilisation near Eryx in times heretofore prehistoric, I reply that as late as 430 B.C. all these things appear to have existed. Letting alone the testimony of Thucydides, surely an Ionian coin is no small historical document in support of an Ionian city. A coin will say more in fewer words and more authoritatively than anything else will. The coin in question cannot belong to an Ionian colony on Mt. Eryx or thereabouts recently established in 430 B.C. We should have heard of such a colony ; how inconceivable again is the bringing in of the " Odyssey " on this supposition. If the city existed at all it can only have done so as a survival of the Phocæan settlement of which Thucydides tells us.

I want no evidence for the survival of such a settlement in later times ; it is not incumbent upon me to show whether it survived or no ; the abundant, I might almost say superabundant, coincidences between all both Scherian and Ithacan scenes in the " Odyssey," and Trapani with its immediate neighbourhood, is enough to demonstrate the Trapanese origin of the poem. Its pre-Syracusan and pre-Sicelian indications fix it as not later than about 1050 B.C., its dialect, Ionic-Æolian, connects it with the Phocæans above referred to. It does not concern me to show what became of these Phocæans after the " Odyssey " had been written ; what I have said about the coin IAKIN is said more in the interests of the coin than of the " Odyssey," which is a more potent and irrefragable proof of its own *provenance* and date than any coin struck some 600 years later can conceivably be. Still, the coin being there, I use it to answer those who demand some evidence external to the

" Odyssey " itself. When they ask me where are my monuments, I answer that they are within the coin, circumscribed by the small cincture of an inch and a half at most. For a coin is a city in little ; he who looks on one beholds a people, an evidence of title, a whole civilisation with its buildings of every kind. Destroy these, but so long as a single one of its coins remains, the city though dead is yet alive, and the fact of its having had buildings that could become ruinous is as palpable as though the ruins themselves had come down to us.

The exact situation of this city Iax, Iacus, or Iace, cannot be determined, but I incline to place it about a mile or a mile and a half East of Trapani at or near a place called Argenteria. This place is said to have yielded silver, but no one believes that it ever did so. It is a quarry and by no means a large one, just at the beginning of the rise to Mt. Eryx. Some say that Argenteria is a corruption of Cetaria and refers to a monster fish that was killed here, though how it got so far from the sea is not apparent ; I think it much more likely, however, that it is a corruption of Iacinteria and that Iax, or Iace, was a quasi-autonomous suburb of Drepanum to which the Greek inhabitants were permitted to retire when the Carthaginians took possession of the parts of the town bordering on the harbour.

My friend Signor Sugameli of Trapani, whose zeal in this matter so far outstrips even my own, that I would gladly moderate it if I knew how to do so, assures me that in his younger days he used to employ a stone in building that the mason told him came from a quarry at the foot of Mt. Eryx called Dacinoi or D'Acinoi. This was years before any one thought of bringing Ionians to Trapani. Signor Sugameli suggested that possibly the name might be a corruption of D'Alcinoo—but we may be sure that whatever else Alcinous's name may have been it was not Alcinous. I asked Signor Sugameli to produce the mason, but he could neither find him nor hear of the quarry Dacinoi. Nevertheless I feel sure that he was told what he said he was, and as the quarry cannot have been far from the Argenteria, I think it probable that its name was a corruption of *degli Iacinoi*.

Whether this is sound or not, I do not doubt that the Iacenses who figure so largely in Sicilian history during the Eleventh Century of our own era are to be connected with the Ionian settlement that produced the " Odyssey." The Iacenses were then settled chiefly about forty miles East of Trapani, but the interval of some 1400 years and more between the date of the coin Iakin and the conquest of Sicily by the Normans will leave plenty of time for them to have spread or migrated.

Chapter XIV

It remains for me to show that the writer of the " Odyssey "
had the " Iliad " before her to all intents and purposes as we
now have it, and to deal with the manner in which the poem
grew under her hands.

In my own copies of the " Iliad " and " Odyssey " I have
underlined all the passages that are common to both poems,
giving the references. It is greatly to be wished that one or
other of our University presses would furnish us with an
" Odyssey " in which all the Iliadic passages are printed in a
slightly different type and with a reference, somewhat in the style
of the extracts from " Il." I. and XXIV. here given. The passages
are to be found at the end of Dunbar's *Concordance to the
Odyssey,* but the marking of them as they occur in the course
of the poem will be more instructive. In my translations of the
poems (now finished) I have translated identical passages as
nearly as possible in identical words. In the " Odyssey " I
propose to print them in another type and give the references to
the " Iliad." In the translation of the " Iliad " there is no use
in doing this, for no one supposes that Homer took anything
from the " Odyssey." The publication, however, of these
translations must, I fear, be postponed, but I will give in this
Chapter as many instances as I think will be sufficient to satisfy
the reader that the " Iliad " of the writer of the " Odyssey " was
our own " Iliad."

I will begin by giving two passages from the " Iliad," one
from Book I., and the other from Book XXIV., the references
in all cases being to the " Odyssey." These are perhaps fuller of
lines adopted by the writer of the " Odyssey " than any others
in the " Iliad," though there are some that run them closely.
Lines or parts of lines in the smaller type do not occur in the
" Odyssey."

The first passage that I will call attention to is " Iliad " I.
455–485, which is as follows :—

ἠδ' ἔτι καὶ νῦν μοι τόδ' ἐπικρήηνον ἐέλδωρ·   cf. iii. 418
ἤδη νῦν Δαναοῖσιν ἀεικέα λοιγὸν ἄμυνον."

cf. iii. 385   ὣς ἔφατ' εὐχόμενος τοῦ δ' ἔκλυε Φοῖβος Ἀπόλλων.

iii. 447   αὐτὰρ ἐπεί ῥ' εὔξαντο καὶ οὐλοχύτας προβάλοντο,   cf. xii. 359–361
αὐέρυσαν μὲν πρῶτα καὶ ἔσφαξαν καὶ ἔδειραν,
μηρούς τ' ἐξέταμον κατά τε κνίσῃ ἐκάλυψαν
δίπτυχα ποιήσαντες, ἐπ' αὐτῶν δ' ὠμοθέτησαν.
κᾶιε δ' ἐπὶ σχίζῃς ὁ γέρων, ἐπὶ δ' αἴθοπα οἶνον

cf. iii. 456–462   λεῖβε· νέοι δὲ παρ' αὐτὸν ἔχον πεμπώβολα χερσίν.

αὐτὰρ ἐπεὶ κατὰ μῆρα κάη καὶ σπλάγχνα πάσαντο,   cf. xii. 364, 365

xiv. 430, 431 cf. also xix. 423   μίστυλλόν τ' ἄρα τἆλλα καὶ ἀμφ' ὀβελοῖσιν ἔπειραν,
ὤπτησάν τε περιφραδέως, ἐρύσαντό τε πάντα.

αὐτὰρ ἐπεὶ παύσαντο πόνου τετύκοντό τε δαῖτα,   cf. xvi. 478–480

xix. 425 i. 150 & elsewhere   δαίνυντ', οὐδέ τι θυμὸς ἐδεύετο δαιτὸς ἐΐσης.
αὐτὰρ ἐπεὶ πόσιος καὶ ἐδητύος ἐξ ἔρον ἕντο,

i. 148 iii. 339, 340   κοῦροι μὲν κρητῆρας ἐπεστέψαντο ποτοῖο,   xxi. 271, 272
νώμησαν δ' ἄρα πᾶσιν ἐπαρξάμενοι δεπάεσσιν   vii. 183
οἱ δὲ πανημέριοι μολπῇ θεὸν ἱλάσκοντο,
καλὸν ἀείδοντες παιήονα, κοῦροι Ἀχαιῶν,
μέλποντες ἑκάεργον· ὁ δὲ φρένα τέρπετ' ἀκούων.

cf. xix. 426–428   ἦμος δ' ἠέλιος κατέδυ καὶ ἐπὶ κνέφας ἦλθεν,   cf. iii. 329
δὴ τότε κοιμήσαντο παρὰ πρυμνήσια νηός.   cf. xii. 31, 32
ἦμος δ' ἠριγένεια φάνη ῥοδοδάκτυλος Ἠώς,............   20 times in Od. only twice in Il.
καὶ τότ' ἔπειτ' ἀνάγοντο μετὰ στρατὸν εὐρὺν Ἀχαιῶν·

cf. ii. 420 xv. 292   τοῖσιν δ' ἴκμενον οὖρον ἵει ἑκάεργος Ἀπόλλων.
οἱ δ' ἱστὸν στήσαντ' ἀνά θ' ἱστία λευκὰ πέτασσαν·   iv. 783

ii. 427–429   ἐν δ' ἄνεμος πρῆσεν μέσον ἱστίον, ἀμφὶ δὲ κῦμα
στείρῃ πορφύρεον μεγάλ' ἴαχε νηὸς ἰούσης·
ἡ δ' ἔθεεν κατὰ κῦμα διαπρήσσουσα κέλευθον.
αὐτὰρ ἐπεί ῥ' ἵκοντο κατὰ στρατὸν εὐρὺν Ἀχαιῶν,

xvi. 325   νῆα μὲν οἵ γε μέλαιναν ἐπ' ἠπείροιο ἔρυσσαν

I should perhaps tell the reader that the first Book of the
" Iliad " is one of the few which modern criticism allows to
remain in the possession of the poet who wrote what Professor
Jebb calls the " primary " " Iliad."

The second of the two passages above referred to is " Iliad "
XXIV. 621–651, which runs :—

ἢ καὶ ἀναΐξας ὄιν ἄργυφον ὠκὺς Ἀχιλλεὺς
σφάξ᾽· ἕταροι δ᾽ ἔδερόν τε καὶ ἄμφεπον εὖ κατὰ κόσμον,

cf. xiv. 430– {μίστυλλόν τ᾽ ἄρ᾽ ἐπισταμένως πεῖράν τ᾽ ὀβελοῖσιν,
431 & xix.
422, 423 {ὤπτησάν τε περιφραδέως ἐρύσαντό τε πάντα.

Αὐτομέδων δ᾽ ἄρα σῖτον ἑλὼν ἐπένειμε τραπέζῃ
καλοῖς ἐν κανέοισιν· ἀτὰρ κρέα νεῖμεν Ἀχιλλεύς.

i. 149, 150 & {οἱ δ᾽ ἐπ᾽ ὀνείαθ᾽ ἑτοῖμα προκείμενα χεῖρας ἴαλλον.
many other
places {αὐτὰρ ἐπεὶ πόσιος καὶ ἐδητύος ἐξ ἔρον ἕντο,

ἢ τοι Δαρδανίδης Πρίαμος θαύμαζ᾽ Ἀχιλῆα,
ὅσσος ἔην οἷός τε· θεοῖσι γὰρ ἄντα ἐῴκει·
αὐτὰρ ὁ Δαρδανίδην Πρίαμον θαύμαζεν Ἀχιλλεύς,
εἰσορόων ὄψιν τ᾽ ἀγαθὴν καὶ μῦθον ἀκούων.

αὐτὰρ ἐπεὶ τάρπησαν ἐς ἀλλήλους ὁρόωντες,   *cf.* iv. 47 &
                                                                         x 181
τὸν πρότερος προσέειπε γέρων Πρίαμος θεοειδής,
,,λέξον νῦν με τάχιστα, διοτρεφές, ὄφρα καὶ ἤδη
ὕπνῳ ὕπο γλυκερῷ ταρπώμεθα κοιμηθέντε·   *cf.* iv. 294, 295
                                                                         & xxiii. 254, 255
οὐ γάρ πω μύσαν ὄσσε ὑπὸ βλεφάροισιν ἐμοῖσιν,
ἐξ οὗ σῆς ὑπὸ χερσὶν ἐμὸς πάις ὤλεσε θυμόν,
ἀλλ᾽ αἰεὶ στενάχω καὶ κήδεα μυρία πέσσω,
αὐλῆς ἐν χόρτοισι κυλινδόμενος κατὰ κόπρον.
νῦν δὴ καὶ σίτου πασάμην καὶ αἴθοπα οἶνον
λαυκανίης καθέηκα· πάρος γε μὲν οὔ τι πεπάσμην.''

ἢ ῥ᾽, Ἀχιλεὺς δ᾽ ἑτάροισιν ἰδὲ δμωῇσι κέλευσεν   ⎫   iv. 296–300
δέμνι᾽ ὑπ᾽ αἰθούσῃ θέμεναι καὶ ῥήγεα καλὰ   ⎪
πορφύρε᾽ ἐμβαλέειν, στορέσαι τ᾽ ἐφύπερθε τάπητας,   ⎬
cf. vii. 336– χλαίνας τ᾽ ἐνθέμεναι οὔλας καθύπερθεν ἔσασθαι.   ⎪
340   αἱ δ᾽ ἴσαν ἐκ μεγάροιο δάος μετὰ χερσὶν ἔχουσαι,   ⎪
                αἶψα δ᾽ ἄρα στόρεσαν δοιὼ λέχε᾽ ἐγκονέουσαι.   ⎭

cf. xxii. 194 τὸν δ᾽ ἐπικερτομέων προσέφη πόδας ὠκὺς Ἀχιλλεύς·
,,ἐκτὸς μὲν δὴ λέξο, γέρον φίλε, μή τις Ἀχαιῶν
ἐνθάδ᾽ ἐπέλθῃσιν βουληφόρος, οἵ τέ μοι αἰεὶ
....

Professor Jebb is disposed to attribute " Il." XXIV. to the
writer of " Il." IX., which he does not ascribe to Homer. I regret
that I can go no further with him than that " Il." XXIV. and
" Il." IX. are by the same hand.

It is beyond my scope to point out the slight and perfectly unimportant variations from the " Iliad " which are found in some of the Odyssean lines to which I have given a reference ; they are with hardly an exception such as are occasioned by difference of context. Though unimportant they are not uninteresting, but I must leave them for the reader to examine if he feels inclined to do so.

He will observe that some lines are nearly and some quite common to the two extracts above given, and I should add that not a few other lines are repeated elsewhere in the " Iliad," but enough remains that is peculiar to either of the two extracts to convince me that the writer of the " Odyssey " knew them both. And not only this, but they seem to have risen in her mind as spontaneously, and often no doubt as unconsciously, as passages from the Bible, Prayer-book, and Shakespeare do to ourselves.

If, then, we find the writer so familiar with two such considerable extracts from the first and last Books of the " Iliad " —for I believe the reader will feel no more doubt than I do, that she knew them, and was borrowing from them—can we avoid thinking it probable that she was acquainted, to say the least of it, with the intermediate Books ? Such surely should be the most natural and least strained conclusion to arrive at, but I will proceed to shew that she knew the intermediate Books exceedingly well.

I pass over the way in which Mentor's name is coined from Nestor's (*cf.* " Il." II. 76–77 and " Od." ii. 224, 225, and 228), and will go on to the striking case of Ulysses' servant Eurybates. In " Od." xix. 218, 219 Penelope has asked Ulysses (who is disguised so that she does not recognise him) for details as to the followers Ulysses had with him on his way to Troy, and Ulysses answers that he had a servant named Eurybates who was hunched in the shoulders (xix. 247). Turning to " Il." II. 184 we find that Ulysses had a servant from Ithaca named Eurybates, but he does not seem to have been hunched in the shoulders ; on reading further, however, we immediately come to Thersites, " whose shoulders were hunched over his chest " (" Il." II. 217, 218). Am I too hasty in concluding that the writer of the "Odyssey," wanting an additional detail for Penelope's greater assurance, and not finding one in the "Iliad," took the hunchiness off the back of the next man to him and set it on to the back of Eurybates? I do not say that no other hypothesis can be framed in order to support a different conclusion, but I think the one given above will best commend itself to common sense; and the most natural inference from it is that the writer of the "Odyssey" knew at any rate part of "Il." II. much as we have it now.

I often wondered why Menelaus should have been made to return on the self-same day as that on which Orestes was holding the funeral feast of Ægisthus and Clytemnestra; the Greek which tells us that he did so runs :—

αὐτῆμαρ δέ οἱ ἦλθε βοὴν ἀγαθὸς Μενέλαος ("Od." iii. 311).

I did not find the explanation till I remembered that in "Iliad" II. 408, when Agamemnon has been inviting the Achæan chieftains to a banquet, he did not ask Menelaus, for Menelaus came of his own accord :—

αὐτόματος δέ οἱ ἦλθε βοὴν ἀγαθὸς Μενέλαος,

on remembering this I observed that it would be less trouble to make Menelaus come home on the very day of Ægisthus' funeral feast than to alter αὐτόματος in any other way which would leave the rest of the line available. I should be ashamed of the writer of the "Odyssey" for having done this, unless I believed it to be merely due to unconscious cerebration. That the Odyssean and Iliadic lines are taken the one from the other will approve itself to the instincts of any one who is accustomed to deal with literary questions at all, and it is not conceivable that Menelaus should, in the "Iliad," have been made to come uninvited because in the "Odyssey" he happened to come back on the very day when Orestes was holding Ægisthus' funeral feast; the Iliadic context explains why Menelaus came uninvited—it was because he knew that Agamemnon was too busy to invite him. I infer, therefore, that the writer of the "Odyssey" again shows herself familiar with a part of "Il." II.

I can see no sufficient reason for even questioning that the
catalogues of the Achæan and Trojan forces in the second Book
of the " Iliad " were part of the " Iliad " as it left Homer's
hands. They are wanted so as to explain who the people are of
whom we are to hear in the body of the poem ; their position
is perfectly natural ; the Achæan catalogue is prepared in Nestor's speech (II. 360–368) ; Homer almost tells us that he has had
assistance in compiling it, for he invokes the Muse, as he does
more than once in later Books, and declares that he knows
nothing of his own knowledge, but depends entirely upon what
has been told him*; the lines quoted or alluded to in the
" Odyssey " are far too marked to allow of our doubting that
the writer knew both catalogues familiarly ; I cannot within my
limits give them, but would call the reader's attention to " Il."
II. 488, *cf.* " Od." iv. 240 ; to the considering Sparta and
Lacedæmon as two places (" Il." II. 581, 582) which the writer of
the " Odyssey " does (iv. 10), though she has abundantly shown
that she knew them to be but one ; to " Il." II. 601, *cf.* " Od." iii.
386 ; to the end of line 614, θαλάσσια ἔργα μεμήλει, *cf.* " Od."
v. 67, θαλάσσια ἔργα μέμηλεν ; to 670, *cf.* " Od." ii. 12 ; to 673,
674, *cf.* " Od." xi. 469, 470 ; to " Il." II. 706, αὐτοκασίγνητος
μεγαθύμου Πρωτεσιλάου, which must surely be parent of the
line αὐτοκασιγνήτη ὀλοόφρονος Αἰήταο, " Od." x. 137 ; to " Il."
II. 707, ὁπλότερος γένεῃ· ὁ δ' ἅμα πρότερος καὶ ἀρείων, *cf.*
" Od." xix. 184, where the same line occurs ; to " Il." II. 721,
ἀλλ' ὁ μὲν ἐν νήσῳ κεῖτο κρατέρ' ἄλγεα πάσχων, *cf.* " Od." v.
13, where the same line occurs, but with κεῖται instead of κεῖτο
to suit the context ; *cf.* also " Od." v. 395, where we find πατρός,
ὅς ἐν νούσῳ κεῖται, κρατέρ' ἄλγεα πάσχων, a line which shows
how completely the writer of the " Odyssey " was saturated
with the " Iliad " ; to " Il." II. 755, Στυγὸς ὕδατός ἐστιν
ἀπορρώξ, *cf.* " Od." x. 514, where the same words end the line ;
to " Il." II. 774, δίσκοισιν τέρποντο καὶ αἰγανέῃσιν ἱέντες
cf. " Od." iv. 626, and xvii. 168, where the same line occurs ; to
" Il." II. 776, where the horses of the Myrmidons are spoken of
as λωτὸν ἐρεπτόμενοι, *cf.* " Od." ix. 97, where the same words

---

* ἡμεῖς δὲ κλέος οἶον ἀκούομεν, οὐδέ τι ἴδμεν, " Il." ii. 486.

are used for Ulysses' men when with the Lotus-eaters ; to " Il."
II. 873, νήπιος, οὐδέ τί οἱ τό γ' ἐπήρκεσε λυγρὸν ὄλεθρον, cf.
"Od." iv. 292, ἄλγιον, οὐ γάρ οἵ τι τά γ' ἤρκεσε λυγρὸν ὄλεθρον.

None of the passages above quoted or referred to are to be
found anywhere else in the " Iliad," so that if from the " Iliad "
at all, they are from the catalogues. But having already shown,
as I believe, that the writer of the " Odyssey " knew lines 76, 77,
78, 184, 216, 217, and 408 of Book II., and accepting the rest
of the Book as written by Homer, with or without assistance,
I shall not argue further in support of my contention that the
whole Book II. was known to, and occasionally borrowed from,
by the writer of the " Odyssey."

Perhaps the prettiest example of unconscious cerebration in
the " Odyssey " is to be found in the opening line of " Od." iii.,
which runs ἠέλιος δ' ἀνόρουσε λιπὼν περικαλλέα λίμνην,
which is taken from " Il." v. 20, Ἰδαῖος δ' ἀπόρουσε λιπὼν
περικαλλέα δίφρον. One is at a loss to conceive how a writer so
apparently facile should drift thus on to an Iliadic line of such
different signification except as the result of saturation. It is
inconceivable that she should have cast about for a line to say
that the sun was rising, and thought that Idæus jumping off his
chariot would do. She again has this line in her mind when in
Book xxii. 95 she writes Τηλέμαχος δ' ἀπόρουσε λιπὼν δολιχόσ-
κιον ἔγχος.

The same kind of unconscious cerebration evidenced by the
lines last referred to leads her sometimes to repeat lines of her
own in a strange way, without probably being at all aware of
it. As for example :—

βασιλῆες......εἰσὶ καὶ ἄλλοι
πολλοὶ ἐν ἀμφιάλῳ Ἰθάκῃ νέοι ἠδὲ παλαιοί,

(i. 394, 395).

This passage in the following Book becomes :—

εἰσὶ δὲ νῆες
πολλαὶ ἐν ἀμφιάλῳ Ἰθάκῃ νέαι ἠδὲ παλαιαί·

(ii. 292, 293).

Another similar case is that of the famous line about

Sisyphus' stone bounding down hill in a string of dactyls, " Od." xi. 598, it runs :—

> αὖτις ἔπειτα πέδονδε κυλίνδετο λᾶας ἀναιδής.

" The cruel stone came bounding down again on to the plain." I believe this to be nothing but an unconscious adaptation from the one dactylic line that I can remember in the " Iliad," I mean :—

> ἀμφοτέρω δὲ τένοντε καὶ ὀστέα λᾶας ἀναιδὴς
> ἄχρις ἀπηλοίησεν.
>
> " Il." IV. 521, 522.

" The cruel stone shattered the bones of the ancle, tendons and all." Granted (which is very doubtful) that there may be an accommodation of sound to sense in the Odyssean line, I contend that the suggestion came from the Iliadic line.

I would gladly go through the whole " Iliad " calling attention to the use the writer of the " Odyssey " has made of it, but to do this would require hardly less than a book to itself. I will therefore ask the reader to accept my statement that no one Book in the " Iliad " shows any marked difference from the others as regards the use that has been made of it, and will limit myself to those Books that have been most generally declared to be later additions—I mean Book x. and Book XVIII.—for I consider that I have already sufficiently shown the writer of the " Odyssey " to have known Books I., XXIV., and the Catalogues in Book II. It may be well, however, to include Book XI. in my examination, for this is one of the most undoubted, and it will be interesting to note that the writer of the " Odyssey " has both the most doubted and undoubted Books equally at her fingers' ends. I shall only call attention to passages that do not occur more than once in the " Iliad," and will omit the very numerous ones that may be considered as common form.

In " Il." x. 141, 142 we find :—

> τίφθ' οὕτω ;......
> Νύκτα δι' ἀμβροσίην, and in " Od." ix. 403, 404.
> τίπτε τόσον......
> Νύκτα δι' ἀμβροσίην.

In "Il." x. 142, ὅτι δὴ χρειὼ τόσον ἵκει; cf. "Od." ii. 28, τίνα χρειὼ τόσον ἵκει.

"Il." x. 158 begins with the words λὰξ ποδὶ κίνησας. So also does "Od." xv. 45.

"Il." x. 214 has, ὅσσοι γὰρ νήεσσιν ἐπικρατέουσιν ἄριστοι, this line is found "Od." i. 245, xvi. 122, xix. 130, but with νήσοισιν instead of νήεσσιν.

"Il." x. 220 ends with ὀτρύνει κραδίη καὶ θυμὸς ἀγήνωρ, so also does "Od." xviii. 61.

"Il." x. 221 has ἀνδρῶν δυσμενέων δῦναι στράτον ἐγγὺς ἐόντων; cf. "Od." iv. 246, ἀνδρῶν δυσμενέων κατέδυ πόλιν εὐρυάγυιαν·

"Il." x. 243, 244 have, πῶς ἂν ἔπειτ' Ὀδυσῆος ἐγὼ θείοιο λαθοίμην, οὗ περὶ μὲν.........

In "Od." i. 65, 66 we find the same words only with ὅς instead of οὗ. This is a very convincing case, for the ἔπειτα, which is quite natural in the Iliadic line, is felt to be rather out of place in the Odyssean one, and makes it plain that the Odyssean passage was taken from the Iliadic, not *vice versâ*.

"Il." x. 255 ends with μενοπτόλεμος Θρασυμήδης, so also does "Od." iii. 442.

"Il." x. 278, 279, ...ἥ τέ μοι αἰεὶ
ἐν πάντεσσι πόνοισι παρίστασαι......
cf. "Od." xiii. 300, 301, ...ἥ τέ τοι αἰεὶ
ἐν πάντεσσι πόνοισι παρίσταμαι......

"Il." x. 292–295, σοὶ δ' αὖ ἐγὼ ῥέξω βοῦν ἦνιν εὐρυμέτωπον
ἀδμήτην, ἣν οὔ πω ὑπὸ ζυγὸν ἤγαγεν ἀνήρ.
τήν τοι ἐγὼ ῥέξω χρυσὸν κέρασιν περιχεύας.
ὣς ἔφαν εὐχόμενοι, τῶν δ' ἔκλυε Παλλὰς Ἀθήνη.

The first three of these four lines is repeated verbatim in "Od." iii. 382–384. In "Od." iii. 385 the fourth line becomes
ὣς ἔφατ' εὐχόμενος τοῦ δ' ἔκλυε Παλλὰς Ἀθήνη.ʼ

"Il." x. 351......ὅσσον τ' ἐπὶ οὖρα πέλονται ἡμιόνων, cf. "Od." viii. 124 ὅσσον τ' ἐν νείῳ οὖρον πέλει ἡμιόνοιιν.

"Il." x. 400, τὸν δ' ἐπιμειδήσας προσέφη πολύμητις Ὀδύσσευς this line occurs "Od." xxii. 371.

"Il." x. 429 ends with δῖοί τε Πελασγοί, so also does "Od." xix. 177.

" Il." x. 457, φθεγγομένου δ' ἄρα τοῦ γε κάρη κονίῃσιν ἐμίχθη, this line is found " Od." xxii. 329.

" Il." x. 534, ψεύσομαι ἦ ἔτυμον ἐρέω; κέλεται δέ με θυμός. In " Od." iv. 140 this line is found.

"Il." x. 556, ῥεῖα θεός γ' ἐθέλων καί, κ.τ.λ. Cf. "Od." iii. 231.

" Il." x. 576 ἔς ῥ' ἀσαμίνθους βάντες εὐξέστας λούσαντο. See " Od." iv. 48, xvii. 87.

Here, then, are seventeen apparent quotations from Book x., omitting any claim on lines which, though they are found in the " Odyssey," are also found in other Books of the " Iliad," from which, and not from Book x., it may be alleged that the writer of the " Odyssey " took them. This makes the writer of the " Odyssey " to have taken about one line in every 33 of the 579 lines of which Book x. consists. Disciples of Wolf—no two of whom, however, are of the same opinion, so it is hard to say who they are—must either meet my theory that the " Odyssey " is all written at one place, by one hand, and in the eleventh century B.C., with stronger weapons than during the last six years they have shown any signs of possessing, or they must full back on some Laputan-manner-of-making-books theory, which they will be able to devise better than I can.

I do not forget that the opponents of the genuineness of " Il." x. may contend that the passages above given were taken from the " Odyssey," but this contention should not be urged in respect of Book x. more than in respect of the other Books, which are all of them equally replete with passages that are found in the " Odyssey," and in the case given above of " Il." x. 243, 244 and " Od." i. 65, 66, it is not easy to doubt that the Iliadic passage is the original, and the Odyssean the copy.

I will now deal with the undoubted Book xi., omitting as in the case of Book x. all lines that occur in other Books, unless I call special attention to them.

The first two lines of Book xi. are identical with the first two of Book v. of the " Odyssey," but " Il." xi. 2 occurs also in " Il." xix. 2.

" Il." xi. 42, 43, ἵππουριν· δεινὸν δὲ λόφος καθύπερθεν ἔνευεν, εἵλετο δ' ἄλκιμα δοῦρε δύω, κεκορυθμένα χαλκῷ.

These two lines are found " Od." xxii. 124, 125, but the first of them occurs three or four times elsewhere in the " Iliad."

" Il." XI. 181, ἀλλ' ὅτε δὴ τάχ' ἔμελλεν ὑπὸ πτόλιν αἰπύ τε
τεῖχος
cf. " Od." iv. 514, 515, ἀλλ' ὅτε δὴ τάχ' ἔμελλε Μαλείαων ὄρος αἰπὺ
ἵξεσθαι τότε δή.........

" Il." XI. 201, προέηκε τεῖν τάδε μυθήσασθαι, cf. " Od." iv. 829, where the same words occur.

" Il." XI. 253, ἀντικρὺς δὲ διέσχε φαεινοῦ δουρὸς ἀκωκή. cf. " Od." xix. 453, where the same line occurs but with διῆλθε for διέσχε.

" Il." XI. 531, ὣς ἄρα φωνήσας ἵμασεν καλλίτριχας ἵππους cf. " Od." xv. 215, where the same line occurs but with ἔλασεν instead of ἵμασεν.

" Il." XI. 624–639. The mess which Hecamede cooked for Patroclus and Machaon was surely present to the mind of the writer of the " Odyssey " when she was telling about the mess which Circe cooked for Ulysses' men, " Od." x. 234, 235.

" Il." XI. 668, 669..................οὐ γὰρ ἐμὴ ἲς
ἔσθ', οἵη πάρος ἔσκεν ἐνὶ γναμπτοῖσι μέλεσσιν
cf. " Od." xi. 393, 394, ἀλλ' οὐ γάρ οἱ ἔτ' ἦν ἲς ἔμπεδος οὐδέ τι κῖκυς
οἵη περ πάρος ἔσκεν ἐνὶ γναμπτοῖσι μέλεσσιν.

" Il." XI. 678, 679..................ἀγέλας, τόσα πώεα οἰῶν
τόσσα συῶν συβόσια, τόσ' αἰπόλια πλατέ' αἰγῶν.
These lines occur " Od." xiv. 100, 101 but with ἀγέλαι instead of ἀγέλας.

" Il." XI. 742, τὸν μὲν ἐγὼ προσιόντα βάλον χαλκήρεϊ δουρί·
This line is found " Od " xiii 267 but with κατιόντα for προσιόντα.

" Il." XI. 777, στῆμεν ἐνὶ προθύροισι ταφὼν δ' ἀνόρουσεν Ἀχιλλεύς, cf. " Od " xvi. 12, ἔστη ἐνὶ προθύροισι ταφὼν δ' ἀνόρουσε συβώτης.

Here we have only eleven well-marked passages common to both poems, in spite of the fact that Book XI is nearly 300 lines longer than Book x., but I am precluded from referring to any passages that occur also in any other Book of the " Iliad." Running my eye over the underlined lines in my copy of the " Iliad," I do not find much, though I admit that there is some difference between their frequency in Book XI., and in the other

Books. Furthermore I own to finding Book XI. perhaps the least interesting and the most perfunctorily written in all the " Iliad," and can well believe that the writer of the " Odyssey " borrowed from it less because she was of the same opinion, but however this may be, the number of common passages above collected is ample to establish the fact that the writer of the " Odyssey " had Book XI. in her mind as well as Book X.

I will now go on to examine the passages in " Il." XVIII. which the writer of the " Odyssey " has wholly or in part adopted. They are :—

"Il." XVIII. 22–24, ὣς φάτο τὸν δ' ἄχεος νεφέλη ἐκάλυψε μέλαινα
ἀμφοτέρῃσι δὲ χερσὶν ἑλὼν κόνιν αἰθαλόεσσαν·
χεύατο κὰκ κεφαλῆς χαρίεν δ' ᾔσχυνε πρόσωπον.

These lines are found " Od." xxiv. 315–317 except that as they refer to an old man, instead of, as in the " Iliad," to a young one, χαρίεν δ' ᾔσχυνε πρόσωπον has become πολιῆς ἀδινὰ στεναχίζων. The first of the three lines occurs also in " Il." XVII. 591.

"Il." XVIII. 108, καὶ χόλος ὅς τ' ἐφέηκε πολύφρονά περ χαλεπῆναι,

cf. "Od." xiv. 464, ἠλεός, ὅς τ' ἐφέηκε πολύφρονά περ μάλ' ἀεῖσαι.

"Il." XVIII. 250, Πανθοΐδης· ὁ γὰρ οἶος ὅρα πρόσσω καὶ ὀπίσσω;

cf. "Od." xxiv. 452, where however Πανθοΐδης becomes Μαστορίδης.

"Il." XVIII. 344–349,
ἀμφὶ πυρὶ στῆσαι τρίποδα μέγαν ὄφρα τάχιστα
Πάτροκλον λούσειαν ἄπο βρότον αἱματόεντα.
οἱ δὲ λοετροχόον τρίποδ' ἵστασαν ἐν πυρὶ κηλέῳ,
ἐν δ' ἄρ' ὕδωρ ἔχεαν, ὑπὸ δὲ ξύλα δαῖον ἑλόντες·
γάστρην μὲν τρίποδος πῦρ ἄμφεπε, θέρμετο δ' ὕδωρ
αὐτὰρ ἐπεὶ δὴ ζέσσεν ὕδωρ ἐνὶ ἤνοπι χαλκῷ,

cf. "Od." viii. 434–437, ὄφρα τάχιστα becomes ὅττι τάχιστα.

"Il." XVIII. 345 is omitted. In the following line οἱ becomes αἱ, and in the one after this ἑλόντες becomes ἑλοῦσαι·

The last line of the Iliadic passage is not given in " Od." viii., but appears without alteration in " Od." x. 360.

"Il." XVIII. 363, ὅς περ θνητός τ' ἐστὶ καὶ οὐ τόσα μήδεα οἶδεν.
This line occurs " Od." xx. 46.

"Il." XVIII. 385-387,

τίπτε Θέτι τανύπεπλε, ἱκάνεις ἡμέτερον δῶ
αἰδοίη τε φίλη τε ; πάρος γε μὲν οὔ τι θαμίζεις,
ἀλλ' ἕπεο προτέρω ἵνα τοι πὰρ ξείνια θείω·

"Il." XVIII. 424-427,

τίπτε Θέτι τανύπεπλε, ἱκάνεις ἡμέτερὸν δῶ
αἰδοίη τε φίλη τε ; πάρος γε μὲν οὔ τι θαμίζεις·
αὔδα ὅ τι φρονέεις· τελέσαι δέ με θυμὸς ἄνωγεν
εἰ δύναμαι τελέσαι γε καὶ εἰ τετελεσμένον ἐστίν.

The "Odyssey" (v. 87-91) has both these passages combined as follows :—

Τίπτε μοι, Ἑρμεία χρυσόρραπι, εἰλήλουθας
αἰδοῖός τε φίλος τε ; πάρος γε μὲν οὔ τι θαμίζεις
αὔδα ὅ τι φρονέεις· τελέσαι δέ με θυμὸς ἄνωγεν
εἰ δύναμαι τελέσαι γε καὶ εἰ τετελεσμένον ἐστίν.
ἀλλ' ἕπεο προτέρω, ἵνα τοι πὰρ ξείνια θείω.

"Il." XVIII. 389, 390 .... ἐπὶ θρόνου ἀργυροήλου
καλοῦ δαιδαλέου· ὑπὸ δὲ θρῆνυς ποσὶν ἦεν·

These lines will be found "Od." x. 314, 315.

"Il." XVIII. 431, ὅσσ' ἐμοὶ ἐκ πασέων Κρονίδης Ζεὺς ἄλγε' ἔδωκεν,
cf. "Od." iv. 722, 723 ....πέρι γάρ μοι Ὀλύμπιος ἄλγε' ἔδωκεν
ἐκ πασέων,

"Il." XVIII. 457, τούνεκα νῦν τὰ σὰ γούναθ' ἱκάνομαι αἴ κ'
ἐθέλῃσθα.

This line occurs "Od." iii. 92 and "Od." iv. 322.

"Il." XVIII. 463, θάρσει, μή τοι ταῦτα μετὰ φρεσὶ σῇσι μελόντων.
This line occurs "Od." xiii. 362, xvi. 436, and xxiv. 357.

"Il." XVIII. 486-489 πληιάδας θ'.........................
ἄρκτον θ', ἣν καὶ ἄμαξαν ἐπίκλησιν καλέουσιν,
ἥ τ' αὐτοῦ στρέφεται καί τ' Ὠρίωνα δοκεύει
οἴη δ' ἄμμορός ἐστι λοετρῶν Ὠκεάνοιο·

These lines occur "Od." v. 272-275.

"Il." XVIII. 533, 534, στησάμενοι δ' ἐμάχοντο μάχην ποταμοῖο
παρ' ὄχθας
βάλλον δ' ἀλλήλους χαλκήρεσιν ἐγχείῃσιν·

These lines are found "Od." ix. 54, 55 with παρὰ νηυσὶ θοῇσιν
instead of ποταμοῖο παρ' ὄχθας.

" Il." XVIII. 604–606,

> τερπόμενοι· μετὰ δέ σφιν ἐμέλπετο θεῖος ἀοιδὸς
> φορμίζων· δοίω δὲ κυβιστητῆρε κατ' αὐτοὺς
> μολπῆς ἐξάρχοντες ἐδίνευον κατὰ μέσον.

These lines occur " Od." iv. 17–19.

To meet the possible objection that " Il." XVIII. was written later than the " Odyssey," and might therefore have borrowed from it, I will quote the context of line 108 as well as the line itself. The passage runs (XVIII. 107–110) :—

> ὡς ἔρις ἔκ τε θεῶν ἔκ τ' ἀνθρώπων ἀπόλοιτο
> καὶ χόλος ὅς τ' ἐφέηκε πολύφρονά περ χαλεπῆναι,
> ὅς τε πολὺ γλυκίων μέλιτος καταλειβόμενοιο
> ἀνδρῶν ἐν στήθεσσιν ἀέξεται ἠΰτε καπνός.

The context of the Odyssean line which I suppose to be derived from this noble passage is as follows (xiv. 462–465) :—

> κέκλυθι νῦν Εὔμαιε, καὶ ἄλλοι πάντες ἑταῖροι·
> εὐξάμενός τι ἔπος ἐρέω· οἶνος γὰρ ἀνώγει
> ἠλεός, ὅς τ' ἐφέηκε πολύφρονά περ μάλ' ἀεῖσαι
> καί θ' ἁπαλὸν γελάσαι, καί τ' ὀρχήσασθαι ἀνῆκεν,

Which is the most likely—that the magnificent Iliadic lines were developed from " Od." xiv. 464, or that this line is an unconscious adaptation from " Il." XVIII. 108 ? For that the two lines are father and son will hardly be disputed.

Which again commends itself best—that the writer of " Il." XVIII. took the heating of Ulysses' bath water to heat water for Patroclus, or that the writer of the " Odyssey " omitted the line about Patroclus, and used the rest of the passage to heat water for Ulysses' bath ?

As regards the two salutations to Thetis (" Il." XVIII. 385–387, and 424–427), is it more likely that the writer of " Il." XVIII. made two bites of the Odyssean cherry of v. 87–91, or that the writer of the " Odyssey," wanting but a single salutation, combined the two Iliadic ones as in the passage above given ?

Lastly, is the list of constellations which Vulcan put on to the shield of Achilles more likely to have been amplified from " Od." v. 272–275, or these last-named lines to have been taken with such modification as was necessary, from " Il." XVIII, 486–489 ? Whatever may be the date of the " Odyssey," I cannot doubt that " Il." xviii. must be dated earlier ; and yet there is no Book of the " Iliad " about which our eminent Homeric scholars are more full of small complaints, or more unanimous in regarding as an interpolation. If there is one part of the " Iliad " rather than another in which Homer shows himself unapproachable, it is in his description of the shield of Achilles.

I will again assure the reader that all the Books of the " Iliad " seem drawn from with the same freedom as that shown in those which I have now dealt with in detail, and also that I can find no part of the " Odyssey " which borrows any less freely from the " Iliad " than the rest of the poem ; here and there difference of subject leads the writer to go three or four pages without a single Iliadic cento, but this is rare. One or two, or even sometimes three or four, Iliadic passages in a page is nearer the average, but of these some will be what may be called common form.

Their frequency raises no suggestion of plagiarism any more than the Biblical quotations in *Pilgrim's Progress* would do if the references were cut out. They are so built into the context as to be structural, not ornamental ; and to preclude the idea of their having been added by copyists or editors. They seem to be the spontaneous outcome of the fullness of the writer's knowledge of the " Iliad." It is also evident that she is not making a *résumé* of other people's works ; she is telling the story *de novo* from the point of view of herself, her home, her countrymen, and the whole island of Sicily. Other peoples and places may be tolerated, but they raise no enthusiasm in her mind.

Nevertheless, a certain similarity of style and feeling between the " Odyssey " and all the poems of the Epic cycle is certain to have existed, and indeed can be proved to have existed from the fragments of the lost poems that still remain. In all art, whether literary, pictorial, musical, or architectural, a certain character will be common to a certain age and country. Every age has its stock subjects for artistic treatment ; the reason for this is that it is convenient for the reader, spectator, or listener, to be familiar with the main outlines of the story. Written literature is freer in this respect than painting or sculpture, for it can explain and prepare the reader better for what is coming. Literature which, though written, is intended mainly for recitation before an audience few of whom can read, exists only on condition of its appealing instantly to the understanding, and will, therefore, deal only with what the hearer is supposed already to know in outline. The writer may take any part of the stock national subjects that he or she likes, and within reasonable limits may treat it according to his or her fancy, but it must hitch on to the old familiar story, and hence will arise a certain similarity of style between all poems of the same class that belong to the same age, language, and people. This holds just as good for the medieval Italian painters as it does for the Epic cycle. They offer us a similarity in dissimilarity and a dissimilarity in similarity.

When we remember, however, that the style of the " Odyssey " must not only perforce gravitate towards that of all the other then existing epic poems, but also that the writer's mind is as strongly leavened with the mind of Homer, let alone the other Cyclic poets, as we have seen it to be, it is not surprising that the veneer of virility thus given to a woman's work should have concealed the less patent, but far more conclusive, evidence that the writer was not of the same sex as the man, or men, from whom she was borrowing.

At the same time, in spite of the use she makes of Homer, I think she was angry with him, and perhaps jealous ; on which head I will say more in my next Chapter. Possibly the way he laughs at women and teases them, not because he dislikes them, but because he enjoys playing with them, irritates her ; she was not disposed to play on such a serious subject. We have seen how she retorts on him for having made a tripod worth three times as much as a good serviceable woman of all work. His utter contempt, again, for the gods, which he is at no pains to conceal, would be offensive to a writer who never permits herself to go beyond the occasional mild irreverence of the Vicar's daughter. Therefore, she treats Homer, as it seems to me, not without a certain hardness ; and this is the only serious fault I have to find with her.

For example, she takes the concluding lines of Hector's farewell to Andromache, a passage which one would have thought she would have shrunk from turning to comn on uses, and puts it into the mouth of Telemachus when he is simply telling his mother to take herself off. She does this in i. 356–359 and again in xxi. 350–353. This is not as it should be. Nor yet again is her taking the water that was heated to wash the blood from the body of poor Patroclus ("Il." xviii. 344 &c.) and using it for Ulysses' bath ("Od." viii. 434–437). Surely the disrespect here is deeper than any that can be found in Homer towards the gods.

But, whatever the spirit may have been in which the writer of the "Odyssey" has treated the "Iliad," I cannot doubt that she knew this poem exceedingly well in the shape in which we have it, and this is the point which I have thought it worth while to endeavour to substantiate at such length in the foregoing Chapter.

Chapter XV

THE ODYSSEY IN ITS RELATION TO THE OTHER POEMS OF THE
TROJAN CYCLE, AND ITS DEVELOPMENT IN THE HANDS OF THE
AUTHORESS.

THE writer of the " Odyssey " appears to have known most of
those lost poems of the Epic cycle—eight in number—that
relate to Troy, but as all we know about them is from the
summaries given in the fragment of Proclus, and from a few
lines here and there quoted in later authors, we can have no
irrefragable certainty that she had the poems before her even
when she alludes to incidents mentioned by Proclus as being
dealt with in any given one of them. Nevertheless, passages
in " Od." i. and iii. make it probable that she knew the Nosti
or the Return of the Achæans from Troy, and we may suppose
that Nestor's long speeches (" Od." iii. 102–200 and 253–328) are
derived mainly from this source, for they contain particulars
that correspond closely with the epitome of the Nosti given
by Proclus.

We can thus explain the correctness of the topography of the
Ægæan sea that is manifested in Nestor's speeches, but no
where else in the poem beyond a bare knowledge of the existence
of Apollo's shrine in Delos (" Od." vi. 162) and an occasional
mention of Crete. I see Professor Jebb says that the " Odyssey "
" shows a familiar knowledge of Delos ; "* but there is no
warrant for this assertion from anything in the poem.

The writer of the " Odyssey " seems, in Book iv., to have also
known the Cypria, which dealt with the events that led up to
the Trojan war.

Book xxiv. of the " Odyssey " (35–97) suggests a knowledge
of the " Æthiopis." So also does the mention of Memnon
(" Od." xi. 522).

---

* *Introduction to Homer*, Macmillan, 1888, p. 172.

Knowledge of the " Little Iliad " may be suspected from " Od." iv. 271–283, where Helen seems to be now married to Deiphobus, and from xi. 543–562 ; as also from xi. 508, 509, where Ulysses says that he took Neoptolemus to Scyrus. Ulysses entering Troy as a spy (" Od." iv. 242–256) is also given by Proclus as one of the incidents in the "Little Iliad." I do not see, therefore, that there can be much doubt about the writer of the " Odyssey " having been acquainted with the " Little Iliad," a poem which was apparently of no great length, being only in four Books.

From the two Books of the " Sack of Troy " we get the account of the council held by the Trojans over the wooden horse (" Od." viii. 492–517).

We have seen how familiar the authoress of the " Odyssey " was with the " Iliad " ; there only remains, therefore, one of the eight Trojan poems which she does not appear to have known— I mean the " Telegony," which is generally, and one would say correctly, placed later than the " Odyssey " ; but even though it were earlier we may be sure that the writer of the " Odyssey " would have ignored it, for it will hardly bear her out in the character she has given of Penelope.

In passing I may say that though Homer (meaning, of course, the writer of the " Iliad ") occasionally says things that suggest the Cypria, there is not a line that even suggests knowledge of a single one of the incidents given by Proclus as forming the subjects of the other Books of the Trojan cycle ; the inference, therefore, would seem to be that none of them, except possibly, though very uncertainly, the Cypria, had appeared before he wrote. Nevertheless we cannot be sure that this was so.

The curious question now arises why the writer of the " Odyssey " should have avoided referring to a single Iliadic incident, while showing no unwillingness to treat more or less fully of almost all those mentioned by Proclus as dealt with in the other poems of the Trojan cycle, and also while laying the " Iliad " under such frequent contributions.

I remember saying to a great publisher that a certain book was obviously much indebted to a certain other book to which no reference was made. "Has the writer," said the publisher in question, "referred to other modern books on the same subject?" I answered, "Certainly." "Then," said he, "let me tell you that it is our almost unvaried experience that when a writer mentions a number of other books, and omits one which he has evidently borrowed from, the omitted book is the one which has most largely suggested his own." His words seemed to explain my difficulty about the way in which the writer of the "Odyssey" lets the incidents of the "Iliad" so severely alone. It was the poem she was trying to rival, if not to supersede. She knew it to be far the finest of the Trojan cycle; she was so familiar with it that appropriate lines from it were continually suggesting themselves to her—and what is an appropriate line good for if it is not to be appropriated? She knew she could hold her own against the other poems, but she did not feel so sure about the "Iliad," and she would not cover any of the ground which it had already occupied.

Of course there is always this other explanation possible, I mean that traditions about Homer's private life may have been known to the writer of the "Odyssey," which displeased her. He may have beaten his wife, or run away with somebody else's, or both, or done a hundred things which made him not exactly the kind of person whom Arētē would like her daughter to countenance more than was absolutely necessary. I believe, however, that the explanation given in the preceding paragraph is the most reasonable.

And now let me explain what I consider to have been the development of the "Odyssey" in the hands of the poetess. I cannot think that she deliberately set herself to write an epic poem of great length. The work appears to have grown on her hands piecemeal from small beginnings, each additional effort opening the door for further development, till at last there the "Odyssey" was—a spontaneous growth rather than a thing done by observation. Had it come by observation, no doubt it would have been freer from the anomalies, inconsistencies, absurdities, and small slovenlinesses which are inseparable from the development of any long work, the plan of which has not been fully thought out beforehand. But surely in losing these it would have lost not a little of its charm.

From Professor Jebb's *Introduction to Homer*, Ed. 1888, p. 131, I see that he agrees with Kirchhoff in holding that the "Odyssey" contains "distinct strata of poetical material from different sources and periods," and also that the poem owes its present unity of form to one man ; he continues :

But under this unity of form there are perceptible traces of a process by which different compositions were adapted to one another.

In a note on the preceding page he tells us that Kirchhoff regards the first 87 verses of Book i. as having formed the exordium of the original Return of Ulysses.

My own conclusions, arrived at to the best of my belief before I had read a word of Professor Jebb's *Introduction*, agree in great part with the foregoing. I found the "Odyssey" to consist of two distinct poems, with widely different aims, and united into a single work, not unskilfully, but still not so skilfully as to conceal a change of scheme. The two poems are : (1) The visit of Ulysses to the Phæacians, with the story of his adventures as related by himself. (2) The story of Penelope and the suitors, with the episode of Telemachus's voyage to Pylos. Of these two, the first was written before the writer had any intention of dealing with the second, while the second in the end became more important than the first.

I cordially agree with Kirchhoff that the present exordium belongs to the earlier poem, but I would break it off at line 79, and not at 87. It is a perfect introduction to the Return of Ulysses, but it is no fit opening for the "Odyssey" as it stands. I had better perhaps give it more fully than I have done in my abridgement. It runs :

Tell me, O Muse, of that ingenious hero who travelled far and wide after he had sacked the strong citadel of Troy. He saw many cities and learned the manners of many nations ; moreover, he suffered much by sea while trying to save his own life and bring his men safely home ; but do what he might he could not save his men, for they perished through their own sheer folly in eating the cattle of the Sun-God Hyperion ; so the god prevented them from ever getting home. Tell me too about all these things, O daughter of Jove, from whatever source you may know them (i. 1–10).

Then follows the statement that Ulysses was with the nymph Calypso, unable to escape, and that his enemy, Neptune, had gone to the Ethiopians (i. 11–21). The gods meet in council and Jove makes a speech about the revenge taken by Orestes on Ægisthus (i. 26–43) ; Minerva checks him, turns the subject on to Ulysses, and upbraids Jove with neglecting him (i. 44–62). Jove answers that he had not forgotten him, and continues :

" Bear in mind that Neptune is still furious with Ulysses for having blinded an eye of Polyphemus, king of the Cylopes. Polyphemus is son to Neptune by the nymph Thoösa, daughter to the sea-king Phorcys, but instead of killing him outright he torments him by preventing him from getting home. Still, let us lay our heads together and see how we can help him to return. Neptune will then be pacified, for if we are all of a mind he can hardly hold out against us unsupported " (i. 68–79).

Let us now omit the rest of Book i., Books ii. iii. and iv. and go on with line 28 of Book v., which follows after a very similar council to the one that now stands at the beginning of Book i. Continuing with line 28 of Book v. we read :

When he had thus spoken he said to his son Mercury : " Mercury, you are our messenger, go therefore and tell Calypso we have decreed that poor Ulysses is to return home. He is to be conveyed neither by gods nor men, but after a perilous voyage of twenty days upon a raft he is to reach fertile Scheria, &c." (v. 28–34).

From this point the poem continues with only one certain, and another doubtful, reference to the suitors and Penelope, until (according to Kirchoff) line 184 of Book xiii. I had thought that the point of juncture between the two poems was in the middle of line 187, and that the ἔγρετο in the second half of the line had perhaps been originally εὗδεν ; but it must be somewhere close about this line, and I am quite ready to adopt Kirchhoff's opinion now that I have come to see why Ulysses was made to sleep so profoundly on leaving Scheria.

Till I had got hold of the explanation given on page 173, I naturally thought that the strange sleep of Ulysses had been intended to lead up to something that was to happen in Ithaca, and which had been cancelled when the scheme was enlarged and altered ; for without this explanation it is pointless as the poem now stands.

I do not now think that there was ever any account of what happened to Ulysses on his waking up in Ithaca, other than what we now have, but rather that the writer was led to adopt a new scheme at the very point where it became incumbent upon her to complete an old one. For at this point she would first find herself face to face with the difficulty of knowing what to do with Ulysses in Ithaca after she had got him there.

She could not ignore the suitors altogether ; their existence and Penelope's profligacy were too notorious. She could not make Ulysses and Penelope meet happily while the suitors were still in his house ; and even though he killed them, he could never condone Penelope's conduct—not as an epic hero. The writer of the "Odyssey" had evidently thought that she could find some way out of the difficulty, but when it came to the point she discovered that she must either make Ulysses kill his wife along with the suitors, or contend that from first to last she had been pure as new fallen snow. She chose the second alternative, as she would be sure to do, and brazened it out with her audience as best she could. At line 187, therefore, of Book xiii. or thereabouts, she broke up her Return camp and started on a new campaign.

To bring the two poems together she added lines xi. 115-137, in which Teiresias tells Ulysses about the suitors and his further wanderings when he shall have killed them. I suppose Teiresias' prophecy to have originally ended where Circe's does when she repeats his warning about the cattle of the Sun-god verbatim (xii. 137-140) with the line

$$\text{ὀψὲ κακῶς νεῖαι ὀλέσας ἄπο πάντας ἑταίρους·}$$

The first line of the addition to Teiresias' original prophecy (xi. 115) is also found with a slight variant in ix. 535, but it merely states that Ulysses will find trouble in his house, without mentioning what the trouble is to be.

With the two exceptions above noted, there is not only nothing in the original poem (*i.e.*, Book i. 1–79 and v. 28–xiii. 187 or thereabouts) to indicate any intention of dealing with the suitors, but there are omissions which make it plain that no such intention existed. In the proem the Muse is only asked to sing the Return of Ulysses. In the speech of Jove at the council of the gods (i. 32–43), he is not thinking about the suitors, as he would assuredly do if the writer had as yet meant to introduce them. In repeated speeches of the gods, and especially in Book v. which is Book i. of the original poem (see lines 36–42, 288, 289, and 345),* it seems that Ulysses' most serious troubles were to end when he had reached Scheria. So again Calypso (v. 206–208) tries to deter him from leaving her by saying that he little knows what he will have to go through before he gets home again, but she does not enforce her argument by adding that when he had got to Ithaca the worst was yet to come. I have already dealt with the silence of Ulysses' mother in Hades.

Noting, therefore that omission is a more telling indication of scheme than lines which, when a new subject is being grafted on to an old one, are certain to be inserted where necessary in order to unify the work, I have no hesitation in believing that Books i. 1–79 and v. 28–xiii. 187 or thereabouts, formed as much as the authoress ever wrote of the original poem ; I have the less hesitation in adopting this conclusion because, though I believe that I came to it independently as any one must do who studies the " Odyssey " with due attention, I find myself in substantial agreement with Kirchhoff in spite of much difference of detail, for I cannot admit that the two poems are by two or more separate people.

The introduction of lines xi. 115–137 and of line ix. 535, with a writing of a new Council of the gods at the beginning of Book v. to take the place of the one that was removed to Book i. 1–79, were the only things that were done to give even

---

* None of these three passages will be found in my abridgement.

a semblance of unity to the old scheme and the new, and to conceal the fact that the Muse after being asked to sing of one subject spends two thirds of her time in singing a very different one, with a climax for which no one had asked her. For, roughly, the Return occupies eight Books and Penelope and the suitors sixteen.

That lines xi. 115–137 were non-existent when Book xiii. was being written is demonstrated by the fact of Ulysses' saying to the Phæacians that he hoped he should find his wife living with her friends in peace (xiii. 42, 43). He could not have said this if Teiresias had already told him that his house would be full of enemies who were eating up his estate, and whom he would have to kill. He could hardly forget such a prophecy after having found Teiresias quite correct about the cattle of the Sun-god. Indeed he tells Penelope about his visit to Hades and his interview with Teiresias (xxiii. 323), so it is plain he remembered it. It is plain, again (from xiii. 382, &c.), that Ulysses was then learning from Minerva about the suitors for the first time—which could not be if Teiresias' prophecy had been already written.

It is surprising, seeing what a little further modification would have put everything quite straight, that the writer should have been content to leave passages here and there which she must have known would betray the want of homogeneity in her work, but we should be very thankful to her for not having tidied it up with greater care. We learn far more about her than we should do if she had made her work go more perfectly upon all fours, and it is herself that we value even more than her poem. She evidently preferred cobbling to cancelling, and small wonder, for if, as was very probably the case, the work was traced with a sharply pointed style of hardened bronze, or even steel,* on plates of lead, alteration would not be so easy as it is with us. Besides, we all cobble rather than cancel if we can. It is quite possible, but I need hardly say that it is not more than a mere possibility, that the abruptness of the interpolation in Book iv.

---

* Cf. " Od." ix. 391–393.

lines 621–624, may be due simply to its having been possible to
introduce four lines without cutting the MS. about very badly,
when a longer passage would have necessitated a more radical
interference with it.

We look, then, for the inception of the poem in Books i.
1–79 and v. 28–xiii. 187 or thereabouts, or more roughly in
Books v.—xii. inclusive. These Books, though they contain
no discrepancies among themselves, except the twenty lines
added to the prophecy of Teiresias above referred to, are not
homogeneous in scope, though they are so in style and treatment. They split themselves into two groups of four, *i.e.*,
v.–viii. and ix.–xii. The first group is written to bring Ulysses
to Scheria and to exhibit the Phæacians and the writer herself—
the interest in Ulysses being subordinate ; the second is written
to describe a periplus of Sicily.

Book ix.–xii. appear to have been written before Books
v.–viii. We may gather this from the total absence of Minerva.
It is inconceivable that having introduced the Goddess so
freely in Books v.–viii. the writer should allow her to drop out
from the story when there was such abundant scope for her
interference. These Books are certainly by the same hand
as the rest of the poem. They show the same amount of Iliadic
influence ; nowhere does a woman's hand appear more plainly ;
nowhere is Sicily, and more particularly Trapani, more in
evidence, direct or indirect. It is from the beginning of Book ix.
that we get our conviction that the Ionian islands were drawn
from the Ægadean, and the voyages of Ulysses, as I have
already shown, begin effectively with Mt. Eryx and end with
Trapani. We may, therefore, dismiss all idea that Books ix.–
xii. are by another writer.

Not only is the absence of Minerva inexplicable except by
supposing that at the time these Books were written it was no
part of the writer's scheme to make her such a *dea ex machinâ*
as she becomes later, but the writer shows herself aware that
the absence of the goddess in Books ix.–xii. requires apology,
and makes Ulysses upbraid her for having neglected him from
the time he left Troy till she took him into the city of the
Phæacians (xiii. 314–323). The goddess excuses herself by

saying she had known all the time that he would get home quite safely, and had kept away because she did not want to quarrel with her uncle Neptune—an excuse which we also find at the end of Book vi., in which Book she has, nevertheless, been beautifying Ulysses and making herself otherwise useful to him. I suppose Neptune did not mind how much his niece helped Ulysses, provided she did not let him see her.

I know how my own books, especially the earlier ones, got cut about, rearranged, altered in scheme, and cobbled to hide alteration, so that I never fairly knew what my scheme was till the book was three-quarters done, and I credit young writers generally with a like tentativeness.

I have now, I believe, shown sufficient cause for thinking that Books ix.–xii., *i.e.*, the voyage of Ulysses round Sicily, were the part of the " Odyssey " that was written first. I am further confirmed in this opinion by finding Ulysses fasten his box with a knot that Circe had taught him (viii. 448)—as though the writer knew all about Circe, though the audience, of courses, could not yet do so. A knowledge of Book ix., moreover, is shown in Book ii. 19, a passage which does not appear in my abridgement. Here we learn how Antiphus had been eaten by Polyphemus ; Book ix. is also presupposed in i. 68, which tells of the blinding of the Cyclops by Ulysses.

We may also confidently say that Books v.–viii. were written before i.–iv. and xiii.–xxiv. (roughly), but what the vicissitudes of Books v.–viii. were, and whether or no they drew upon earlier girlish sketches—as without one shred of evidence in support of my opinion I nevertheless incline to think —these are points which it would be a waste of time to even attempt to determine.

It is in Books v.–viii., and especially in the three last of these books, that the writer is most in her element. Few will differ from Col. Mure, who says of Scheria :

There can be little doubt from the distinctive peculiarities with which the poet has invested its inhabitants, and the precision and force of the sarcasm displayed in his portrait of

their character, that the episode is intended as a satire on the
habits of some real people with whom he was familiar.

> (*Language and Literature of Ancient Greece*, Vol. I.,
> p. 404).

Speaking on the same page of the obviously humorous
spirit in which the Phæacian episode is conceived, Col. Mure
says :

> This episode is, perhaps, the most brilliant specimen of the
> poet's combined talent for the delineation of character and for
> satirical humour. While there is no portion of his works a right
> understanding of which is so indispensable to a full estimate of
> his genius, there is none, perhaps, which has been so little
> understood. Appeal may be made to the tenor of the most
> esteemed commentaries, still more, perhaps, to the text of the
> most popular translations, where the gay sarcastic tone of
> description and dialogue which seasons the whole adventure,
> is replaced by the tragic solemnity of the gravest scenes of the
> " Iliad."

People find what they bring. Is it possible that eminent
Homeric scholars have found so much seriousness in the more
humorous parts of the " Odyssey " because they brought it
there ? To the serious all things are serious. Coleridge, so I
learn from the notes at the end of Mr. Gollancz's *Temple
Shakespeare*, saw no burlesque in the speeches of the players
which are introduced into *Hamlet*. He says :

> The fancy that a burlesque was intended sinks below
> criticism ; the lines, as epic narrative, are superb.

As Mr. Gollancz has given no reference, so neither can I.
Mr. Gollancz continues that if Coleridge had read Act II.
Scene i. of *Dido and Æneas*—a play left unfinished by
Marlowe—he would have changed his mind, but I do not
believe he would.

At the same time I take it that the writer was one half
laughing and the other half serious, and would sometimes
have been hard put to it to know whether she was more in
the one vein than in the other. So those who know the cantata
" Narcissus " will admit that there are people who are fully
aware that there is no music in this world so great as Handel's,
but who will still try to write music in the style of Handel,

and when they have done it, hardly know whether they have been more in jest or earnest, though while doing it they fully believed that they were only writing, so far as in them lay, the kind of music which Handel would have written for such words had he lived a hundred years or so later than he did.

We may note, without, however, being able to deduce anything from it as regards the dates at which the various parts of the poem were composed, that in the first four Books of the " Odyssey " the season appears to be summer rather than winter. In all the other Books (of course excluding those in which Ulysses tells his story) the season is unquestionably winter, or very early spring. It is noticeable also that snow, which appears so repeatedly in the " Iliad," and of which Homer evidently felt the beauty very strongly, does not appear, and is hardly even mentioned, in the " Odyssey." I should perhaps tell some readers that winter is long and severe in the Troad, while on the West coast of Sicily snow is almost unknown, and the winter is even milder than that of Algiers.

I ought also perhaps hardly to pass over the fact that amber, which is never mentioned in the " Iliad," appears three times in the " Odyssey."* This may be mere accident, nevertheless Sicily was an amber-producing country, and indeed still is so ; a large collection of Sicilian amber exists in the museum of Castrogiovanni, the ancient Enna, and I have been assured on good authority, but have not verified my informant's statement, that some fine specimens may be seen in the South Kensington Museum. Speaking of Sicilian amber the *Encyclopædia Britannica* says :

The most beautiful specimens are, perhaps, those which are found at Catania. They often possess a beautiful play of purple not to be observed in the product of other places.

I cannot make out whether the first four Books were written before the last twelve or after ; probably they were written first, but there is something to be said also on the other side.

---

* iv. 73, xv. 460, xviii. 296.

I will not attempt to settle this point, and will only add that when we bear in mind how both the two main divisions of the "Odyssey"—the Phæacian episode with the Return of Ulysses, and the story of Penelope and the suitors, show unmistakeable signs of having been written at one place, by a woman, by a woman who is evidently still very young, and that not a trace of difference in versification, style, or idiom can be found between the two divisions, the only conclusion we should come to is that the poem was written by one and the same woman from the first page to the last. I think we may also conclude in the absence of all evidence to the contrary—for assuredly none exists that deserves the name of evidence—that we have the poem to all intents and purposes in the shape which it had assumed in the hands of the authoress.

Chapter XVI

CONCLUSION.

BEFORE I quit my subject, I should perhaps answer a question which the reader has probably long since asked himself. I mean, how it is conceivable that considerations so obvious as those urged in the foregoing Chapters should have been overlooked by so many capable students for so many hundreds of years, if there were any truth in them. For they lie all of them upon the surface ; they are a mere washing in the Jordan and being clean ; they require nothing but that a person should read the " Odyssey " as he would any other book, noting the physical characters described in the Scherian and Ithacan scenes, and looking for them on some West coast of the Mediterranean to the West of Greece.

The answer is that the considerations which I have urged have been overlooked because, for very obvious reasons, it never occurred to any one to look for them. " Do you suppose, then," more than one eminent scholar has said to me directly or indirectly, " that no one has ever read the ' Odyssey ' except yourself ? " I suppose nothing of the kind, and know that it was only possible for the truth when once lost (as it soon would be on the establishment of the Phœnicians at Drepanum) to be rediscovered, when people had become convinced that the " Odyssey " was not written by the writer of the " Iliad." This idea has not yet been generally accepted for more than a hundred years,* if so long, but until it was seized and held firmly, no one was likely to suspect that the " Odyssey " could have come from Sicily, much less that it could have been written by a woman, for there is not one line in the " Iliad " which even hints at the existence of Sicily, or makes the reader suspect the

* I see that my grandfather, Dr. Butler, of Shrewsbury, accepts it in his *Antient Geography*, published in 1813, but I do not know where he got if from.

author to have been a woman, while there are any number of passages which seem absolutely prohibitive of any other opinion than that the writer was a man, and a very strong one.

Stolberg in the last century, and Colonel Mure in this, had the key in the lock when they visited Trapani, each of them with the full conviction that the Cyclops incident, and the hunting the goats, should be placed on Mt. Eryx and the island of Favognana—but they did not turn it. Professor Freeman, Schliemann, and Sir H. Layard, all of them visited Trapani and its immediate neighbourhood either as students or excavators, and failed to see that there was as splendid a prize to be unburied there without pick and shovel, outlay, or trouble of any kind, as those of Nineveh, Mycene, and Hissarlik—and why? Because they were still hampered by the long association of the " Iliad " and " Odyssey " as the work of the same person. Knowing that the " Iliad " could hardly have been written elsewhere than in the Northern half of the West coast of Asia Minor, if would never occur to them to look for the " Odyssey " in a spot so remote as Trapani. They probably held it to be the work of some prehistoric Herodotus, who would go on from scene to scene without staying longer than he could help in any one place, instead of feeling sure, as I believe they should have done, that it was the work of one who was little likely to have travelled more than a very few miles from her own home. Moreover, Admiralty charts are things of comparatively recent date, and I do not think any one would have been likely to have run the " Odyssey " to ground without their help.

But however this may be, I do not doubt that the habit of ascribing the " Odyssey " to Homer has been the main reason of the failure to see the obvious in connection with it. Surely it is time our eminent Iliadic and Odyssean scholars left off misleading themselves and other people by including the " Odyssey " in their " Introductions " to the work of " Homer." It was permissible to do this till within recent years ; anything else, indeed, would have been pedantic, but what would have been pedantic a hundred years ago, is slovenly and unscholarly now.

Turning from her commentators to the authoress herself, I am tempted to wonder whether she would be more pleased or angry could she know that she had been so long mistaken for a man—and that man Homer. It would afford her an excellent opportunity for laughing at the dullness of man. Angry, however, as she would no doubt be, she could hardly at the same time help being flattered, and would perhaps console herself by reflecting that poets as great as she was are bound to pay the penalty of greatness in being misunderstood.

Horace tells us that mediocrity in a poet is forbidden alike by gods, men, and publishers, but, whether forbidden or no, there are a good many mediocre poets who are doing fairly well. So far as I can see, indeed, gods, men, and more par-ticularly publishers, will tolerate nothing in a poet except mediocrity, and if a true poet by some rare accident slips in among the others, it is because gods and publishers' readers did not find him out until it was too late to stop him. Horace must have known perfectly well that he was talking nonsense.

And after all it is well that things are as they are ; for the mediocre poet, though he may hang about for many years, does in the end die, or at any rate become such a mere literary Struldbrug as to give plain people no trouble, whereas the true poet will possess himself of us, and live on in us whether we will or no, and unless the numbers of such people were severely kept in check they would clog the wheels of the world. Half a dozen first-class poets in prose or verse are as many as the world can carry in any comfort ; twenty Shakespeares, twenty Homers, twenty Nausicaas would make literature im-possible, yet we may be sure that every country in every century could yield two or three first-class writers, if genius were to be known at once, and fostered by those who alone know how to foster it. Genius is an offence ; like all other offences it must needs come, but woe to that man or woman through whom it comes, for he or she must pass through the Scylla and Charybdis of being either torn in pieces on the one hand, or so misunderstood on the other as to make the slipping through with life in virtue of such misrepresentation more mortifying than death itself.

Do what we may we cannot help it. Dead mind like dead body must, after a decent interval, be buried out of our sight if living mind is to have fair play, and it might perhaps not be a bad thing if our great educational establishments had more of the crematorium and less of the catacomb about them than they have at present. Our notions of intellectual sanitation are deplorably imperfect, and unless the living become more jealous of letting dead mind remain unconsumed in their system, a fit of intellectual gout must ere long supervene, which, if not fatal, will still be excruciatingly painful. Since, therefore, there are such insuperable difficulties in the way of eliminating geniuses when we have once absorbed them, and since also, do what we may, we can no more detect the one genius who may be born among a multitude of good average children, than Herod could detect the King of the Jews among the babes of Bethlehem, we have no course but to do much as Herod did, and lay violent hands upon all young people till we have reduced every single one of them to such mediocrity as may be trusted to take itself off sooner or later. To this end we have established schools and schoolmen ; nor is it easy to see how we could more effectually foster that self-sufficiency which does so much towards helping us through the world, and yet repress any exuberance of originality or independence of thought which may be prejudicial to its possessor during his own life, and burdensome to posterity when he is dead and gone.

Obviously wise, however, and necessary as our present system is, we nevertheless grumble at it. We would have any number of first-class geniuses in art, literature and music, and yet have plenty of elbow room for ourselves. Our children too ; they cannot show too many signs of genius, but at the same time we blame them if they do not get on in the world and make money as genius next to never does. Like the authoress of the " Odyssey " we are always wanting to have things both ways ; we would have others be forgotten, and yet not be forgotten ourselves ; when we have shuffled off this mortal coil, we would fain shuffle on another that shall be at once less coil and less mortal, in the good thoughts of coming generations, but if this desire is so universal as to be called natural, it is one which the best and sanest of us will fight against rather than encourage ; such people will do their work as well and cheerfully as they can, and make room for others with as little fuss as possible when they have had their day.

If, however, any man resents the common course of nature and sets himself to looking upon himself and cursing his fate that he was not born to be of the number of them that enter into life eternal even in this world, let him console himself by reflecting that until he is long dead, there is no certain knowing whether he is in life or no, and also that though he prove to be an immortal after all, he cannot escape the treatment which he is the more sure to meet with according as he is the more immortal—let alone the untold misery which his works will inflict upon young people.

If ever a great classic could have been deterred from writing by a knowledge of how posterity would treat her, the writer of the " Odyssey " should have been so, for never has poem more easy to understand failed more completely of being understood. If she was as lovely as I should like to think her, was ever sleeping beauty hidden behind a more impenetrable hedge of scholasticism ?   How could it be otherwise ?   The " Odyssey," like the " Iliad," has been a school book for nearly 3000 years, and what more cruel revenge could dullness take on genius ? What has the erudition of the last 2500 years done for the " Iliad " and the " Odyssey " but to emend the letter in small things and to obscure the spirit in great ones ?

There was indeed, as I said in my opening Chapter, a band of scholars a century or two before the birth of Christ who refused to see the " Iliad " and " Odyssey " as the work of the same person, but erudition snubbed them and snuffed them out so effectually that for some 2000 years they were held to have been finally refuted.   Can there be any more scathing satire on the value of scholastic criticism ?   It seems as though Minerva had shed the same darkness over both the poems that she shed over Ulysses, that they might go in and out among eminent Homeric scholars from generation to generation, and none should see them.

The world does indeed know little of its greatest men and women, and bitterly has it been reproached for its want of penetration, but there are always two sides, and it should be remembered that its greatest men and women commonly know very little of the world in its more conventional aspects. They are continually flying in the face of all that we expect of greatness, and they never tell us what they are ; they do not even think that they are great ; if they do we may be sure that they are mistaken ; how then can we be expected to appreciate people correctly till we have had plenty of time to think them over ?

And when we have thought them over, how little have our canons of criticism to do with the verdict which we in the end arrive at. Look at the " Odyssey." Here is a poem in which the hero and heroine have been already married many years before it opens ; from the first page to the last there is no young couple in love with one another, there is in fact nothing amatory in the poem, for though the suitors are supposed to be madly in love with Penelope, they never say or do anything that carries conviction as to their being so. We accept the fact, as we do the sagacity of Ulysses, because we are told it, not because we see it. The interest of the poem ostensibly turns mainly on the revenge taken by a bald middle-aged gentleman, whose little remaining hair is red, on a number of young men who have been eating him out of house and home, while courting his supposed widow.

Moreover, this subject, so initially faulty, is treated with a carelessness in respect of consistency and plausibility, an ignorance of commonly known details, and a disregard of ordinary canons which it would not be easy to surpass, and yet, such is the irony of art that it is not too much to say that there is only one poem which can be decisively placed above it. If the " Odyssey " enforces one artistic truth more than another, it is that living permanent work in literature (and the same holds good for art and music) can only be done by those who are either above, or below, conscious reference to any rules or canons whatsoever—and in spite of Shakespeare, Handel, and Rembrandt, I should say that on the whole it is more blessed to be below than above. For after all it is not the outward and visible signs of what we read, see, or hear, in any work, that bring us to its feet in prostration of gratitude and affection ; what really stirs us is the communion with the still living mind of the man or woman to whom we owe it, and the conviction that that mind is as we would have our own to be. All else is mere clothes and grammar.

As regards the mind of the writer of the " Odyssey " there is nothing in her work which impresses me more profoundly than the undercurrent of melancholy which I feel throughout it. I do not mean that the writer was always, or indeed generally, unhappy ; she was often, at any rate let us hope so, supremely happy ; nevertheless there is throughout her work a sense as though the world for all its joyousness was nevertheless out of joint—an inarticulate indefinable half pathos, half baffled fury, which even when lost sight of for a time soon re-asserts itself. If the " Odyssey " was not written without laughter, so neither was it without tears. Now that I know the writer to have been a woman, I am ashamed of myself for not having been guided to my conclusion by the exquisitely subtle sense of weakness as well as of strength that pervades the poem, rather than by the considerations that actually guided me.

The only approach to argument which I have seen brought forward to show that the " Odyssey " must have been written by a man, consists in maintaining that no woman could have written the scene in which Ulysses kills the suitors. I cannot see this ; to me it seems rather that no man could have brought himself to disregard probability with so little compunction ; moreover a woman can kill a man on paper as well as a man can, and with the exception of the delightful episode in which Ulysses spares the lives of Phemius and Medon, the scene, I confess, appears to me to be the most mechanical and least satisfactory in the whole poem. The real obstacle to a general belief that the " Odyssey " was written by a woman is not anything that can be found in the poem, but lies, as I have already said, in the long prevalence of an opinion that it was written by the same person as the " Iliad " was. The age and respectability of this opinion, even though we have at length discarded

it, will not allow us to go beyond ascribing the " Odyssey " to another man—we cannot jump all at once to the view that it was not by a man at all. A certain invincible scholasticism prevents us from being able to see what we should see at once if we would only read the poem slowly and without considering anything that critics have said concerning it.

This, however, is not an easy thing to do. I know very well that I should never have succeeded in doing it if I had not passed some five-and-thirty rebellious years during which I never gave the " Odyssey " so much as a thought. The poem is so august : it is hallowed by the veneration of so many ages ; it is like my frontispiece, so mysterious, so imperfect, and yet so divinely beyond all perfection ; it has been so long associated with the epic poem which stands supreme—for if the " Odyssey " be the Monte Rosa of literature, the " Iliad " must, I suppose, for ever remain as the Mont Blanc ; who can lightly vivisect a work of such ineffable prestige as though it were an overlooked *parvenu* book picked up for a few pence at a second hand book stall ? Lightly, no, but inexorably, yes, if its natural health and beauty are to be restored by doing so.

One of our most accomplished living scholars chided with me in this sense a year or two ago. He said I was ruthless. " I confess," he said, " I do not give much heed to the details on which you lay so much stress : I read the poem not to theorise about it, but to revel in its amazing beauty."

It would shock me to think that I have done anything to impair the sense of that beauty which I trust I share in even measure with himself, but surely if the " Odyssey " has charmed us as a man's work, its charm and wonder are infinitely increased when we see it as a woman's. Still more must it charm us when we find the writer to be an old friend, and see no inconsiderable part of her work as a reflection of her own surroundings.

Have we, then, a right in sober seriousness so to find her ? I have shown that in the earliest known ages of Greek literature poetesses abounded, and gained a high reputation. I have shown that by universal consent the domestic and female interest in the " Odyssey " predominates greatly over the male.

I have shown that it was all written in one place, and if so—
even were there no further reasons for thinking so—presumably
by one hand: I have shown that the writer was extremely
jealous for the honour of woman, so much so as to be daunted
by no impossibilities when trying to get rid of a story that she
held to be an insult to her sex. These things being so, is it
too much to ask the reader to believe that the poem was not
written, as Bentley held, by a man for women, but for both
men and women, by one who was herself a woman?

And now as I take leave of the reader, I would say that if
when I began this work I was oppressed with a sense of the
hopelessness of getting Homeric scholars to take it seriously
and consider it, I am even more oppressed and dismayed when
I turn over its pages and see how certain they are to displease
many whom I would far rather conciliate than offend. What
can it matter to me where the "Odyssey" was written, or
whether it was written by a man or a woman? From the
bottom of my heart I can say truly that I do not care about the
way in which these points are decided, but I do care, and very
greatly, about knowing which way they are decided by sensible
people who have considered what I have urged in this book. I
believe I have settled both points sufficiently, but come what
may I know that my case in respect of them is amply strong
enough to justify me in having stated it. And so I leave it.

Index

Nothing will be Indexed which can be found readily by referring to the Table of Contents.